The Cyber Intelligence Handbook:

An Authoritative Guide for the C-Suite, IT Staff, and Intelligence Team

By David M. Cooney, Jr.

Content of this book was cleared for public release by the Department of Defense's Office of Prepublication Security Review on 08 January 2019

Copyright © 2019 David M. Cooney, Jr

All Rights Reserved

ISBN: 9781082404382

To Kathy, whose love, support, and ceaseless hard work have defined and enriched my life for the last 37 years. You enabled me to have the career that spawned this book by your unselfish commitment to our family and personal sacrifice. You have always inspired me to aspire and encouraged me when I need it the most.

Acknowledgements

This book is a labor of love and a byproduct of seizing an opportunity rather than executing the next step in a master plan. As I set about to write this acknowledgement, I compiled a list of people who had made meaningful contributions in shaping me as an intelligence professional and leader, and my first list was over 50 names in length. I am certain that if I were to write something about each person on that list I would think of 50 more. Suffice to say that I have been blessed throughout my career to be surrounded by bright people who were passionate about their jobs and who shaped me as a person and as an intelligence professional. So to all of my shipmates and teammates who gave of themselves to contribute to my professional journey, thank you.

There are three individuals and a small group of key contributors who deserve special recognition, however, because without their contribution, this book might still be a future consideration rather than a completed work.

The first person on the list is my late father, Rear Admiral David Cooney, US Navy Retired, who set me on my path that has led me to where I am today. His guidance and advice were what led me to choose to seek a navy commissioning program as a component of my college education, and he was the person who suggested that I consider intelligence as a career field. My father was a competitive debater in his youth, and he taught my sisters and me how to present logical and unemotional arguments, to challenge popular opinion and to recognize biases in our own thinking. He emphasized to me the need to continue my education throughout my life, and he repeatedly told me that a hallmark of successful leaders was their ability to formulate the right questions. He imparted his belief that the difference between an undergraduate and graduate education was that the former taught one how to answer the questions one was presented, while the latter taught one how to evaluate whether the questions being asked were relevant to addressing the problems one was trying to solve. He instilled in me a strong contrarian analytic approach, an appreciation for the importance of civil discourse and precise use of words, and a recognition of the centrality of beginning all journeys with a destination in mind. Those three practices guided me throughout my career and are all clearly present in the content and construct of this book.

The second person I must recognize is my friend, colleague, and coconspirator in this project Muireann O'Dunlaing Parker. Muireann and I were teammates on the GE Capital IT security team for an all too brief 16 months, during which time she had a significant positive impact in shaping the way I thought about my job and how my team could broaden our value. She combined a disciplined academic problem solving approach with a rather infectious "why the hell not" attitude toward the application of unconventional ideas. When I told her that I was writing this book, she told me that she wanted to help, and she was good to her word. She has been a driving force in shaping the book's organization, dramatically improving the precision of the presentation of stakeholder roles, clarifying relationships between multiple processes, and creating the name 4E for the simplified intelligence process. Muireann's perspectives, professional experience, and ability to ask penetrating questions touched every aspect of the finished product.

I turned to my life-long friend Dr. Mark McGibbon late in this project to pick his brain on a variety of topics and to ask him to write the Foreword. Henry (as he is known to his friends) and I have been friends, shipmates, roommates, running mates, and kindred spirits for 30 years. We can go five years without talking and pick up our last conversation like it was yesterday. Henry is one of the most talented and energetic people I have ever met. He has an impressive academic background that he has applied to teaching and business, but what sets Henry apart is that he has a knack for establishing really high goals then going out and exceeding them.

From the moment Henry became aware of what I was doing he has offered ideas and encouragement, and I have no doubt that he will be a major force going forward as I try to socialize my ideas and market this book and its message.

Finally, I need to recognize a small, but important group of people who played critical roles in helping me to transition from a senior military intelligence officer to the cyber intelligence leader for a systemically important financial institution. I want to thank Mark Clark for finding a home for me on his team at Booz Allen and Al Pollard and Marty Greene for helping me to develop marketable cyber skills and for creating opportunities for me to grow. I also need to recognize John Hibbs and Paul Shaw for taking the leap of faith to hire me to establish a cyber intelligence capability at GE Capital. John opened the door for me and encouraged me to push the envelope with new ideas and to be a disruptive force and catalyst for change. Paul committed countless hours of his time to tutor me and to keep my early efforts on track, and his fingerprints are all over the successes my team enjoyed. My GE Capital team, particularly the group that was with me for the two plus years we were growing something special, Justin Sherenco, Aaron Varrone, Garrett Carstens, Marcus Ruffin, and George Dodd, all contributed immensely to my professional education. I suspect that each will recognize their influence on my professional understanding the content of the book. Thank you.

David Cooney
March 2019

Table of Contents

Dedication	*i*
Acknowledgements	*iii*
Table of Contents	*vi*
Foreword	*viii*
Introduction	*xii*
Section One – Understand Intelligence	**1**
Chapter 1.1 – Intelligence Lexicon	7
Chapter 1.2 – Cyber Intelligence Roles	18
Chapter 1.3 – Doctrinal Intelligence Process	29
Chapter 1.4 – Literate Stakeholders	39
Chapter 1.5 – Educated Stakeholders	53
Section Two – Understand Threats	**66**
Chapter 2.1 – Establishing a Threat Framework	72
Chapter 2.2 – Applied Threat Understanding	89
Chapter 2.3 – Future Threats	108

Section Three – Understand Your Needs   **117**

Chapter 3.1 – Cyber Intelligence Economics   122
Chapter 3.2 – Cyber Intelligence Establishment Planning Process 129
Chapter 3.3 – Application Case Studies   150

Section Four – The Simplified Cyber Intelligence Process   **171**

Chapter 4.1 – The Establish Phase   177
Chapter 4.2 – The Enable Phase   188
Chapter 4.3 – The Execute Phase   215
Chapter 4.4 – The Evaluate Phase   241

Section Five – Sustaining and Improving Cyber Intelligence Capabilities   **259**

Chapter 5.1 – Institutionalizing Stakeholder Driven Process Improvements   263
Chapter 5.2 – Measuring Performance   277
Chapter 5.3 – Analytic Frameworks   288
Chapter 5.4 – Applied Intelligence   310
Chapter 5.5 – Advanced Concepts for Cyber Intelligence Operations   324

Afterword   **344**

Appendix A – List of Acronyms   **349**

Appendix B – Contemplating Future Threats   **351**

Appendix C – Execution-Level Proficiency Matrix   **356**

Foreword

The author of this book, Captain Dave Cooney (USN – Retired), is a highly respected leader in the cyber intelligence field. Cooney is a visionary with deep analytical skills. His strategic-level leadership experiences and drive to educate the world were the catalyst for him to author this book. He made a difference while serving in the United States Navy (USN) because he respectfully challenged old school thinking while introducing new and innovated ways to think, plan and execute cyber intelligence related strategies, tactics and initiatives. This book follows in that same vein.

As a friend and admirer of Cooney of 30 years, I respect his decision to write this book and educate the world on cyber intelligence. Cooney's pragmatism and ability to capture his thoughts in cogent models based upon his cyber intelligence and information technology (IT) leadership experiences during his employment in government and corporate industries. Under his leadership, Cooney managed billions of US dollars' worth of IT equipment ranging from mainframe computers to handheld devices, which allowed him to reflect on human behaviors and processes that are now dependent upon technology.

While serving as an USN Cryptologic Officer, I had the unique privilege to work directly and indirectly for one of the most highly respected Intelligence Officers in the USN, Lieutenant Commander Cooney in the late 1980's, and then Captain Cooney in the early 2000's. In both instances, I was fortunate to observe Cooney's approach to challenging traditional ways of handling cyber intelligence problem solving. While serving in the USN, Cooney had the ability to grasp the holistic perspective of cyber intelligence related problem by capturing the problem in models based upon empirical and new factual data while simultaneously including hypotheticals. These hypotheticals helped determine options along with the "givens" to answer a series of questions for best-option decision-making. After reading Cooney's book, he continues to present his thoughts in an articulate manner, which in turn will help implement and institutionalize his cyber intelligence related ideas, which are often expressed in models throughout government and businesses.

I consider Cooney's unselfish act of sharing this timely and important piece of intellectual property with readers, his contribution to assist government and corporate leaders in the improvement of their cyber security operations. As previously mentioned, Cooney has the ability to collectively observe and interpret human behavior, processes and technology for improved decision-making. Further, within this book, Cooney will identify cyber intelligence field deficiencies within: (a) in-house intelligence expertise, (b) materials to inform decision makers on cyber intelligence capabilities, and (c) effective cyber intelligence models for timely cyber intelligence related decision-making. In my opinion, as a business leader and former USN Officer, Cooney's book is the missing reference guide that can enable conscientious leaders to professionalize their cyber intelligence operations.

Cooney provides readers with a straightforward approach of employing cyber intelligence to institutionalize threat-driven IT security operations within organizations. He introduces readers to practical lexicons, taxonomies, and frameworks that cyber security operational professionals can adopt and tailor within their respective organizations to overcome the aforementioned cyber intelligence and security deficiencies.

Additionally, readers will learn Cooney's three cyber intelligence prerequisite conditions for a successful sustainment of cyber intelligence operations: (1) possess a critical mass of knowledgeable and engaged stakeholders; (2) share a commonly recognized framework for characterizing threats and threat actors; and (3) be able to articulate realistic performance expectations for cyber intelligence aligned with and prioritized by organizational needs. Cooney also coined the phrase, Cyber Intelligence Fire

Triangle, to describe the collective impact of the three conditions on operational capability. Just as a fire can only burn if all three elements of the fire triangle (heat, fuel, and oxygen) are present, cyber intelligence operations can only be sustained when all three conditions described by the cyber intelligence fire triangle are present.

Returning to Cooney's experiences, he brings a unique balance of government and corporate intelligence experience within the passages of this book. He was the Director of Intelligence Operations for 1 of the 9 major US Military Combatant Commands, as well as, the Cyber Intelligence & Incident Detection Leader for 1 of the 9 financial institutions, GE Capital, which was created by Dodd-Frank legislation.

His 29-year US Navy intelligence career involved 15 assignments afloat and ashore. Cooney was an all-source analyst, admirals' aide, manager, leader, policy developer, planner, and doctrine developer. His private sector experience includes 4-years at BAH as the senior intelligence professional in their cyber practice for the US Navy, and 4-years as the Cyber Intelligence and Incident Detection Leader for GE Capital.

Many of the cyber intelligence approaches presented in this book were developed and tested during Cooney's employment at GE Capital, and most have their roots derived from his Navy experience. He benefited greatly from being a General Electric Team Member, which allowed him exposure to unique cyber threats categorized by industry and geography. Cooney's participation in a range of government and academia cyber related conferences and symposia helped him to refine his Cyber Intelligence Fire Triangle and reinforce its centrality as an organizing principle.

Finally, as a President and CEO of a public/private medium-sized IT business, experienced entrepreneur, former computer-science and business management graduate-school professor, and retired USN Officer, I am acutely aware of the costs being imposed on businesses by malicious cyber actors. I view cyber intelligence as an important tool for reversing the current security dynamic that all too frequently favors the attacker over the defender. Applying my background as a business leader, academic, IT professional, and former USN Officer, I recognize the importance of creating a cadre of professionals who can understand the complexities of both the IT and intelligence fields, and who have the business acumen to apply their actions in a manner that support enterprise-level goals.

I most strongly recommend this book to any leader and professional who desires to begin or complete their cyber intelligence or IT related education.

H. Mark McGibbon, Ph.D. & D.B.A.
President & CEO
Virgin Islands Next Generation Network

Introduction

Background

Although I did not realize it until many years later, I got one of the most important pieces of feedback in intelligence my career about two months into my first job. I was assigned as the intelligence officer for a carrier-based anti-submarine warfare squadron. My squadron was about four days into an intense week-long certification process called the Operational Readiness Exam, when my over-stressed and sleep-deprived commanding officer stopped me in the middle of a crowded ship's passageway and provided me with a blunt critique of the inadequacies of the performance of the intelligence team in general and my performance in particular. The gist of his feedback was that we were making him work too hard to get what he needed. He presented his logic in a linear fashion: he was a pilot, which meant that he flew airplanes; I was an intelligence officer, which meant I provided intelligence; so henceforth, I was to give him the gouge (naval aviation speak for the definitively correct answer in the simplest format possible), and I was to cease pestering him with questions because my job was to give answers.

Thirty-nine years have passed since that first unsolicited feedback session, and in that time I learned that my commanding officer's heartfelt feedback was more than one man's opinion; it represented an almost universal expectation for the wide range of intelligence customers I would meet throughout my career. Simply stated, people want the definitively correct/actionable answers to all relevant threat questions (including the ones they did not ask.)

The concept of the existence of the gouge, therefore, serves as both a cautionary note and a logical starting point for introducing this book. Organizations led by people waiting for someone to provide the gouge will find that approach to be a losing strategy. Consistently successful cyber intelligence outcomes are the byproduct of creating/sustaining a critical mass of informed stakeholders who are willing to take ownership of their roles and accept the ambiguities associated with operating in a threat environment in which threat actors can exercise their own freewill.

My purpose in writing this book is to publish a cyber intelligence primer that can be used as a reference by people charged with acquiring new or improving existing cyber intelligence capabilities in their organizations. The book is intended to fill a void in the existing body of open source literature, i.e. the absence of writings focused on private sector cyber intelligence operations that were not written by security firms seeking to market their cyber intelligence products and services. The content represents the application of nearly four decades of intelligence experience supporting a wide range of technical and operational functions to the unique challenges associated with establishing and executing cyber intelligence operations in private sector organizations with little or no previous exposure to the intelligence profession.

I had more than three decades of intelligence experience in the defense sector prior to taking on the role of establishing a cyber intelligence capability in a highly regulated financial company in which there were only a few people who had ever been exposed to intelligence concepts. It took me some time to recognize the range of challenges I was facing in my efforts to provide useful intelligence to people who neither understood what they needed nor their role in articulating the questions they wanted intelligence to address. After months of working to understand the operational functions I needed to support, mastering my customers' technical lexicons, developing an understanding of the organizational culture in which I operated, and refining my intelligence products to address threats to the organization, I came to the realization that my team's outputs were not influencing business or IT security decisions.

This realization stimulated months of experimentation and outreach to both internal customers and external contacts I had met at professional forums. My analysis of data collected in this outreach identified a number of common factors that were imposing limits on the ability of cyber intelligence operations to contribute to positive security outcomes in organizations in which stakeholder had no experience working with intelligence. Among the most significant of these factors were the lack of a shared understanding of what cyber intelligence was and what it could do; no common lexicon for communicating ideas and needs; the absence of examples of successful process models that could be emulated; undefined stakeholder roles; and poorly developed threat frameworks for defining threats and threat actors.

Taken together, the factors enumerated above constitute the problems this book was written to solve. This book organizes the factors limiting cyber intelligence success into three capability buckets: (1) understand intelligence, (2) understand threats, and (3) understand your needs. Each of these capability buckets represents a side on a visual model that I refer to as the cyber intelligence fire triangle. The original fire triangle expresses physical law that fire can only exist if three factors are present: heat, fuel, and oxygen. The requirement is absolute and forms the basis for firefighting (i.e. remove one element and the fire is extinguished.) Applied to cyber intelligence, the fire triangle analogy expresses the idea that sustained and responsive cyber intelligence operations are only possible in organizations in which the three prerequisite conditions of the cyber intelligence fire triangle are met.

This introduction presents an overview of the cyber intelligence fire triangle and the key supporting concepts that readers need to have in place to be able to make full use of the content of this book.

The Cyber Intelligence Fire Triangle

Figure I.1 provides a visualization of the cyber intelligence fire triangle and the three capability buckets that define it.

Figure I.1 – The Cyber Intelligence Fire Triangle

Capability Bucket One: Understand Intelligence

Overview:

The intellectual cornerstone of this book is that cyber intelligence is the application of intelligence to the cybersecurity/information technology (IT) security field for the purpose of providing improved awareness and understanding of threats to networks and data that will enable security professionals to make better informed and timelier decisions, an outcome I call "threat-driven IT security operations." With the exception of companies in the cybersecurity business that are acquiring cyber intelligence capabilities as part of a business plan to sell intelligence products and services, organizations acquiring cyber intelligence capabilities are doing so as a means of enhancing the capabilities of specifically identified IT security functions (henceforth referred to as supported functions.) The people executing the supported functions are the frontline cyber intelligence customers, and those customers must inform cyber intelligence planning by defining how increased threat understanding will enhance their ability to perform their roles.

Section One of this book addresses four conditions that need to be met before organizations will have sufficient understanding of intelligence to be able to execute consistently productive cyber intelligence operations: a common intelligence lexicon [Chapter 1.1]; an understanding of the primary roles of intelligence [Chapter 1.2]; a defined and repeatable intelligence process [Chapter 1.3]; and a clear understanding of stakeholder roles [Chapters 1.4 and 1.5.]

Key Supporting Concepts:

Intelligence Integration: Cyber intelligence is not a capability that can be purchased as an aftermarket add-on and connected to one's network to run in the background with no inputs or updates. It is a participatory team activity that requires continuous inputs and feedback, and stakeholder satisfaction with cyber intelligence outputs will be directly related to their process participation. Given the importance of active stakeholder participation, people charged with establishing/improving cyber intelligence capabilities must not only clearly define stakeholder roles, they must also socialize and market them during the establishment process to encourage stakeholder buy-in.

Cyber Intelligence Stakeholders: Given the large number of different functions impacted by cyber intelligence and the absence of universal position description standards from one organization to the next, I chose to develop a stakeholder taxonomy that bins stakeholder roles into three responsibility groupings. This taxonomy is employed throughout the book; each chapter begins with an overview of stakeholder roles employing this taxonomy. The three cyber intelligence stakeholder groupings are:

(1) Literate Stakeholders: are leaders outside of IT who will be held accountable to a board, stockholders, regulators, or their own personal standards of integrity should their organization be successfully attacked by malicious cyber actors. Literate stakeholders need to have a macro understanding of how intelligence operations work and what cyber intelligence capabilities their organization has in place. They need to understand when decisions they make have the potential to alter IT security dynamics, and they need to hold themselves accountable when their decisions generate greater IT and enterprise risk. [*Chapter 1.4 provides a more detailed discussion on the specific desired contributions of six different groups of literate stakeholders.*]

(2) Educated Stakeholders: are composed of IT professionals, particularly Chief Information Officers (CIO), Chief Information Security Officers (CISO), and individuals in positions that report directly to them. Educated stakeholders need to have a solid working knowledge of intelligence processes and command of the intelligence lexicon. They are responsible for playing an active role in articulating and prioritizing the intelligence requirements designed to drive cyber intelligence operations, for providing feedback to refine cyber intelligence actions, and for establishing the performance standards they expect cyber intelligence to meet. In addition, they need recognize when organizational decisions have the potential to change the organizations' attack surface, and they need to be able to portray associated risks accurately. [*Chapter 1.5 provides a detailed discussion on the specific roles of* *key educated stakeholders in driving focused cyber intelligence operations.*]

	Literate Stakeholders	Educated Stakeholders	Intelligence Practitioners
Primary Roles	1. Maintain awareness of existing cyber intelligence capabilities 2. Know how to communicate questions and concerns 3. Maintain awareness of primary threats to the organization and the industry in which it operates	1. Understand cyber intelligence process and lexicon/taxonomies 2. Drive cyber intelligence requirements and performance feedback processes 3. Advocate for the role of cyber intelligence and impact of cyber threats to literate stakeholders	1. Master key elements of professional knowledge 2. Be proficient in ability to conduct cyber intelligence operations 3. Drive continuous improvement in operational performance and organizational impact
Group Members	• C-level Executives • Privacy and External Relationships • People engaged in procurement, vendor selection/management, and supply chain management • Business Development Team • Fraud Team • People with authority to execute financial transactions	• Chief Information Officer • Chief Information Security Officer • Chief Technology Officer • Information Technology Security Process Owners	• Cyber Intelligence Leader • Technical Intelligence Exploitation Team • Cyber Intelligence Analysis Team • Network Hunters

Table I.1 – Sample Stakeholder Identification and Role Assignment Matrix

(3) Intelligence Practitioners: are people filling positions that have intelligence tasks listed in their position descriptions and who are responsible for executing cyber intelligence operations to predict, prevent, and detect cyber-attacks. Intelligence practitioners need to master their understanding of cyber intelligence processes and attain a deep knowledge of the operational and security functions they are responsible for supporting. In addition, they are responsible for ensuring the integrity of all cyber intelligence processes and for driving continuous self-learning and process improvement to keep pace with evolving threats.

Operational Definitions: In addition to the term stakeholders, some discussions employ the terms leaders and customers. To avoid any confusion that might create, I wanted to provide operational definitions for those terms upfront:

(1) Leaders: are the people who have decision-making authorities in the organization. There are leaders in all three stakeholder groups, so when I use the word leader, I am talking about decision-makers and no stakeholder grouping should be inferred.

(2) Customers: refers to the collective of literate and educated stakeholders. Customers are the stakeholders for whom cyber intelligence is produced.

Capability Bucket Two: Understand Threats

Overview:

The primary role of intelligence, regardless of the function it is supporting, is to provide customers with threat awareness and understanding. Intelligence practitioners must not only master their own craft, but they must also engage in continuous conversations with their key stakeholders to understand how organizational business decisions might impact potential threat actors' perception of the organization's attack surface.

Section Two presents three topics intended to provide readers with a taxonomy and supporting lexicon designed to enhance their ability to discuss threats precisely. The section opens with the presentation of a threat framework that provides cyber intelligence stakeholders with a common set of reference points for classifying threat actors, defining their motivations, characterizing the threats they present, and identifying the effects they are trying to create [*Chapter 2.1*]. The threat framework is then applied to nine real-world cyber-attack case studies to demonstrate how its taxonomy and lexicon promote common understanding [*Chapter 2.2*]. The discussion is concluded by offering eight future cyber-threat trends employing two prediction methodologies [*Chapter 2.3*].

Key Supporting Concepts:

Attack Surface: The term attack surface used in this book is derived from military operations in the physical domain. I use the term throughout the book to describe the collective factors threat actors consider when looking at a given organization as a potential target. Attack surfaces in the cyber domain encompass vulnerabilities in both the physical and cyber spheres that include architecture, policy, legal, geographical, and human factors. Business decisions alter attack surfaces, and cyber intelligence stakeholders must work together to capture the impacts of changes to attack surfaces in real time and apply them to impacted IT and enterprise risk models.

Tactics, Techniques, Procedures, and Tools (TTPTs): The acronym TTPT is used throughout the book to describe the range capabilities threat actors possess. Threat actor capabilities are a byproduct of the tools they have and their proficiency and imagination in applying them. Mature cyber intelligence practices will routinely address capability, proficiency, and opportunity attributes of threat actors in their analysis.

Threat Actor Constraints: The concept of threat-driven IT security operations is that informed professionals can employ threat understanding to improve the quality and timelines of IT security decisions designed to deter and/or defeat future attacks. Cyber intelligence supporting threat-driven IT security operations must be able to assess the challenges faced by potential attackers from the perspective of the attacker. Kill-chain methodologies and system of systems analysis [*Chapter 5.3.1*] are useful tools for analyzing the challenges and constraints threat actors face in their attack planning. Leaders can leverage that understanding to harden their networks and data against malicious actors targeting them.

Capability Bucket Three: Understand Your Needs

Overview:

There is an old joke shared among military intelligence professionals that there are only two possible outcomes to any operation; it will either be an operational success or an intelligence failure. Like most old jokes, it has endured because it contains elements of truth. After nearly four decades of studying intelligence lessons learned and intelligence failures (both real and imagined), I have isolated a single thread that is evident in almost every case study; the most common form of intelligence failure is unmet expectations. Sadly, the most common reason that expectations are not met is that they were not articulated.

Section Three offers three topics to assist cyber intelligence stakeholders engaged in processes designed to define enterprise cyber intelligence needs and realistic expectations. The section opens with a discussion of the economics of cyber intelligence. It builds a theoretical cost versus proficiency curve and defines four operating environments along that curve that can be used to define proficiency goals and to measure process maturity [*Chapter 3.1*]. It then presents a three-step process (operational design, establishment planning, and selection/refinement) designed to identify expectations for cyber intelligence within the context of organizational culture and to translate those expectations into planning guidance to direct the development of an executable cyber intelligence plan [*Chapter 3.2*]. The section concludes by offering three approaches for establishing and/or improving cyber intelligence capabilities designed to address the adopting organizations' most important intelligence needs. The discussion for each approach addresses strengths, challenges, in-sourcing/outsourcing tradeoffs, and organizational considerations. Each approach includes two theoretical application scenarios to present challenges associated with establishing a new capability versus refining an existing practice [*Chapter 3.3*].

Key Supporting Concepts:

Defining Cyber Intelligence Success: Any discussion of cyber intelligence success needs to begin by recognizing that it can never be measured in absolute terms. The best intelligence products one can generate will still contain elements of ambiguity, and world class intelligence organizations can only address a subset of the intelligence requirements they are working at any given time. Despite these challenges, it is essential for high performing organizations to develop methodologies for articulating performance expectations to refine and improve cyber intelligence outcomes.

(1) Requirements-based Measurements of Success: One of the best ways to measure cyber intelligence success is to evaluate intelligence performance against customers' stated requirements. A universally accepted intelligence best practice is for organizations to develop a finite number of priority intelligence requirements (PIRs) that express the enterprise's most compelling intelligence needs. That best practice applies to private sector cyber intelligence operations, and it provides a sound basis for stakeholders to measure the impact of cyber intelligence in the context of what they need it to provide. Using the requirements as a baseline for measuring success demands some thoughtful analysis, however. A binary approach of measuring whether questions were or were not answered will seldom be an accurate measure of intelligence performance, because that approach does not isolate cyber intelligence contributions as an independent variable in a multivariate process. For example, the absence of reporting may reflect threat actor inactivity rather than poor performance by the cyber intelligence team.

(2) Measuring Success Against Predefined Definitions: An alternate approach would be for leaders to develop a finite number of success definitions that measure cyber intelligence contribution to supported processes. Table I-2 presents a generic example of this approach; it offers sample success conditions at three different levels of operation (e.g. strategic, operational, and tactical.) Strategic-level success definitions correspond to enterprise-level impact and literate stakeholders needs. The operational-level success conditions correspond to cyber intelligence contributions to educated stakeholder needs. Tactical-level success conditions address cyber intelligence impact at the working level of IT operations and security and the performance of cyber intelligence practitioners.

Strategic Level	• Cyber threats are a component of the enterprise risk process • Literate stakeholders contribute to the requirements process • Regulators judge cyber intelligence capabilities to exceed standards
Operational Level	• Cyber intelligence has an executable strategy to address all of the issues identified in a specific plan • Cyber intelligence is a major input to information technology risk assessment processes • Cyber intelligence reporting is routinely causing educated consumers to submit requests of information or update intelligence requirements
Tactical Level	• Vulnerability management efforts are being prioritized by intelligence • Increased user reporting of suspicious email following awareness training that employed realistic threat actor tactics • Intelligence cued search finds malware on a network that should have been detected by anti-virus software

Table I.2 – Sample Success Conditions

(3) Measuring Cyber Intelligence Success as a Component of Customer and Practitioner proficiency Levels: This approach recognizes that cyber intelligence success requires all stakeholders to be proficient in their roles, and seeks to measure cyber intelligence outcomes in the context of the performance of all stakeholders.

Figure I.2 provides a visualization of this alternative method and addresses the interrelationship between intelligence customers' and practitioners' proficiency levels in a simple two by two matrix.

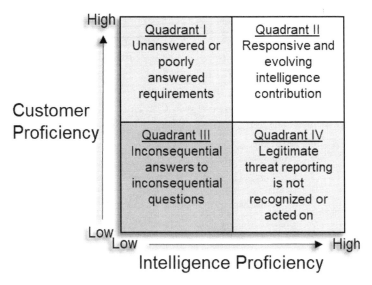

Figure I.2 – Intelligence Success Matrix

The variable "customer proficiency" on the y-axis is a composite measurement of how well the primary intelligence customers interacting with the intelligence team understand their operational needs, the threat environment, and the subtleties of the intelligence process. The variable "intelligence proficiency" on the x-axis is also a composite measure, and it addresses the intelligence team's knowledge of both their profession and the operations they are supporting, as well as their capabilities to perform their roles.

Beyond the Cyber Intelligence Fire Triangle

The second half of the book is focused on process and process improvement. One of the greatest challenges facing organizations acquiring cyber intelligence capabilities is how to apply those capabilities in a repeatable process in which tasks and stakeholder roles are defined and documented. The doctrinal intelligence process present in Chapter 1.3 is the closest thing to a universal standard for intelligence process in the world today, but it was developed for military intelligence operations in the physical world, and it was optimized to be run in large hierarchal organizations with deep process understanding. The doctrinal process is labor intensive; it does not scale well to smaller organizations, and it is difficult to maintain over long periods of time.

Section Four presents a simplified cyber intelligence process that maintains the essential elements of process flow and the discipline of the doctrinal process but with a reduced number of steps and fewer requirements for labor intensive documentation. The simplified process, which is also referred to as the 4E process, because the names of all four of its steps (establish, enable, execute, and evaluate) begin with the letter "e," defines clear and unique roles for each step and articulates tasks and subtasks associated with three lines of intelligence operation (information and intelligence acquisition management, planning and executing intelligence operations, and intelligence management) for each step. Table I.3 provides an overview of the 4E process.

Cyber threat actors and the threats they pose are dynamic, and organizations that are not improving and refining their cyber intelligence and IT security programs are losing ground. Section Five presents approaches for both sustaining and improving cyber intelligence capabilities. Topics include building an effective performance review cycle [*Chapter 5.1*], measuring performance [*Chapter 5.2*], employing advanced analytic frameworks [*Chapter 5.3*], leveraging intelligence as an operational function [*Chapter 5.4*], and advanced concepts [*Chapter 5.5*].

	Intelligence and Information Acquisition Management	Planning and Executing Intelligence Operations	Intelligence Management
Establish	Document what you know and what your customers need to know - consolidate and prioritize	Convert planning guidance, feedback, and learning into executable actions - document and assign actions	Evaluate the performance of management processes and refine/update them based on experience
Enable	Develop the tools and processes needed to acquire the threat data, information, and intelligence identified in the establish phase	Refine and document product and dissemination templates, warning problems, and preplanned responses	Produce workforce utilization targets, strategies for managing external partnerships, and metrics for measuring performance
Execute	Collect threat data, respond to alerts, conduct research, and track the performance of published requirements against customer expectations	Process and exploit threat data, analyze, produce, disseminate, and integrate intelligence	Manage analyst capacity, production activities, and external relationships; monitor KPIs, and both solicit and provide feedback
Evaluate	Review requirements process to measure performance and effectiveness; review/refine key performance indicators (KPIs), and conduct customer outreach	Assess intelligence impact on supported operations and decision-makers; conduct alternative and post event analysis, and update threat assessment product(s)	Evaluate the performance of existing performance measures, external relationships, return on investment, and process feedback; compile/share lessons learned

Table I.3 – 4E Process Overview

IT Security versus Cybersecurity

One of the issues that I struggled with at different points in writing this book was what naming convention to employ to describe the range of security functions that cyber intelligence exists to support. I defaulted to the traditional term "IT security" over the increasing popular term "cybersecurity" early in the drafting process, but I found myself questioning that decision at multiple points in the editing and prepublication review processes.

Given that a primary theme throughout the book is building and employing a precise professional lexicon, I felt compelled to do additional research on the two security terms to determine if there was an authoritative source for settling the naming issue. My research produced four findings worth sharing:

> (1) no authoritative definitions for either IT security or cybersecurity exist;
> (2) many of the definitions for IT security suggest that it is a synonym for information security;[1]
> (3) the term cybersecurity is still evolving – there is not even broad concurrence whether it is a compound word (cybersecurity) or two words (cyber security); and
> 4) one can cite sources that state that IT security and cybersecurity are interchangeable terms,[2] that cybersecurity is a subset of IT security,[3] and that IT security is a subset of cybersecurity.[4]

Falling back on my academic training, I concluded that I could choose whichever naming convention I wanted as long as I defined my terms. I chose to stick with my original decision to use IT security, and I chose to define IT security and cybersecurity as synonyms. I also added operational definitions for information security, IT security, and cybersecurity to Chapter 1.1 to provide readers with the definitions I used in this book.

---

[1] https://www.sans.org/it-security/
[2] https://usa.kaspersky.com/resource-center/definitions/what-is-cyber-security
[3] http://business.gmu.edu/blog/tech/2016/06/30/cyber-securit-it-security-difference/
[4] https://www.cisco.com/c/en/us/products/security/what-is-information-security-infosec.html

Section I
Understand Intelligence

Section Overview

This section addresses the first side of the cyber intelligence fire triangle, *"understand intelligence."* It introduces the essential knowledge elements for *"understand intelligence"* that must be present before any organization can hope to build a sustainable cyber intelligence capability focused on the threats of greatest consequence to that organization. At a macro-level, *"understand intelligence"* requires stakeholders to acquire a common understanding of four concepts: what intelligence is; what it can do; what processes must be performed; and what actions must take place to shape favorable outcomes. This section presents the critical knowledge elements required to convert that macro-level understanding into actionable cyber intelligence operations: a precise professional intelligence lexicon; specific roles cyber intelligence can perform; a defined and repeatable intelligence process to guide execution; and articulated stakeholder roles and responsibilities for shaping cyber intelligence outcomes.

Chapter 1.1 – *Intelligence Lexicon* develops an operational definition for the term cyber intelligence and presents definitions for twenty-six additional words and processes used by intelligence professionals and employed in the remainder of the book.

Chapter 1.2 – *Intelligence Roles* develops the three principal roles cyber intelligence can play in private sector organizations, and it provides readers with a successful model they can apply regardless of their industry or the maturity of their cyber intelligence program.

Chapter 1.3 – *The Doctrinal Intelligence Process* offers a high-level overview of the traditional six step intelligence process employed by most government agencies. The purpose of this overview is to introduce readers to the range of actions organizations must consider when designing/enabling end-to-end cyber intelligence operations.

Chapter 1.4 – *Literate Stakeholders* and Chapter 1.5 – *Educated Stakeholders* expand upon the stakeholder discussions in the introduction. The chapters are designed to assist individual stakeholders to acquire a better understanding of how they can contribute to successful cyber intelligence outcomes.

For Your Consideration

Given some years of experience, most thoughtful intelligence professionals will begin to recognize that there are a number of predictable and recurring constants present in intelligence operations that they can leverage to improve intelligence performance in both planning and execution. Building on the physical science analogy present in the cyber intelligence fire triangle, this introduction identifies five ubiquitous constants in intelligence operations that govern the art of the possible and presents them as the five laws of intelligence. The five laws of intelligence apply to cyber intelligence, and they provide stakeholders with a solid foundation for understanding the limits of intelligence that they need to account for in their planning and expectation setting processes.

Law One: Omniscience is Unattainable

This simple law governs all intelligence operations and is at once the least complicated concept in this book and the most frequently ignored in real-world application. The primary focus of effective cyber intelligence operations will be to predict future threats to one's networks and data. The future is always uncertain, and predicting future actions by people one does not know is never going to produce anything more accurate that "most likely" and "most dangerous" threat predictions. Leaders who develop comfort levels with what they can and cannot expect from cyber intelligence will consistently navigate the uncertainty with agility, while leaders who consistently holdout for more information will tend to be frustrated by and distrusting of intelligence.

This law drives the imperative for cyber intelligence stakeholders to identify and prioritize their threat concerns and intelligence needs in the form of intelligence and information requirements. Relevant and actionable requirements are only possible in organizations in which members of all stakeholder groups share an understanding of relevant threats and intelligence capabilities. A best practice for creating that shared understanding is for organizations to employ priority intelligence requirements (PIRs) to articulate the threat concerns that matter most to the organization, and to establish relative priorities among those concerns.

Law Two: Quality is Inversely Proportional to Speed

When a new threat or attack is first detected, the initial indicator represents only a small percentage of the information one will need to have to be able to understand fully what has occurred. Most intelligence reporting regimes place a high degree of importance on event notifications, which means that intelligence practitioners are obligated to report event indicators that are essentially unevaluated threats at the data level. This common practice has spawned the two great truisms of the intelligence profession: (1) "the first report is always wrong;" and (2) "if you want it bad, you get it bad."
Successful cyber intelligence outcomes require that all parties in the intelligence notification chain have the same context regarding what is being reported. A good starting point for most organizations would be to adopt Colin Powell's four-step approach for communicating intelligence accurately: "Tell me what you

know. Tell me what you don't know. Then tell me what you think. Always distinguish which is which."5

Law Three: Threat Actors Always get a Vote

There is an old military adage that no plan survives first contact with the enemy, and that adage is applicable to non-military situations as well. Competent threat actors will collect intelligence on intended targets, and they will apply the outputs of their intelligence to develop attack plans to take advantage of weaknesses they detect. Sophisticated threat actors will seek to be unpredictable so that even if their target detects their activity, they may not recognize it as being malicious in nature.

A good strategy for achieving successful cyber intelligence outcomes is to ensure that the cyber intelligence team develops potential threat actor courses of action that take into account the actors' capabilities and intentions. Actions supporting this process do not have to be terribly sophisticated or detailed; what they require is that analysts make an effort to analyze threats from the perspective of what information is likely available to threat actors and what decisions will make the most sense and provide the greatest benefit to those actors. As cyber intelligence capabilities mature, intelligence teams can cultivate more sophisticated approaches for developing increasingly accurate and detail courses of action that can drive better threat detection operations. [Chapter 5.3 presents two analytic frameworks readers will find useful as starting points for more advanced analytic efforts.]

Law Four: Failing to Plan is Planning to Fail

One of the prominent recurring themes in post-event analysis of successful cyber-attacks is that the victim organization had not engaged in contingency planning for the attacks they suffered. In

---

[5] Colin Powell, Opening Remarks before the Senate Governmental Affairs Committee on Intelligence Reform,
https://fas.org/irp/congress/2004_hr/091304powell.html September 13, 2004.

many cases, somebody in the organization had information that could have led to quicker recognition of the attack and more effective responses, but that person either did not know that information had value or they did not know who needed it.

A best practice for overcoming this problem is to leverage the threat actor courses of action (developed in Law Three) to drive contingency planning, which can be used to generate preplanned responses for cyber-attacks [addressed in Chapter 4.2]. In addition to developing threat scenarios that can be used for planning, cyber intelligence leaders need to develop collection, analysis, production, and dissemination plans for each scenario. High performing organizations will not only develop preplanned responses but will also develop practices for testing them with red teams or tabletop wargames. These testing venues can both validate contingency planning and identify gaps that constitute future IT risk.

Law Five – Irrelevant Questions Produce Irrelevant Answers

Cyber intelligence is a customer-driven business, and contrary to the old adage, the customer is not always right. Many newly established cyber intelligence teams share the problem of having large portions of their limited capabilities being diverted toward tangential lines of inquiry. Common examples of this behavior are demands for reporting of historic events and a misplaced emphasis on threat actor attribution. These behaviors not only divert cyber intelligence resources from more useful activities, they also generate products of dubious value to decision-makers engaged in actions designed to improve the organization's IT security environment. While unstructured intelligence tasking creates inefficiencies during normal operations, the real harm imposed by this approach occurs during stressing events, like an actual cyber-attack. Limited cyber intelligence capacity can easily become fully taxed responding to questions, the answers to which do not contribute to blocking the ongoing attack and preserving data for analysis to prevent future attacks.

There are a number of best practices organizations can employ to detect and eliminate the friction imposed by irrelevant demands. One proven approach is for the cyber intelligence team to build and maintain a product catalog and to have regular (at least quarterly) stakeholder review sessions to determine the return on investment of each product. Products should be rank ordered by educated stakeholders and a cut line should be drawn where available resources are fully consumed. Preplanned responses developed during contingency planning and refined by wargaming should include a list of PIRs for each class of contingency (e.g. data breach, ransomware attack, distributed denial of service attack). Those PIRs should be employed during the real-world events, and any questions not covered in the plan need to be vetted by the CISO or CIO prior to being assigned to the intelligence team.

Chapter 1.1
Intelligence Lexicon

Key Points

- Like all professions, the intelligence profession has a unique professional lexicon that enables people to communicate with a high degree of clarity and precision.
- This chapter presents the intelligence lexicon used throughout the book. That lexicon has five key components:
  - an operational definition for the term cyber intelligence;
  - a precise delineation between the words data, information, and intelligence;
  - a discussion of the awareness, knowledge, and understanding continuum;
  - definitions for terms employed in cyber intelligence operations; and
  - operational definitions of functions supported by cyber intelligence.

Stakeholder Roles

Literate Stakeholders	Educated Stakeholders	Intelligence Practitioners
• Demonstrate a deep understanding of the definition for cyber intelligence • Be able to apply the terms "critical organizational data and information" and "priority intelligence requirements"	• Demonstrate command of all of the definitions in this chapter • Be able to differentiate between the elements of the data/information/intelligence and awareness/knowledge/understanding continuums	• Master all of definitions and concepts of this chapter • Apply the correct words to convey precise meanings in all communications • Assist other stakeholders in mastering the lexicon

Context

The intelligence profession has a well-developed professional lexicon. Stakeholder mastery of the specific definitions of key words and terms in that lexicon and their ability to employ them in precise, two-way communications with other stakeholders are foundational requirements for competent cyber intelligence operations. This chapter presents a subset of the professional intelligence lexicon in broad use in most western militaries and intelligence services to provide readers with an intelligence dictionary for their use as a reference.

Developing an Operational Definition for Cyber Intelligence

One of the first things people seeking to acquire cyber intelligence capabilities will discover is that there is no single authoritative definition for cyber intelligence among people selling cyber intelligence products and services. The variation in definitions creates confusion and inhibits peoples' ability to share precise meanings. This section employs the old school academic construct of developing an operational definition for a term for which no authoritative definition exists. The operational definition developed for cyber intelligence in this chapter provides the standard definition used throughout the book.

The root word "intelligence" has two applications; it describes both the process and the output of the process of the same name. The operational definition for cyber intelligence developed in this chapter recognizes both.

US joint military doctrine writers provide the most universally quoted definition for intelligence in use today in the keystone joint intelligence doctrine document *Joint Publication 2.0* (JP 2.0). JP 2.0 defines intelligence as:

> *"the product resulting from the collection, processing, integration, evaluation, analysis, and interpretation of available information concerning foreign nations, hostile or potentially hostile forces or elements, or areas of actual or potential operations."[6]*

There are a couple of elements of this definition worth retaining in the operational definition: (1) intelligence is the product of a specifically defined process, and (2) intelligence specifically addresses threats. The weaknesses of this definition are that it uses a random series of process descriptors rather than a more rigorous process description and that it uses very nation-state/military centric descriptors of threat that do not translate well to private sector cyber intelligence operations.

As intelligence practices began being applied in private industry to deal with cyber threats, many organizations seeking to sell intelligence services developed unique definitions for intelligence to help describe their service offerings. Research found many different definitions for intelligence, but the most frequently cited was produced by the firm Gartner. Gartner's definition for threat intelligence is:

> *"evidence-based knowledge, including context, mechanisms, indicators, implications and actionable advice about an existing or emerging menace or hazard to assets that can be used to inform decisions regarding the subject's response to that menace or hazard."[7]*

The Gartner definition has currency, and it is widely cited by IT security writers in the media. In addition to its currency, the Gartner definition has the advantage of having been developed specifically to support the sales of products and services to private sector enterprises to support their efforts to mitigate cyber-threats.

---

[6] Joint Publication 2.0, Joint Intelligence, p. GL8.
[7] Gartner, Definition: Threat Intelligence, May 16, 2013.

That said, it has some real drawbacks. For instance, the word "knowledge" at the outset of the definition sets the bar pretty high for intelligence. Intelligence can create knowledge, but more often, it generates awareness that contributes to knowledge. In addition, the phrase "menace or hazard" seems to be a needlessly clumsy way to avoid using the word "threat." Lastly, Gartner's use of the word "actionable" has inadvertently created a false narrative among people in the cybersecurity field that suggests that analyzed threat information is not intelligence if it cannot drive a specific action. Like the use of the word knowledge, defining intelligence as actionable over promises and establishes unrealistic expectations for users. Cyber intelligence will consistently provide consumers with greater threat awareness, which can contribute to their ability to make better informed decisions regarding future actions to counter threats (i.e. threat-driven IT security operations), but it will seldom provide unambiguous actionable knowledge.

Building on the JP 2.0 and Gartner definitions, the following is the operational definition for cyber intelligence that will be employed for the remainder of the book:

Cyber intelligence is the output of a deliberately executed process of the same name that is designed to create threat awareness, knowledge and understanding. Cyber intelligence is the product of analysis of information created by the exploitation of data collected in response to vetted intelligence requirements. Cyber intelligence may enrich understanding of existing and/or identify new threats to one's networks and data or threats in the environment in which one operates.

Key Definitions in the Professional Intelligence Lexicon for People Engaged in Conducting Intelligence Operations

This section defines key intelligence terms used throughout the book.

Data/Information/Intelligence Continuum

Data: within this continuum, data is the output of the collection process, and as such it is unevaluated and single source; the term data is applied to representations of facts, concepts, or instructions in a structured manner so that they can be communicated, processed, and/or exploited.

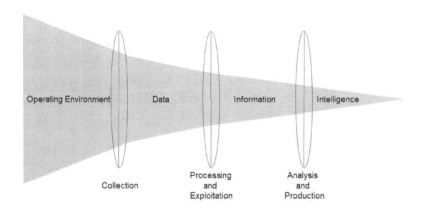

Figure 1.1.1 – Visualization of the Data/Information/Intelligence Continuum[8]

---

[8] Joint Publication 2.0, Joint Intelligence, 22 October 2013, p. I-2.

Information: within this continuum, information is the output of processing and exploitation of threat data – information is evaluated data that can be single source or can be correlated to other information; information can be actionable; it can create or increase knowledge, and it is a primary input to intelligence analysis.

Intelligence: Defined above.

Awareness/Knowledge/Understanding Continuum

Awareness: is the lowest level within the continuum – it conveys that the possessor has a perception of events or conditions but no ability to validate or apply those perceptions

Knowledge: is the middle level of the continuum – a person with knowledge has acquired information and has the ability to recall it – knowledge can be both theoretical and practical

Understanding: is the highest level of cognitive performance within the continuum – understanding is achieved when a person has a grasp or comprehension of information or intelligence to a level of proficiency that they can apply it

Intelligence Operations Definitions

Analysis: the process of converting processed and exploited information and previously produced intelligence into new intelligence – analysis encompasses a number of sub-tasks, among the most common of which are to evaluate, validate, integrate, interpret, and contextualize information [*See Section 4.3.2.2*]

Collection: the process of acquiring data in response to intelligence and information requirements

Collection Management: the process of converting intelligence requirements into collection requirements, establishing priorities, tasking or coordinating with appropriate collection sources or partner organizations, and monitoring collection results to adjust the collection plan in response to real-world performance. In more mature intelligence organizations, collection management is divided into two sub disciplines:

> **Collection Requirements Management (CRM):** addresses identifying what data needs to be collected to answer the questions being posed to cyber intelligence analysts by their stakeholders – actions conducted within CRM involve converting intelligence and information requirements into intelligence collection requirements, mapping those collection requirements to collection capabilities, and evaluating how well those actions address stakeholder needs [*See Section 4.2.1.2*]

> **Collection Operations Management (COM):** addresses tasking collection assets in response to requirements identified in the CRM process – actions may include updating logging requirements, deploying signatures to sensors, tasking network hunters, and submitting requests for information to partners to leverage externally accessible collection capabilities [*See Section 4.3.1*]

Collection Plan: a systematic scheme for optimizing available collection resources in a time phased approach to satisfy assigned intelligence and information requirements

Critical Organizational Data and Information (CODI): refers to data and information about the organization (its operations, products, services, people, and customers) of sufficient sensitivity or value that having it released outside the organization or losing access to it would impose significant consequences and/or costs – CODI is a private sector replacement for the military term *essential elements of friendly information*, and CODI should define the data and information that needs to be addressed by information classification policies

Dissemination: actions associated with delivering intelligence products to customers in manner that satisfies their requirements – dissemination actions will vary by product format, timeliness considerations, and available communications paths [*See Section 4.3.2.7*]

Essential Elements of Information (EEIs): are the most critical information requirements regarding threats that need to be addressed in collection planning – EEIs are normally formatted as questions and are derived in the CRM process by analyzing what actions might constitute indicators of activities relevant to addressing specifics PIR (defined below) [*See Section 4.2.1.1*]

Exploitation: human cognitive actions applied to data to convert it into information – dominant activities include correlation (associating/combining data on a single subject to improve the reliability or credibility of the information) and collation (identifying and grouping related items of information for critical comparison) [*See Section 4.3.2.1*]

Integration: actions designed to apply disseminated intelligence to previous awareness, knowledge, and/or understanding [*See Section 4.3.2.8*]

Intelligence and Information Acquisition Management (IIAM): encompasses all actions involving collecting, refining, and prioritizing intelligence and information requirements (customer-driven and internally identified), converting them into a format in which they can be applied to an intelligence collection process, and executing intelligence collection operations

Priority Intelligence Requirement (PIR): within cyber intelligence operations, PIRs constitute the organization's most important threat questions – PIRs define and prioritize the most critical questions that cyber intelligence operations must address, and they are vetted and approved by a person in the organization designated as the PIR approving authority – cyber intelligence practitioners may nominate changes to the approving authority, but only that person can make changes to the PIRs [*See Section 4.2.1.1*]

Production: actions that convert analysis into a format that can be disseminated to intelligence customers – intelligence products can range from highly polished peer reviewed papers and briefings at one end of the production spectrum to a phone call or text message at the other end [*See Section 4.3.2.6*]

Requests for Information (RFI): is a structured process by which intelligence stakeholders can ask questions about threats or about issues raised in intelligence products – RFIs are normally serialized and tracked to completion, and in most cases, they are not closed until the person who submitted the RFI acknowledges that the response they received satisfied their needs [*See Section 4.2.2.3*]

Operational Definitions for Functions Supported by Cyber Intelligence

The final section of the Introduction addresses the absence of authoritative definitions for the descriptors that are routinely employed to describe the collection of security disciplines cyber intelligence is generally assigned to support (e.g. information security, IT security, and cybersecurity.) The large number of and wide variance in existing definitions creates confusion and presents barriers to the development of the broadly recognized standards that are a prerequisite to the creation of impactful information and intelligence sharing programs. The following operational definitions both define the terms and the relationship between them within the body of this book:

Cybersecurity (aka Cyber Security): see IT Security below.

Defense In-Depth: is an approach to IT security that seeks to optimize cyber intelligence to detect, deter, and defeat actions by malicious actors by as many means as possible at multiple steps along a defined cyber-threat kill-chain. Defense in-depth begins with identifying the most likely actions threat actors will need to take from the moment they are motivated to attack one's organization to the point they have achieved their goals. It then applies that knowledge to maximize the number of opportunities cyber intelligence will have to detect indicators of malicious activity. Effective defense in-depth operations include application of IT security practices to shape the organization's attack surface in ways that increase the number and complexity of actions attacker must take so as to deter attacks and increase the likelihood of detecting attackers' actions. [*See Table 5.5.1.1*]

Information Security (InfoSec): is the professional discipline concerned with identifying and protecting the confidentiality, integrity, and availability of organizations' most important information (referred to in this book by the term CODI.) The InfoSec discipline is concerned with identifying information that requires protection, developing a classification schema for different categories of protected information, developing controls for each class of protected information, seeking to understand and address vulnerabilities (either through specific security actions or by accounting for vulnerabilities within a risk management framework), detecting and responding to and assessing damage from security incidents, providing InfoSec training to the workforce, and refining policies and controls in the face of changing threats. [*Important Note*: InfoSec is concerned with all CODI regardless of format, i.e. it is broader than the IT department and includes protecting information in physical formats by employing physical security and controls governing access and storage.]

Information Technology Security (IT Security): is the security discipline tasked with protecting endpoints, servers, networks, and data from a full range of malicious actions ranging from misuse through cyber-attacks. IT security, also called cybersecurity, applies people, technology, processes, and controls to protect the confidentiality, integrity, and availability of digital information identified by InfoSec. IT security employs a range of security approaches to include: security architecture, cyber intelligence, security operations, incident management (i.e. detect, respond, and recover), policy/training (e.g. user access, mobile devices, personal use), and IT security risk.

Threat-Driven IT Security Operations: are operations characterized by security decisions being made in anticipation of rather than in response to threats to one's networks and data. They are the byproduct of a deliberate decision to establish interdependent relationships between cyber intelligence as a supporting function and specific supported IT security functions. Threat-driven IT security operations leverage cyber intelligence generated awareness, knowledge, and understanding to focus finite security capabilities where they can have the greatest payoff.

Chapter 1.2
Cyber Intelligence Roles

Key Points

- Organizations seeking to align cyber intelligence operations to address the cyber-threats of greatest consequence to their operations must first understand the primary ways that cyber intelligence can contribute to enterprise and IT security.
- The three primary roles of cyber intelligence operations are:
    - Predictive Threat Warning
    - Threat Awareness
    - Support to Security Operations

Stakeholder Roles

Literate Stakeholders	Educated Stakeholders	Intelligence Practitioners
• Develop an understanding of the three roles and how they contribute to the organization's security posture	• Develop the skills to discuss cyber intelligence operations in the context of specific roles • Understand the best practices and challenges associated with each role	• Master all three roles • Individuals need to be able to maintain awareness of how they are contributing to each of the roles at any given time • Assist other stakeholders in maintaining context

Context

This chapter presents three primary roles for cyber intelligence for private sector organizations to consider:

- **Predictive Threat Warning:** intelligence actions focused on detecting and reporting changes in the threat environment that either directly threaten the organization or impact the threat calculus for the organization, the

industry in which it operates, its employees, customers, and/or suppliers
- **Threat Awareness:** intelligence actions designed to build and maintain situational awareness and understanding of threats in the operational environment in which the organization operates
- **Support to Security Operations:** intelligence operations driven by, and integrated into security functions of the IT security team that are designed to enhance the effectiveness of security operations

By defining intelligence roles in this manner, stakeholders will have a basis for understanding how their intelligence operations are driving the balance between current and future threat analysis by cyber intelligence practitioners. This kind of awareness is especially important in organizations with small intelligence teams and/or immature cyber intelligence capabilities, in which a single labor intensive task might consume all of the capability present in the organization.

This role-based taxonomy provides a useful approach for making informed decisions regarding how to increase cyber intelligence capabilities over time or to cease performing specific intelligence actions that do not enhance operations or security. Organizational intelligence needs evolve continuously, and each organization's needs are unique at any point in time. Organizations engaged in establishing new cyber intelligence practice will find that their intelligence needs exceed existing capacity to address those needs, while organizations seeking to improve existing capabilities will often find they do not have specific skills in their existing workforce. Leaders who understand the three primary roles have a basis for planning an evolutionary path that is best suited to their needs and culture. They can establish priorities among the roles, and focus on building core capabilities based on those priorities.

Primary Cyber Intelligence Roles

1. Predictive Threat Warning

Predictive threat warning encompasses intelligence activities referred to as indications and warning in traditional intelligence parlance. As the name implies, the role is concerned with providing advanced warning to cyber intelligence customers of changes in the threat environment that bear on the organization's security posture. Of the three roles described in this section, this is the most strategic and most challenging, because successful execution is directly related to active participation by senior leadership (both literate and educated stakeholders), and consistently successful outcomes require a high degree of organizational maturity.

A best practice for ensuring that predictive threat warning actions are aligned to threats of greatest concern is to develop and maintain PIRs. EEIs, developed by the cyber intelligence team by analyzing articulated PIRs, will guide cyber intelligence operations by identifying what the most critical indications of threat activity are and by developing collection and reporting strategies to ensure requirements owners are notified when events bearing on their requirements are detected. Both the substance of and the relative priorities among the intelligence requirements are dynamic, which means that maintaining effective intelligence requirements is a continuously ongoing process. The cyber intelligence leader will likely drive the requirements process in immature organizations, but their role should decrease as stakeholders become more comfortable with their roles and become more comfortable making process inputs and offering feedback.

(a) Best practices:

- No single factor plays a greater role in determining the effectiveness of cyber intelligence in this role than the quality of stakeholder driven PIRs. Organizations focused

by PIRs are far more likely to succeed than those who do not. [*The PIR process is presented in detail in subtask 4.2.1.1 of Chapter 4.2.*]
- Articulate a reporting matrix as a component of the requirements process to ensure that impacted stakeholders are notified in a timely fashion and in a reliable manner when relevant threat indicators are detected. The discovery of indicators that one's network is under attack is not the time to stop and ask the question; who do I need to tell?
- Mature intelligence teams will find that creating a finite number of intelligence warning problems is a useful, high payoff activity for defining intelligence actions for addressing enduring strategic threats. Intelligence warning problems are not only useful for helping to track ongoing actions, they also provide a good visualization tool for presenting where intelligence coverage is good and where gaps exist. [*Subtask 4.2.2.2 in Chapter 4.2 develops the concept of intelligence warning problems.*]

(b) Challenges:

- **Thinking Beyond Articulated Requirements:** Regardless of how much effort any organization expends on building and maintaining intelligence requirements the outputs will be imperfect. Threat actors always have a vote, and they will strive to be unpredictable; thus they will routinely change their tactics, techniques, procedures, and tools (TTPT) as a means of bypassing static security and unimaginative cyber intelligence operations. Cyber intelligence teams need to engage in practices designed to drive thinking about future threat actor behaviors not addressed in articulated intelligence requirements and to communicate their findings as a catalyst for updating requirements.
- **Respecting Ambiguity:** Intelligence operations rarely generated unambiguous indicators or the true intentions of

malicious actors, so analytic findings must be based on secondary indicators like the preponderance of evidence or the absence of data that should be present. Given that uncertainty is ever present, it is critical that the cyber intelligence team presents its analysis precisely and accurately. This is especially true in the high stakes role of predictive threat warning in which actions taken (or not taken) in response to intelligence have large potential costs. This need for accuracy reinforces the importance of stakeholder participation, not just in identifying the threats that matter to them, but also in becoming sufficiently well informed on cyber intelligence to be able to factor the ambiguity present in most time sensitive intelligence reporting into their decision making process.

2. Threat Awareness:

The threat awareness function encompasses a broad range of actions designed to ensure that key stakeholders understand the threats facing the organization (its employees, customers and partners) and the industry in which it operates. In contrast to predictive threat warning, which is focused on addressing evidence of future threats that are either targeting or likely to target one's organization, threat awareness employs a broader threat aperture designed to create awareness of current threat activities and emerging threat trends regardless of whether those threats pose any near-term danger to the organization. Consequently, threat awareness products are often great sources for refining intelligence requirements, but they seldom drive near-term changes in cyber intelligence or IT security operations.

The core functions associated with threat awareness are encompassed in what intelligence doctrine calls "current intelligence," but they also include elements of "general" and "scientific and technical intelligence." The purpose of threat awareness is to create a core group of well-informed stakeholders. Intelligence analysis and production activities in support of this role must be guided by stakeholders' intelligence and information requirements, but analysts engaged in threat awareness are not limited to addressing articulated requirements; they can and should report on all cyber threats they consider to be relevant, even if those threats are not responding to an existing requirement.

(a) Best practices:

- Whenever possible, analysts should employ multiple intelligence sources. When that is not possible, they should state clearly that the intelligence is single source, and they should cite source reliability based on previous reporting. Analysts must track reporting biases and potential conflicts of interest in reporting (e.g. malware analysis on a new malware variant was produced by an anti-virus company that has a product it is selling that can detect and block the threat.)
- Analysts should always provide context in their reports. They should address why the threat they reported is relevant and what it means to the customer.
- Cyber intelligence operations must be supported by knowledge management capabilities that allow analysts to access previous relevant reporting to add value and context to current reporting.
- Cyber intelligence operations should have a well-defined, easy to use RFI process that encourages stakeholders to ask questions.

(b) Challenges:

- **Production Management:** Threat awareness is a production intensive discipline, and production is the most time consuming and costly of all intelligence activities, so leaders must track production tasks and associated costs carefully. Leaders need to be cautious about establishing new intelligence products; they are easy to start but nearly impossible to stop. Products take on a life of their own, and they tend to develop product advocates within the intelligence team and among customers who will fight tooth and nail to maintain intelligence products beyond their useful lifecycles. [*Subtask 4.3.3.2 in Chapter 4.3 addresses production management in detail.*]

- **Content Management:** Once any organization decides to engage in scheduled production (i.e. daily and weekly intelligence products), the tyranny associated publishing deadlines can displace product content as the driving factor in intelligence production. Analysts tend fall into production routines, which over time increase the impact of practitioners' cognitive analytic biases (pet projects, self-interest, and over reliance on a narrow range of sources) that can reduce the credibility of intelligence products. Cyber intelligence leaders are accountable for conducting routine content management reviews and for creating working environments in which analysts are rewarded for seeking out new sources. [*Subtask 4.3.3.3 in Chapter 4.3 provides additional material on content management.*]
- **Vendor Management:** The threat awareness role is one that lends itself to being outsourced in part or in whole. Organizations desiring a daily cyber intelligence product prior to building an intelligence staff with sufficient critical mass to produce one can purchase products tailored to their industry and/or standing intelligence requirements for prices competitive with adding staff to perform the role. Human nature being what it is, the analyst behaviors present in the content management section above are also present in analysts working for vendors. Depending on the vendor and their customer service team, intelligence quality assurance on vendor products can be a time consuming task, but intelligence leaders who fail to perform that role can easily find their team being fully tasked responding to queries generated by reporting on threats of dubious relevance to their organization. [*Subtask 4.3.3.3. in Chapter 4.3 addresses management external relationships, including vendors.*]

3. Support to Security Operations:

Cyber intelligence is an application of intelligence to IT security, thus the people performing IT security functions are a critical customer set for cyber intelligence. Cyber intelligence actions supporting security operations tend be performed at a tactical-level, thus they emphasize technical intelligence skills. Tactical operations place greater value on threat information (i.e. the output of the processing and exploiting raw data) over finished intelligence (i.e. the output of all-source analysis.) Cyber intelligence operations performed in support of this role are designed to improve the efficiency and effectiveness of security operations. Examples include such things as: vulnerability management teams prioritizing patching based on an understanding of how malicious actors are leveraging vulnerabilities; detection teams being able to focus their efforts on specific known threat signatures; and security operations teams being able to differentiate between alerts that matter and background noise.

Intelligence support to security operations is unique among the three roles in that it is the only role in which many of the primary customers and the cyber intelligence analysts are peers aligned in the same organization. These factors generally simplify the requirements and the feedback processes, both of which are essential to success in this role. In addition, the tactical nature of this role means that a subset of the most critical threat information can be found on one's own network, meaning that some cyber intelligence customers are also cyber intelligence collectors.

(a) Best practices:

- Integrate intelligence and detection roles into an applied intelligence practice. This organizational approach ensures that intelligence is able to play a central role in security logging decisions and prioritizing what signatures are being applied to network sensors. The challenge in

this this organizational schema is finding a leader with a sufficiently strong knowledge of both areas. [*Chapter 5.4 develops the concept of applied intelligence and subsection 5.4.1 addresses the pros and cons of integrating intelligence and detection functions.*]
- Assign functional advocates from the intelligence team to each IT security area. This practice improves the speed and quality of updating customer requirements and feedback to intelligence and ensures that each security discipline has someone on the intelligence team that speaks their language and understands their unique challenges. This practice is only viable for intelligence teams that have at least as many members as they do supported security functions, and it can be difficult to implement in highly dispersed organizations, because its effectiveness is directly related to the trust generated in personal relationships.
- Build a hunt team. Network hunters are the best source for detecting malicious or anomalous/suspicious activity on one's own network. [*Chapter 5.4 develops the concept of network hunting in subsection 5.4.3.*]
- Schedule routine one-on-one meetings between the cyber intelligence leader and the leaders for each supported security discipline. The goal of the meeting is to ensure that the cyber intelligence leader learns about new tasking or shifting priorities in each security discipline and that he/she has an opportunity to discuss how those changes might impact intelligence support requirements.
- Develop two way metrics for each customer that allows both sides to grade each other's performance in a manner that creates greater understanding of the expectations of both teams in the relationship. This is difficult to do well, and it will only work if both intelligence and the supported security functions are at the same maturity level and the organization's culture values/rewards teamwork and continuous improvement.

- Develop a post-event analysis process for capturing and applying lessons learned from security events. Partner with the Computer Incident Response Team (CIRT) to understand what happened, what weaknesses were exploited, and how the security team performed, and apply that learning to improve cyber intelligence contributions to security operations. [*Subtask 4.4.2.4 in Chapter 4.4 addresses post-event analysis in detail.*]

(b) Challenges:

- **Process Maturity:** One of the primary challenges for cyber intelligence teams trying to maximize their impact on supported IT security functions is to figure out how to align cyber intelligence process maturity initiatives to their customers' ability to employ the outputs of those efforts. Figure I.2 in the introduction offers a good visualization of this challenge. Cyber intelligence that cannot be applied by supported IT security disciplines is wasteful, and organizations should avoid committing resources to such activities unless they are being used to drive improvements in the supported processes.
- **Team Trust:** Cyber intelligence analysis does not always provide the answer people want to hear, and changes to threat understanding can sometimes generate a lot of additional work for supported operations. Cyber intelligence analysts live in a world dominated by ambiguity, and they must strive to ensure that their products are intellectually honest and that they are not showing favoritism for one security discipline over another.
- **Going Native:** Young cyber intelligence analysts with technical IT skills, particularly those with previous experience in IT security jobs, can easily fall into their old comfort zones when they are assigned to support a specific IT security discipline. Security and intelligence professionals will often approach the same problems with

different mindsets, and this diversity in approach is a strength. Security outcomes are frequently enhanced by the creative tensions resulting from intelligence analysis that challenges existing security approaches by offering insights into how potential threat actors might view those approaches. Cyber intelligence leaders need to ensure that their intelligence analysts assigned to support IT security functions are thinking like intelligence professionals and sustaining useful creative tensions.

Chapter 1.3
Doctrinal Intelligence Process

Key Points

- The closest thing to a universal standard for planning and executing intelligence operations is published in US joint military intelligence doctrine.
- While the complexity of processes described in this doctrine limit their utility as a model for small scale cyber intelligence operations, the doctrine offers key insights into the actions and phasing/interrelationships between those actions that competent cyber intelligence operations must be able to perform.
- Intelligence is a customer-driven discipline, and customers drive favorable outcomes by providing well-conceived and relevant intelligence requirements that establish intelligence needs, and by offering thoughtful feedback at key points in the intelligence process.

Stakeholder Roles

Literate Stakeholders	Educated Stakeholders	Intelligence Practitioners
• Understand the cyclical nature of intelligence operations • Recognize the importance of senior leadership inputs in achieving successful results	• Understand both the cyclical nature of the intelligence process and the interrelationships/interdependencies between defined actions • Understand how to contribute to planning/problem definition	• Master the key concepts and associated lexicon/taxonomies • Understand and be able to communicate which process actions defined in the doctrinal process need to be retained to execute sustained cyber operations

Context

US military joint intelligence doctrine represents the closest thing there is to a universally recognized gold standard for intelligence operations in the world today. Doctrine presented in the keystone documents like Joint Publication 2.0 and Joint Publication 2-01 represent experience-based best practices that are continuously updated and subjected to extensive peer review by diverse groups of customers and practitioners prior to being published. No other similar body of work on intelligence exists in the public domain today.

Despite its many fine qualities, the doctrinal intelligence process does not lend itself to the kind of scalable and sustainable cyber intelligence operations that most private sector organizations require. <u>The discussion in this chapter is therefore intended to inform stakeholders about how this proven intelligence process works but is not intended to advocate for its adoption</u>. Section Four presents a simplified and scalable cyber intelligence process that respects the fundamentals of the doctrinal process.

In business parlance, military doctrine has more in common with best practices than it does with governance. Military leaders may choose to disregard some element of doctrine when planning or executing an operation if they judge that there is a better way to get the job done. They will be expected to explain their decision to senior commanders, particularly if it results in negative consequences, but they will not be subjected to a legal investigation for failing to comply with doctrine. This flexibility is an attribute that makes doctrine attractive as a baseline for informing organizations wishing to improve their intelligence processes, because it presents an a la carte menu of options that allows them to borrow what they want and disregard the rest.

Doctrinal Intelligence Operations

The term intelligence operations is used to describe activities defined by the intelligence process that produces intelligence (the product). Intelligence professionals world over employ a process in which intelligence needs define collection priorities; collected data is evaluated for applicability; applicable information is analyzed to produce intelligence that is then disseminated to appropriate customers, and customers provide feedback, ask questions, and update their requirements. Those actions have been codified into a six phase doctrinal process that is summarized in this chapter to provide readers with an understanding of the range of tasks involved in executing intelligence operations and the interrelationships and interdependencies between and among them.

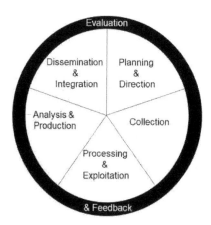

Figure 1.3.1 – The Intelligence Process[9]

Figure 1.3.1 is the standard visualization of the intelligence process from joint doctrine. Among intelligence professionals, the terms intelligence process and intelligence cycle are often used interchangeably. Intelligence cycle is the more traditional term,

---

[9] Joint Publication 2.0, Joint Intelligence, 22 October 2013, p. I.6.

and it emphasizes the interdependent cyclical nature of each phase to the process as a whole. The key takeaway from the figure is that intelligence operations require organizations to integrate multiple complex interdisciplinary steps into a single coherent and commonly understood process.

Phase One – Planning and Direction

Intelligence planning and direction is both the most complex and most important phase of the intelligence process. It is the phase in which organizational leaders develop, refine, and articulate their intelligence requirements, establish priorities among those requirements, and provide planning inputs to guide execution planning.

Doctrinal military planning is initiated by orders from a higher headquarters that assign the tasks that intelligence operations need to be able to support. Intelligence planners analyze the threat environment and engage their leadership in an interactive conversation designed to identify the leaders' top threat concerns and to develop high-level intelligence and information requirements. They also evaluate the resources they have to perform their assigned functions and develop plans for how to prioritize the allocation of those resources across the next four phase (e.g. a collection plan, a processing and exploitation plan, an analysis and production plan, and a dissemination and integration plan.)

Planning and direction actions do not cease when intelligence operations begin. Process participants need to engage in iterative performance reviews, with each planning iteration addressing performance issues discovered during execution. Performance shortfalls and customer feedback will drive changes in the various plans, while evolving operational needs and detected changes in the threat environment will drive refinements in intelligence and information requirements.

Private sector organizations with no previous experience working with intelligence will find this first phase incredible difficult. [*Note: Challenges associated with this phase provided much of the incentive for developing the simplified intelligence process presented in Section Four.*] The primary challenge will be that of defining the problems to be solved and establishing priorities among them. Unlike the military, which has a higher headquarters to define roles and tasks, private sector organizations must identify those things on their own. Work required to refine processes in this phase will likely be very time consuming until the organization's cyber intelligence team is fully in place and is able to establish sustainable operations.

In practice, most military organizations have historically struggled to sustain necessary levels of effort for actions associated with this phase over long periods of routine operations. A considerable amount of effort is needed to maintain plans created in this phase, and the majority of critical inputs need to come from people who are not on the intelligence team and are fully engaged doing other important work. There is a tipping point at which there is insufficient stakeholder participation to sustain this process, and most organizations reach that tipping point fairly quickly.

Phase Two – Collection

The collection phase encompasses the range of activities used to acquire data relevant to addressing questions posed in intelligence and information requirements. This phase has traditionally included both the collection management and execution processes, but in some recently published doctrine, management functions have been pushed back into the previous phase for large organizations.

Collection management activities are divided into two disciplines:

- **Collection Requirements Management (CRM):** CRM consolidates all intelligence and information requirements and translates them into questions that can be answered through the collection process. Questions designed to guide collection to address PIRs are called essential elements of information (EEIs). People conducting CRM will also engage customers to help them revise requirements that are judged to have a low likelihood of being satisfied in the collection process. Figure 1.3.2 provides a flowchart for the CRM process.

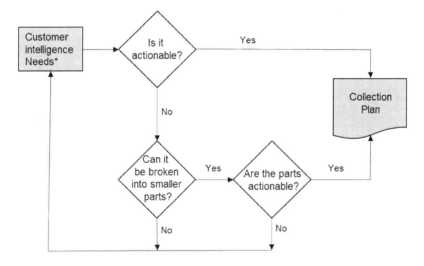

* The term needs covers the full range of requests from PIRs to RFIs

Figure 1.3.2 – The Collection Requirements Management Process

- **Collection Operations Management (COM):** Within the context of this book, COM is a pretty fluid concept. Tasks used to measure COM in current doctrine focus exclusively managing sensors and sensor platforms in the physical world, and in many cases there are no good direct analogs for applying those processes to the cyber domain. That said, COM is a valid construct in the cyber world where it will deal with things like what security data gets logged, what threat signatures need to be active in the sensor grid, and what conditions should trigger alerts. Private sector organizations can use COM to measure the potential impact of acquiring threat data from external sources by identifying whether perspective partnerships or vendor service offerings will provide access to threat data that the organization either cannot collect or cannot collect for the cost of buying it.

Intelligence collection management is among the most highly sophisticated disciplines within intelligence operations. Competent execution demands that practitioners fully understand the deeper questions behind the intelligence and information requirements processes guiding their efforts and that they have a mastery of the actual capability of all available collection systems. Few private sector cyber intelligence teams will be large enough to sustain a designated collection management team, meaning that CRM functions will tend to default to the leadership team, and COM functions will tend to be performed by intelligence analysts.

Phase Three – Processing and Exploitation

Processing describes actions to convert data collected in the collection phase into formats that can be read by humans. Exploitation encompasses a range of actions applied to the data (e.g. decrypt, organize, translate, collate, and/or correlate) by intelligence analysts, the output of which is information. Exploited information can be consumed by intelligence customers as threat information, and it can serve as source material for additional analysis.

This phase is consistently the least understood phase in the intelligence process, which means it is frequently undervalued or ignored. The distinction between exploitation and analysis is useful in intelligence operations. Exploitation involves evaluating data from a single source and deciding whether the data indicates a need for additional actions (e.g. collection, notification, or analysis), whereas analysis seeks to employ multiple sources and is concerned with context and meaning to the organization.

Processing and exploitation actions are key to success in private sector cyber intelligence operations. A practical example would be, an alert (established in the COM step) triggering in the security information and event management (SIEM) console in a security operations center (SOC). The SIEM processes threat data and the alert informs the console operators that an event of interest to the intelligence team has been detected. Actions by the console operator to investigate the source of the alert or an intelligence analyst notified of the alert constitute exploitation.

Phase Four – Analysis and Production

During this phase information generated in the previous phase is converted into intelligence (analysis) and arranged in a format requested by users (production). Analysts integrate new threat information, and they evaluate, analyze, and interpret the new information within their existing understanding and within the context of organizational intelligence requirements. The resulting intelligence is then packaged in accordance with user desires (e.g. slide, brief, paper, email) so it can be disseminated in next phase.

Given that intelligence is the byproduct of analysis, many people will argue that this is the most important phase of intelligence operations, but a more accurate way to characterize it would to say that this is the phase that all of the other phases support. Regardless of how one characterizes it, analysis is the core skill set of intelligence, and one of the primary management challenge for intelligence leaders will be to ensure that analyst capacity is not siphoned off into less important activities.

Analysis best practices include: seeking to fuse information from all available sources (all-source fusion); looking for alternative hypotheses and for information that should be present but is not; contextualizing analytic findings to the supported organization's operations and intelligence requirements; and assessing future implications of newly generated intelligence. Production encompasses a pretty straight forward set of activities, but it can also be the most time consuming intelligence activity for analysts. Cyber intelligence leaders need to manage production requirements carefully to ensure that analysts can maintain a healthy balance between analysis and production activities.

Phase Five – Dissemination and Integration

During this phase intelligence is delivered to the customer (dissemination) and applied to existing intelligence products and threat databases to update knowledge and analytic resources (integration).

Dissemination is the final critical step for intelligence providers; it determines whether relevant intelligence is delivered to the people who most need it. Dissemination planning should be a core component of production design, and well-crafted intelligence and information requirements will include a list of stakeholders who need to be informed when elements of those requirements are satisfied. Operational culture, technology, data handling and classification programs are all important variables in dissemination planning.

Intelligence analysts are responsible for overseeing integration of new intelligence into analytic working aids and standing threat products. Organizations with mature knowledge management practices will generally find integration tasks easier to manage than organizations lacking those capabilities.

Phase Six – Evaluation and Feedback

Performance evaluation and feedback should be continuously ongoing throughout the intelligence process. Every person involved in the intelligence process should provide feedback to the people who precede them and seek feedback from the people who receive their outputs.

Evaluation and feedback is often the most difficult phase for organizations to do well. Measures of effectiveness for intelligence activities are difficult to develop and can often produce ambiguous results. This means that to the extent that most organizations engage in intelligence performance evaluation, their efforts tend be subjective. Feedback also tends to be both emotional and erratic. Intelligence customers tend to be very busy people, and many are reluctant to offer feedback because they are insecure in their understanding of intelligence and are afraid that they will highlight their lack of depth by asking "stupid" questions or suggesting illogical changes.

Cyber intelligence operations that are integrated into defined IT security processes have the potential to do far better with evaluation and feedback than traditional intelligence operations. Intelligence contributions to specific security goals lend themselves to performance measurement, and many key cyber intelligence customers will be peers working in same office rather than senior executives at some distant location.

Chapter 1.4
Literate Stakeholders

Key Points

- Literate stakeholders are people outside of the IT organization who are accountable for creating the conditions under which safe and secure IT operations can be performed.
- Literate stakeholders need to understand how cyber intelligence can contribute to reducing IT and enterprise risk.
- The six primary groupings of people who will be classified as literate stakeholders are:
    - C-level executives
    - Privacy and external relationships
    - People engaged in procurement, vendor selection and management, and supply chain management
    - Business development teams
    - Fraud teams
    - People with the authority to execute financial transactions

Stakeholder Roles

Literate Stakeholders	Educated Stakeholders	Intelligence Practitioners
• Understand individual roles and associated top knowledge objectives and best practices	• Understand the unique challenges for the six groups with sufficient depth to be able to play a constructive role in bridging between cyber intelligence practitioners and literate stakeholders	• Understand the interactions with the six groups identified in the chapter • Develop cyber intelligence practices that respect the challenges literate stakeholders face

Context

This chapter builds a construct for defining who literate stakeholders are, what they need to know about cyber intelligence, and what responsibilities they have.

Literate stakeholders are people outside of the IT organization who are accountable for creating the conditions in which safe and secure IT operations can be performed. In most organizations, the preponderance of cyber intelligence literate stakeholders will be drawn from six groups:

1. C-level executives who are accountable to a board, stockholders, regulators, and/or the people who work for them for the standards and integrity with which they run their organization;
2. Privacy and external relationships addresses actions by people, primarily in the legal and human resources departments, who establish and oversee policies that impact key data, personal privacy issues, and external relationships that have the potential to generate unintended consequences for cyber intelligence operations;
3. People engaged in procurement, vendor selection and management, and supply chain management, who are involved in decisions that define partners with whom the organization shares data;
4. Business development people whose work will shape future operations;
5. Fraud teams; and
6. All employees with the authority to execute financial transactions, because they are primary targets of social engineering and fraud.

Literate stakeholders need to have a macro-level understanding of how cyber intelligence operations work, what cyber intelligence capabilities their organization has in place, how to communicate their needs and concerns to the cyber intelligence team, and what the primary cyber threats facing the organization are and how they manifest themselves. They need to understand when decisions they make have the potential to alter the IT security dynamic, and they need to hold themselves accountable when their decisions generate greater IT and/or enterprise risk.

1. C-Level Executives

In the aftermath of the succession of costly, high profile cyber-attack in the retail, health care and financial sectors in the 2013/2014 timeframe, executives outside of IT have been increasingly held accountable for the actions they took (or more frequently did not take) regarding their organization's resilience in the face of the successful attacks on their networks and data. Despite this trend, many organizations today continue to make decisions on future operations without regard to how those decisions might impact the ability of the their IT staff to secure their networks or how their actions might be viewed by potential threat actors.

Responsible leaders, however, recognize that IT security is an essential element of any successful operation, and they will find ways to factor threats to their networks and data into enterprise risk models. These leaders will become increasingly reliant on having cyber intelligence capabilities in place that can identify threats and threat trends to help inform risk calculus and to inform their decision-making process, but few will have the time necessary to develop deep cyber intelligence expertise. Senior executives need to establish a precedent that threat understanding is an important component of operational planning and hold their leadership teams accountable for being informed.

Top knowledge objectives for C-level executives to be effective literate stakeholders include:

1. **Know that they are targets** – Malicious actors routinely target senior executives to gain access to their accounts as a means of acquiring insider information, and for gaining information they can apply for social engineering.
2. **Know that their organization is being targeted continuously** – There is an emerging conventional wisdom that there are only two kinds of organizations with regard to cyber threats, those that know they have been attacked and those that have not detected the fact that they are under attack. That kind of paranoia is healthy for senior executives.
3. **Know that they can identify and prioritize threat concerns** – Routine PIR generation and review will generally be conducted at the educated stakeholder level, but senior leaders need to know that PIRs exist, what they are, and how they drive cyber intelligence actions.
4. **Know how they can contribute to creating and refining PIRs** – C-level executives have unique perspectives by virtue of their positions and experience, and when those perspectives deal with threat concerns, leader need to know how to go about getting those concerns documented within the intelligence and information requirements processes.
5. **Be conversant in the basic intelligence lexicon** – Consistent with the term literacy, C-level executives performing as literate stakeholders need to have a sufficiently firm understanding of the intelligence lexicon to be able to grasp the subtle nuances of tasking cyber intelligence operations and to understand intelligence products that they consume.
6. **Establish a working knowledge of the common threat framework** – C-level executives should also achieve a working knowledge of the threat framework [*Chapter 2.1*] that enables them to understand the different classes of threat actors, their motivations, threat characterizations, and intended effects. This level of knowledge will enable them to

participate in constructive discussions regarding future threats and how to combat them.
7. **Know the laws of intelligence** – The laws of intelligence presented in the introduction to this section bound the art of the possible, and people who understand them will be superior stewards of their cyber intelligence capabilities.

Best practices to consider are:

1. **Establish regular threat updates** – C-level executives need to maintain a minimum level of threat understanding to be proficient in their roles. Methods for attaining that understanding can vary widely, but it is never a bad idea to ask for threat updates specifically tailored to senior leaders. Establishing a regular update process will enable all participants to achieve a common frame of reference regarding the threats of greatest consequence.
2. **Ask for the bad news** – Every level of review between the cyber intelligence analysts preparing a piece of analysis and the person communicating that analysis will tend to soften bad news, highlight positive events, and become technically less correct. Senior executives who are able to develop mechanisms to combat these tendencies will move their threat understanding closer to ground truth, and to communicate to their subordinates that they want to hear the truth.
3. **Ask other C-level executives what they think about threat reporting** – One of the best ways to cultivate the attributes of a knowledgeable consumer is to seek out insights from one's peers. It offers one valuable insights while encouraging one's peers to consume intelligence products and to think about cyber-threats.

2. Privacy and External Relationships

Two areas where engaged and informed literate stakeholders can enhance cyber intelligence success are creating policies that balance employee rights with employee responsibilities, and defining information sharing policies that balance responsibilities to protect critical organizational data and information with the benefits accrued to organizations that can participate in threat sharing relationships with external partners.

The threat framework presented in Chapter 2.1 identifies insiders as one of the four groups of cyber threat actors undermining network security and data integrity. Insider threat actors are among the least understood threat actor groups because they are a difficult target on which to collect. Skillful insiders can gain legitimate access to data by knowing how to manipulate the rules that govern gaining restricted accesses, and their actions are difficult to detect because they are protected by the appearance of legitimacy. As organizations have increasingly allowed employees the ability to access work networks from personal devices and to access personal accounts on work devices, insiders have been given new capabilities to obscure their illicit behaviors. Policies designed to create worker friendly environments and to protect workers' rights have had the unintended consequences of protecting employees engaged in malicious activities. Leaders charged with keeping organizations in compliance with privacy laws and for designing and executing policies involving workers' rights need to make concerted efforts to understand how insiders are doing harm so that they can play a constructive role in refining policies that protect workers without creating unnecessary restrictions on the ability of IT security teams to collect data to support detecting insider threats. Well-crafted consent agreements for users accessing the network should enable security actions without threatening legitimate privacy issues.

The issue of defining enlightened information sharing policies with respect to external partnerships is a second area where an engaged and knowledgeable legal team can empower cyber intelligence capabilities while protecting organizational data. Legal teams that have not worked with cyber intelligence will tend to view external sharing relationships from the perspective of their potential to expose sensitive data without recognizing their potential for providing greater threat understanding. Legal teams tend to view their role in reviewing the range of agreements used to govern relationships and employee behaviors within those relationships as an opportunity to limit risks associated with employees sharing information of both intrinsic and financial value. This approach often results in checks and balances that limit organizational participation to a point that the organization ceases to derive meaningful benefits from participating in the relationship. Lawyers charged with reviewing artifacts associated with intelligence sharing agreements must possess a sufficient level of knowledge of cyber intelligence to be able to recognize the potential intelligence gains those agreements represent before they begin placing limits on analyst participation.

Top knowledge objectives for literate stakeholders in this category include:

1. **Acquiring threat understanding** – Policy makers need to acquire a working knowledge of the threat matrix [*Chapter 2.1*] and an understanding of current threats and trends bearing on future threats within the context of the threat matrix. This level of understanding will allow them to make better informed risk-based decisions.
2. **Understanding the organization's in-house intelligence collection capabilities** – Informed decisions addressing external relationships will be centered on improving cyber intelligence practitioners' access to threat data. Literate stakeholders who understand what capabilities already exist will be better prepared to weigh the value additional capabilities might bring.
3. **Mastering data classification schema** – Most organization have multi-tiered data classification schema that define classes of organizational data requiring handling safeguards and defining what those safeguards are. Privacy and external relationship policies should be aligned with established data classification policies to provide consistency in developing policy guidance regarding cyber intelligence practices for data collection, retention, and sharing.

Best practices to consider are:

1. **Establish regular program reviews** – Threats and threat actors continuously evolve, and programs designed to address threats will need to be updated at regular intervals. Establishing regular program reviews will allow decision-makers to view their decisions in the context of their impacts on real-world operations.
2. **Adopt a "how can I say yes" approach** – Literate stakeholders engaged in developing policies designed protect workplace privacy rights and external relationships have responsibilities to be honest brokers and to resolve conflicts between parties. The path of least resistance in many instances will appear to be limiting cyber intelligence access to internal threat data and restricting the scope of external relationships, which mean "no" is the easiest answer to requests to expand cyber intelligence authorities. A deeper examination of the facts, however, will frequently result in a determination that potential returns far outweigh risks. That analysis will only take place in cultures in which literate stakeholders' default position is "I want to say yes; provide me with the data and analysis to let me do so."

3. Procurement and Vendor Management

In a world of just-in-time logistics and automated supply chains, many third party business relationships involve granting various network accesses to the external companies providing the contracted service. Ironically, the level of scrutiny described in the cyber intelligence sharing relationship process is not always matched by people reviewing decisions to allow external parties to have network access. Given that the chain is only as strong as the weakest link, the process of granting network access to third parties lowers the effectiveness of one's network security to the level of the least proficient practitioner among one's vendors.

Cyber intelligence should play a role in the risk assessment process for all external relationship in which parties will be granted access to the organization's network, even if that access is nothing more than a finite number of email accounts. The executives overseeing these processes need to achieve a level of threat understanding that will enable them to recognize risk for what it is.

Top knowledge objectives for literate stakeholders in this category include:

1. **Acquiring threat understanding** – Professionals working the various aspects of procurement and vendor/supply chain management need to have a healthy understanding of threats to both their own organization and the industry(s) in which it operates and to the organizations with whom they are contracting and the industries in which they operate.
2. **Gain a historical perspective on threats presented by third party relationships** – Malicious actors routinely employ third party relationships as a threat vector for gaining unauthorized access to targeted networks. People engaged in developing those relationships need to be aware of how relationships have been successfully exploited in the past so that they do not build known vulnerabilities into new relationships.

Best practices to consider are:

1. **Publish a relationship fact guide** – In all cases in which partners are extended privileges to access or connect to one's network, threats to one's partners become threats to one's network. The cyber intelligence team needs to know what external actors have privileges, what those privileges are, and what controls have been put in place to mitigate identified risks.

4. Business Development

People whose roles involve mergers, acquisitions, divestitures, and partnerships in the current cyber-threat environment need to have a high level of threat understanding and need to understand how to engage cyber intelligence for tailored threat products. Any of these actions can create a new threat profile for the organization by adding or subtracting capabilities, people, and systems. Furthermore, cyber-threat actor groups generally view uncertainty and organizational disruptions as fertile ground to apply their craft, so targeting of affected organizations will increase once proposed actions become public.

In publicly held companies, or companies going public, major business transactions involving mergers, acquisitions, divestitures, or partnerships will be conducted in great secrecy. There are few scenarios in which assigning a cyber intelligence analyst early in any process makes sense, but the business development team should consider tasking cyber intelligence to produce assessments covering relevant threats, and if threats merit additional attention, they should assign a senior cyber intelligence analyst to the team and have that person execute the necessary non-disclosure agreements to be brought into the process.

Top knowledge objectives for literate stakeholders in this category include:

1. **Acquire threat understanding** – Professionals working on major business transactions need to have a healthy understanding of threats to their own and future partners' organizations and to the industry(s) in which they operate.
2. **Gain a historical perspective on partners** – Before entering into a relationship with an organization that is likely to involve network and employee integration, planners should seek to determine whether their perspective future partners have a history of IT security related incidents and cyber-attacks. Organizational culture and employee buy-in are often determining factors in proficient network defense, and should therefore to be factors considered in future relationships.

Best practices to consider are:

1. **Develop a framework for identifying relevant threat questions** – With some advanced planning, the business development team can task the cyber intelligence team to create a generic threat assessment that they can use to identify potential threat issues they need to address without bringing a cyber intelligence person into the circle of trust. This framework can be used multiple times and can be refined with experience.
2. **Develop a proficiency for employing the cyber intelligence RFI process** – RFIs are the simplest way for stakeholders to ask relevant questions. Mature cyber intelligence organizations will designate individual analysts to assist customers in stating their RFIs in a manner that can increase the likelihood of producing a successful response. In all cases, having a relationship with the cyber intelligence team and understanding their processes and competing tasking will help customers to improve their own outcomes.

5. Fraud Teams

IT networks and the data they store, process, and transport are targets for people committing frauds and enablers of fraud. Fraud is frequently the means by which malicious cyber-threat actors monetize data they have stolen from organizations they attacked. Dynamic interaction between fraud teams and cyber intelligence teams is mutually beneficial. Cyber intelligence practitioners should be able to leverage improved understanding of threat actor TTPTs into refined intelligence collection strategies, and better targeted collection should increase the ability of organizations to detect evidence they are being targeted or attacked.

Fraud teams are a bit of an outlier among the groups of literate stakeholders. Their role requires them to have a far greater depth of understanding of cyber intelligence processes than any other group. Fraud teams need to have well-defined and near continuous relationships with the cyber intelligence team, and they need to have a firm understanding of day-to-day tactical intelligence processes.

Top knowledge objectives for literate stakeholders in this category include:

1. **Understanding Intelligence and Information Acquisition Management (IIAM)** – Fraud team members need to understand both the processes by which intelligence professionals manage intelligence and information requirements and how they collect data relevant to addressing those requirements.
2. **Understand key cyber intelligence gaps** – All cyber intelligence teams will have gaps in their ability to gain access to threat data, information, and intelligence. Fraud teams often have access to information that can address or mitigate the impact of intelligence gaps, so understanding what those gaps are creates opportunities for the fraud team to contribute to cyber intelligence and IT security.

Best practices to consider are:

1. **Establish a regular coordination process** – Fraud and cyber intelligence teams have unique sources that often provide insights that would be useful to people on the other team, and both will benefit from opportunities to share information and to create a better understanding of what information the other team values.

6. Employees Authorized to Execute Funds Transfers

Over the last several years, sophisticated cybercrime actors have evolved beyond targeting customer accounts and transactions to targeting organizations' payment systems. The most common vulnerabilities targeted in these crimes are those associated with human behavior, and the targets are the people responsible for executing financial transactions. Most attacks involve some form of social engineering designed to persuade or compel their targets to take actions that support the attackers' objectives. The business email compromise (BEC) scam [*addressed in Chapter 2.2*] represents a family of frauds that employ social engineering to convince employees to transfer large sums of money to support a special project for the CEO or CFO or that request changes in account numbers for paying legitimate invoices. Businesses and nonprofits world over have lost billions of dollars to variations of the BEC scam, and the scam continues to work because very few organizations have taken the time to train the people they trust to conduct their financial transactions about the BEC and the variety of threats to the payment systems they operate.

Top knowledge objectives for literate stakeholders in this category include:

1. **Understand threats to payment systems** – All people authorized to execute financial transactions on behalf of the organization should be trained on how to recognize frauds, social engineering, and anomalies in their processes or processing system that might suggest something is amiss.

Best practices to consider are:

1. **Conduct targeted phishing exercises** – Organizations should follow up training with phishing exercises designed to create greater awareness of social engineering threats to people who conduct financial transactions.
2. **Establish a dissemination list for threats to payment systems** – Cyber intelligence will routinely encounter reports addressing threats to payment systems, wire transfer networks, and point-of-sale devices. Organizations with a pathway for disseminating that intelligence to the people most likely to be targeted by the threats will have a means for

creating greater threat awareness among likely targeted employee population.

Chapter 1.5
Educated Stakeholders

Key Points

- Educated stakeholders are IT professionals whose positional responsibilities require them to have a solid working knowledge of cyber intelligence processes and a command of the lexicon employed by cyber intelligence professionals.
- Most IT functions can employ increased threat understanding as a means to improve their effectiveness.
- Some functions require near continuous interactions, while others will have event driven interactions with cyber intelligence.
- Educated stakeholders are the primary customers of cyber intelligence and are the primary sources of input to intelligence and information requirements processes.

Stakeholder Roles

Literate Stakeholders	Educated Stakeholders	Intelligence Practitioners
• Understand the challenges facing educated stakeholders and how top-down driven organizational decisions will impact their ability to drive successful cyber intelligence outcomes	• Individuals need to understand their roles and how to build constructive relationships to drive successful outcomes	• Recognize the unique needs of different educated stakeholder groups • Seek to tailor cyber intelligence processes to help educated stakeholders to play their roles

Context

Educated stakeholders consist of IT professionals, specifically Chief Information Officers (CIO), Chief Information Security Officers (CISO), Chief Technology Officers (CTO), and individuals in positions that report directly to one of the key IT leaders. Educated stakeholders need to have a solid working knowledge of cyber intelligence processes and command of the intelligence lexicon. They are responsible for playing an active role in articulating and prioritizing the intelligence requirements that will drive cyber intelligence operations, and they must provide feedback and create the cyber intelligence performance standards they expect to be met. In addition, they need to recognize when organizational decisions have the potential to change the organization's attack surface, and they need to be able to articulate associated risks accurately.

Given the absence of standardization in IT organizational alignment, roles and functions addressed in this chapter have been kept fairly generic. The chapter begins with addressing four educated stakeholder roles: the CIO, the CISO, the CTO, and a CISO direct report assigned to lead the cyber intelligence effort. It then addresses IT processes that require routine interaction with cyber intelligence, followed by IT processes that will have periodic and event-driven interaction with cyber intelligence. While the supporting discussions focus on the leaders reporting to the CIO, CISO, and CTO (referred to as process owners), one can make a strong argument for the position that all IT professionals working in any of the identified processes need to acquire the knowledge and skills associated with being educated stakeholders.

IT Leadership

For the purposes of this discussion, IT leadership refers to the CIO, CISO, and CTO positions. This approach is not intended to be disrespectful to people filling emerging roles like chief data officers and chief analytic officers; cyber intelligence teams will view people in those positions as highly valued partners and educated stakeholders, but it is too early to define relationships and best practices for those roles at this point. People in those positions can apply the relevant elements of the roles and best practices of the three positions covered in this discussion.

The CIO Position

CIO roles, responsibilities, and knowledge requirements for cyber intelligence will vary from one organization to the next. CIOs charged with running IT organizations that represent profit centers or which are sources of revenue will be responsible for a range of activities that a CIO running a cost center will not have. CIOs whose portfolios include IT security and who have CISOs reporting to them will engage more directly with cyber intelligence than will their counterparts in organizations in which the CISO is a peer rather than a direct report. Their time investment, however, will be a function of the proficiency of their CISO and their cyber intelligence teams, and their expectations for cyber intelligence operations. CIOs with strong CISOs and cyber intelligence leaders and who have realistic expectations for the art of the possible will rarely feel the need to engage in day-to-day management of cyber intelligence operations.

A primary role for all CIOs is to organize and align IT capabilities with their organization's primary operational/business functions. To perform that role effectively, CIOs will need to possess a high degree of understanding of threats to their networks and data, regardless of whether the IT security portfolio is aligned under them or not. They need to understand risks and cost associated with decisions that have impacts on IT security, including when those decision might inhibit the effectiveness of cyber intelligence operations. As the principal advocate for IT within the C-suite, CIOs play a critical role in establishing an environment in which threat awareness is a component of the risk calculus applied to enterprise-level decisions. They also need to be advocates for greater threat awareness, both in the C-suite and among all IT users.
In order to execute their responsibilities, CIOs will need to invest a sufficient level of effort to be able to maintain good situational awareness of threats to their organization and industry, and they will also need to acquire sufficient understanding of their cyber intelligence organization's processes to be able to recognize when proposed changes to their organization's operations and/or

policies will negatively impact those operations. Most CIOs will find value in maintaining awareness of their CISO approved PIRs serving as the centerpiece of intelligence operations.

Best practices CIOs should adopt:

1. Drive the operational design process defined in Chapter 3.3
2. Become honest brokers for the laws of intelligence [*Section One Introduction*] in their interactions in the C-suite
3. Actively consume cyber intelligence situational awareness products
4. Participate in developing and updating strategic-level PIRs

The CISO Position

CISOs will generally be assigned the responsibility for overseeing cyber intelligence operations and integrating those operations into their security portfolios. They play a critical role in extending cyber intelligence capabilities to non-security related IT processes executed by CIO direct reports. As is the case with CIOs, CISO roles and responsibilities can vary considerably among different organizations. CISOs who have designated cyber intelligence leaders aligned directly under them will have significantly more daily interaction than those who have aligned their cyber intelligence portfolio under an incident manager or security operations leader.

Regardless of organizational alignment, CISOs need to play a leadership role in overseeing the PIR process and driving performance metrics, and they need to become critical consumers of cyber intelligence products. CISOs also play an important role in driving the integration of cyber intelligence capabilities into IT security operations. They are responsible for creating and sustaining an IT security culture in which their direct reports employ cyber-threat awareness to improve their teams' effectiveness.

Best practices CISOs should adopt:

1. Read all cyber intelligence products critically and ask questions if there is something they do not understand or with which they disagree.
2. Have the organization's PIRs committed to memory and have ready access to their associated EEIs.
3. Promote cyber intelligence integration by holding their leadership team accountable for threat understanding.
4. Hold their direct reports responsible for participating in the requirements process and for consuming relevant cyber intelligence products.
5. Participate in regularly scheduled analytic forums that include alternative analysis inputs, particularly devil's advocates analysis.
6. Learn to ask why analysts have arrived at a given conclusion and to hold them accountable for well thought out answers.
7. Learn to ask how potential threat actors will view actions made by the organization.
8. Demand thorough after action reviews of incidents and hold people accountable for employing lessons learned.
9. Hold the cyber intelligence team accountable for stating threats in terms of threat actor most likely and most dangerous courses of action.
10. Have the courage to talk about most dangerous courses of action to leadership.
11. Regularly ask questions regarding who is consuming cyber intelligence products and what the return on investment is for individual products.

The CTO Position

CTOs are primarily concerned with building and maintaining the IT infrastructure. They will provide all of the boxes that connect to the network, or establish the standards for and approve the connection of devices they do not provide. They will establish and run asset management programs, run data centers, and in most cases, they will manage vulnerability patching programs.

CTO interaction with cyber intelligence will vary based on their specific portfolios and on the organization's cyber intelligence capabilities. In most cases, cyber intelligence can provide the CTO team with intelligence to support their ability to let real-world threats drive relative priorities for vulnerability patching. Cyber intelligence teams with network hunters can assist the CTO by hunting for unauthorized network connections and by determining whether data flowing between designated devices meets expectations.

CTOs should be consistent contributors to intelligence and information requirement processes that address threats to specific technologies and threat trends.

Best practices CTOs should adopt:

1. Engage cyber intelligence when major vulnerabilities are discovered.
2. Include cyber intelligence as a source when evaluating implementation of third party connections.
3. Contribute to information and intelligence requirements processes.

CISO Direct Report to Whom Cyber Intelligence is Assigned

Many organizations with well-defined intelligence teams and a designated leader have chosen to assign a CISO direct report in the chain between the cyber intelligence leader and the CISO. In relatively immature organizations, particularly those in which the cyber intelligence leader has more intelligence experience than cyber intelligence experience, and/or when that leader was hired from outside of the organization and is still learning how things work, this arrangement makes a great deal of sense. Likewise, organizations with strong incident management and security operations centers that view cyber intelligence primarily as a capability multiplier for those functions would be wise to assign their cyber intelligence team to the person responsible for those functions, until that team is sufficiently capable to begin to support other IT security functions.

For organizations desiring to develop cyber intelligence capabilities that can provide impact beyond the portfolio of a single CISO direct, this organizational alignment creates some challenges that will need to be addressed. The first is that binning cyber intelligence within a subset of the IT security program will have a tendency to cause people to view it in the context of being a component of that program. Human nature and organizational culture both tend to create unofficial bureaucratic tribes within organizations, and the act of aligning cyber intelligence to a subset of security practices can erect barriers. The second is that the best way to learn how to maximize the capabilities of cyber intelligence is to work with it every day. By isolating the CISO from that interaction, organizations will slow the CISO's professional growth in learning how to employ cyber intelligence most effectively by reducing opportunities for regular direct interaction between the cyber intelligence leader and the CISO.

CISO direct reports in this role have to balance the competing demands for developing the cyber intelligence capabilities (and the people who will perform them) for their area of responsibility with providing threat reporting across portions of the organization for which they are not responsible. They must become educated stakeholders then become the focal point for advocating cyber intelligence understanding to other leaders in the IT organization, and they must do this while still performing their primary role.

Best practices include:

1. All of the CISO best practices also apply to leaders in this category.
2. Create an environment in which cyber intelligence can be successful within their area(s) of responsibility.

3. Seek out opportunities among their peers to apply cyber intelligence to their IT security processes.
4. Integrate cyber intelligence operational needs into their budgeting processes.
5. Drive professional development programs for cyber intelligence practitioners.

IT Process Owners

IT process owners are people in leadership positions who are responsible to the CIO, CISO and/or CTO for overseeing processes, the performance of which could be enhanced by greater threat understanding, and who should therefore have a working relationship with the cyber intelligence team. Given the wide variation in how different organizations conduct IT operations and the fact that what peoples' job descriptions say they do and what they actually do are frequent not aligned, there is no universal model one can leverage that can both identify all IT functions that should be employing cyber intelligence capabilities and the roles of the process owners with respect to cyber intelligence operations.

Many IT functions should have routine interaction with cyber intelligence while other functions will have less frequent direct interactions, and those interactions will tend to be event driven. While all IT professionals should develop an understanding of what cyber intelligence can do to support their roles and how to task it, process owners have the primary responsibility for driving relationships.

IT Processes Requiring Routine Cyber Intelligence Interaction

Forensic Investigation – One of the critical capabilities any IT security organization must possess is the capability to analyze what occurred in the aftermath of a cyber incident. Forensic investigators provide that capability, and the outputs from their investigations will enhance threat understanding and provide artifacts that can be applied to detection and hunting operations to improve security. Cyber intelligence can be a resource to investigators, providing them with intelligence on similar events in other organizations and tying discoveries to known threat actor TTPTs. Cyber intelligence is also a key consumer of the outputs from investigations.

Identity and Access Management (IAM) – As the name suggests, IAM deals with a range of tools, processes, and policies created to ensure the integrity of the network and data residing on it. IAM practices are designed to ensure that only authorized users have access to the network and to segmented portions of the network where controlled data resides. Intelligence can support policy and process development and tool selection by providing IAM decision makers with an understanding of how threat actors are attacking and defeating existing IAM approaches in other organizations.

Network Hunting – Network hunting has emerged as a critical capability in recent years. Hunters can apply intelligence to conduct cued searches on one's network to hunt for indications of malicious activities that static, signature-based detection sensors focused on the network perimeter may not detect. They can automate searches that they consider to be worth repeating and move on to the next threat. Hunters bridge cyber intelligence and detection functions, but regardless of where they are aligned in the organization they are a critical cyber intelligence asset for both refining threat understanding and for updating intelligence and information requirements based on real world data.

Security Architecture – Security architects employ design to create defensible networks. Design informed by realistic threat understanding will perform better than designs based solely on theory. Security architects who understand threat actor intentions and TTPTs will have an empirical basis for making design decisions. They can also engage the cyber intelligence team in discussions regarding how to leverage future designs to enhance threat detection efforts.

Security Operations – For the purposes of this discussion, security operations will refer to a wide range of activities designed to prevent, detect, respond to, and recover from malicious activity targeting organizations' network and data. The centerpiece of most security operations is a Security Operations Center (SOC) that will employ a variety of security tools designed to flag activities that may be indicators of threats to networks and data. Cyber intelligence analysts play a critical role in identifying events that need to generate alerts to notify SOC operators that something has occurred that merits their attention, and they will also support process refinements to improve the signal to noise ratio between meaningful and inconsequential events being worked by the SOC. Actions conducted under the headings prevent and recover are multi-disciplinary in nature. Prevent actions can include security architects' designs, IAM teams' policies and tool, and security awareness efforts designed to harden the workforce against social engineering. Recover actions address efforts to restore services and accesses lost during security incidents, most of which have a low probability of requiring cyber intelligence support. Detect and respond functions of security operations should both be major consumers of cyber intelligence:

> **Detect** – The term detect is a euphemism for a range of actions designed to enhance the ability of the security operations team to recognize unauthorized actions. People assigned detection roles conduct a range of actions to include designating: what activities are being logged; what signatures are being loaded into network sensors; and what events are triggering alerts. Detection analysts are increasingly turning to behavioral analytics and network hunting to enhance their abilities to identify and characterize anomalous events. Cyber intelligence can provide both the technical indicators/signatures employed in detection operations and intelligence relevant to new

threats and threat actor TTPTs to enable future detection operations.

Respond – Incident Management/Cyber Incident Response Team (CIRT) – The CIRT construct and the range of activities assigned to incident managers vary widely. In the event of a cyber incident, the CIRT needs to be able to determine what has occurred and whether malicious activities are still ongoing. They need to be able to stop an ongoing attack, to stabilize the situation, to minimize disruption to users, and to restore operational capabilities impacted by the attack (recover/restore.) Cyber intelligence analysts can contribute to CIRT operations during stressing events, and they can support post-event analysis efforts designed to prevent TTPTs employed in the event from being successful in the future.

Security Policy – Security policies address a range of activities involving security processes and procedures. In many cases, security policies provide execution-level detail for implementing a security program directed by higher authority, but in some cases policy may be developed to codify internally developed best practices. Cyber intelligence can play a critical role in reviewing policy documents for completeness, accuracy, and supportability. In addition, documenting cyber intelligence best practices within a CISO-level policy process can provide a number of benefits for both intelligence practitioners and their customers on the security team. Security policies developed in an environment informed by realistic threat understanding will be more effective than policies developed solely to mitigate known vulnerabilities.

Training and Awareness – IT security training and awareness programs offer opportunities to reduce the effectiveness of attacks targeting one's workforce by helping employees to recognize actions targeting them, like social engineering and phishing. Cyber intelligence can play a key role in identifying worthwhile topics, making realistic training materials, and providing inputs for the critical teaching points. In addition, because cyber intelligence is predictive, it can assist awareness programs by introducing material based on likely future threats to increase the likelihood new threats will be recognized for what they are.

Vulnerability Management – Not all system vulnerabilities are equal, and patching priorities should be established to account for both the probability that malicious actors will exploit a given vulnerability and the potential damage they might be able to inflict. In most cases, cyber intelligence teams should be able to provide patching teams with intelligence regarding whether exploits exist for identified vulnerabilities and warning when specific exploits are trending in cybercrime marketplaces.

IT Processes in which Cyber Intelligence Interactions Tend to be Event Driven

Audit/Compliance – Audit and compliance functions exist to ensure that people are following the rules and are executing policies correctly. Very few organizations have developed their cyber intelligence practices to a point where there are policies that need to be audited for compliance, but intelligence inputs to critical processes are increasingly falling into the scope of some audit actions. This is probably a growth area in the future, particularly if cyber intelligence capabilities expand into insider threats or intelligence programs gain access to sources in criminal forums where material protected by privacy laws is being sold.

Data Loss Prevention (DLP) – DLP programs are designed to apply automation to the challenges of tagging and tracking critical data that should not be being moved outside of specific functional areas (or network segments) within any given organization. Cyber intelligence can provide the people who develop the policies for what data and classes of data need to be protected by DLP tools with a greater understanding of what organizational data external threat actors would most like to acquire. Cyber intelligence should also respond to requirements addressing threats to DLP processes and tools.

Insider Threats – Cyber intelligence should play a leading role in supporting insider threat detection operations, but in many cases, insider threat programs are isolated from other security disciplines to protect privacy and workers' rights. As cyber intelligence expands it capabilities in behavioral and big data analytics to detect suspicious actions on the network, it will increasingly detect indicators of insider threat, which will likely drive organizations to review and revise existing policies that restrict relationships between intelligence analysts and insider threat investigators.

IT Risk – IT risk programs can be very bureaucratic with a heavy emphasis on compliance and controls assigned within a designated risk framework (particularly in highly regulated industries.) Items are logged to various risk registers and assigned mitigation actions and controls. Threat is a variable in IT risk calculations, and cyber intelligence should be a primary source for understanding threats, tracking changes in the threat environment, and evaluating the potential effectiveness of proposed controls.

Red Team/Red Cell – Another rapidly maturing discipline with many IT programs is that of red teams or red cells. These groups are primarily concerned with testing the effectiveness of security programs and associated controls. Their capabilities can range from penetration testing all the way up to being able to emulate sophisticated threat actors. Red teams that structure their engagements around employing realistic threats, and whose engagements are designed to address clearly defined objectives can provide CISOs with valuable feedback on security architecture, policy design, operator proficiency, and workforce security awareness. Cyber intelligence can support red team planning and engagement design with real-world threat data and threat actor TTPTs. Red team after action reviews and lessons learned should consistently provide cyber intelligence with realistic feedback on IT system performance that has potential to impact intelligence priorities.

Section Two
Understand Threats

This section addresses side two of the cyber intelligence fire triangle, *"understand threats,"* which expresses the imperative that all cyber intelligence stakeholders have a common understanding of cyber-threats and cyber-threat actors as a precondition for creating and executing responsive cyber intelligence operations. The content of this section provides a taxonomy for classifying threat actors, discussing their motivations, identifying behaviors, and enumerating their intended effects. This taxonomy provides cyber intelligence stakeholders with a reference model that can be employed to create and consume cyber intelligence threat reporting. Organizations that adopt and socialize an authoritative threat framework and share it among all stakeholders will be able to engage in more precise threat conversations and to leverage informed understanding to eliminate wasteful activities driven by fear.

In addition to providing cyber intelligence stakeholders with a threat framework, this section presents case studies for nine actual cyber-attacks that demonstrate how to employ the framework, and it introduces and applies two analytic approaches for predicting future cyber-threats. The content is organized as follows:

Chapter 2.1 – *Establishing a Threat Framework* develops four categories of threat actors, their motivations, their threat characterizations, and the effects they seek to create.

Chapter 2.2 – *Applied Threat Understanding* presents nine case studies of real-world cyber-attacks that apply the framework developed in Chapter 2.1 as an analytic tool for understanding cyber threats.

Chapter 2.3 – *Future Threats* introduces two unique analytic approaches, trend extrapolation and technology driven, and uses them to develop eight cyber-threat predictions.

For Your Consideration

Before discussing how to classify threats and threat actors and how to think about future threats, it is worth spending a few pages quantifying the costs imposed by malicious cyber actors and building a case for how even fairly modest cyber intelligence capabilities might alter the threat dynamic.

Quantifying Costs associated with Cyber-Threat Actors

In a speech at the American Enterprise Institute July of 2012, General Keith Alexander, who was serving as the Director of the US National Security Agency, told an audience that "the loss of industrial information and intellectual property through cyber espionage constitutes the 'greatest transfer of wealth in history'." He quantified intellectual property losses to US businesses from cyber espionage to be $250 billion with another $114 billion in losses due to cybercrime.[10]

As of the publication of this book, there are no authoritative sources for documenting costs created by cyber-threat actors, nor are there any universally accepted methodologies for data collection. In fact, most estimates of cost and forecasts of future costs are published by companies that sell products and services in the cybersecurity and cyber intelligence sectors, which means the authors have financial incentives to avoid being overly conservative in their work. Below are six estimates/forecasts for cybercrime cost published by security firms in recent years:

---

[10] http://foreignpolicy.com/2012/07/09/nsa-chief-cybercrime-constitutes-the-greatest-transfer-of-wealth-in-history/

- CNBC quotes, Hiscox (a UK business insurance firm) as stating that cybercrime cost the global economy over $450 billion in calendar year 2016.[11]
- Microsoft's security stories webpage in early 2018 used the figure $500 billion for worldwide costs attributable to cybercrime.[12]
- Juniper Research published a report in May 2015 that estimated costs created by cyber breaches would reach $2.1 trillion in 2019.[13]
- Juniper followed that up that prediction in May 2017 with an estimate that costs associated with data breaches would reach $8 trillion for the period 2017-2022.[14]
- The most extreme prediction belongs to Cybersecurity Ventures, who in October 2017, predicted that cybercrime will cost the world $6 trillion annually by 2021, which they said is up from $3 trillion in 2015 (a number that is six times higher than Microsoft and Hiscox use.)[15]
- Costs imposed by threat actors are not limited to losses they impose; they also include spending on cybersecurity necessitated by the existence of cyber-threats. *Wired Magazine* estimates that cumulative cybersecurity spending from 2017-2021 may exceed one trillion dollars.[16]

An alternative approach for examining costs imposed by cyber-threat actors is to employ products from government and nonprofit sources that employ real-world data from a small subset of organizations. While these studies are limited in scope, they do

---

[11] https://www.cnbc.com/2017/02/07/cybercrime-costs-the-global-economy-450-billion-ceo.html
[12] https://news.microsoft.com/stories/cybercrime/
[13] https://www.juniperresearch.com/press/press-releases/cybercrime-cost-businesses-over-2trillion
[14] https://www.securitymagazine.com/articles/88049-cybercrime-to-cost-global-business-8-trillion-in-the-next-5-years
[15] https://cybersecurityventures.com/hackerpocalypse-cybercrime-report-2016/
[16] https://www.wired.com/beyond-the-beyond/2017/07/global-cybercrime-costs-trillion-dollars-maybe-3/

provide an empirical basis for examining year over year change. Two good examples are:

- Ponemon Institute and Accenture collected data from 254 companies in seven Countries (Australia, France, Germany, Italy, Japan, United Kingdom and the United States) that addressed the cost of cybercrime in 2017. Data analysis revealed a 23% increase in financial losses from 2016 to 2017 and a 27% growth in the number of cyber-attacks over that same period.[17]
- The FBI's Internet Crime Complaint Center (IC3) has published an annual report since 2013 that provides data on complaints they received and losses associated with those complaints. Table II.1 summarizes data from those reports, the most recent of which was published in May 2018. Of note, the number of complaints is relatively stable, while losses follow a generally upward trend over the period covered by the IC3. This data is interesting, but it only covers a narrow subset of cyber-attacks, i.e. those reported to the IC3.

The key takeaway from all of these reports is that cyber-threat actors are imposing significant costs on the world's economy. Those cost are not limited to any specific geography or industry, and they continue to grow.

---

[17] https://www.accenture.com/t20171006T095146Z__w__/us-en/_acnmedia/PDF-62/Accenture-2017CostCybercrime-US-FINAL.pdf#zoom=50

Year	Number of Complaints	Reported Losses	Cost per Complaint
2012	289K	$ 525 M	$1,817
2013	262K	$ 782 M	$2,985
2014	269K	$ 800M	$2,974
2015	288K	$ 1,070 M	$3,715
2016	298K	$ 1,450 M	$4,866
2017	302K	$1,419 M	$4,699
Total	1,708K	$6,046 M	$3,540

Table II.1 – Data from the FBI Internet Crime Complaint Center 2012-2016[18]

The Case for How Cyber Intelligence Can Make a Difference

What is not reflected in this data, however, is the degree to which the human element drives threat actor decisions regarding who they are going to attack. Cyber-threat actors are human beings, and they engage in a cost/benefit analysis at each stage of their attack. They understand the relative value of the data they are targeting, and they will sometimes choose to abandon an attack if the costs of overcoming security are too great.

Cyber intelligence operations offer the potential to provide understanding of what threat actors need to accomplish at each step of their attack process, commonly referred to as the kill-chain. [*Kill-chains are covered in Chapter 5.3.*] Armed with this understanding, IT security professionals can act to complicate threat actor tasks and to increase the likelihood of detecting their presence at multiple points along the kill-chain, and in so doing, increase costs imposed on attackers. This approach is referred to

---

[18] https://pdf.ic3.gov/2017_IC3Report.pdf

as defense in-depth, and examples of cyber intelligence being applied to create defense in-depth include:

- Network security architects can employ cyber intelligence to develop network designs that complicate access to data of greatest interest to malicious actors and that also increase the likelihood of detecting actions early in the kill-chain.
- Security operations teams can apply identity and access management (IAM) and data loss prevention (DLP) tools more effectively. They can make better informed decisions on logging and alerting actions, and in cases where behavioral analytics are in place, they can write more effective detection rules.
- Cyber intelligence can cue network hunters' searches and can drive security automation.
- Vulnerability management teams can prioritize patching decisions based on cyber intelligence regarding whether exploits exist for malicious actors to employ to take advantage of published vulnerabilities.
- Users can be trained to recognize and report potential social engineering efforts by being exposed to real-world examples of products and techniques.

Chapter 2.1
Establishing a Threat Framework

Key Points

- There are four categories of threat actors:
    - State Actors
    - Criminals
    - Hacktivists
    - Insiders
- Each category can be further subdivided into collectives, organizations, and individuals.
- Threat actors have different motivations and seek to impose different effects on organizations they target.
- Threat actor proficiency can be characterized as:
    - Opportunistic
    - Targeted
    - Sophisticated
    - Persistent

Stakeholder Roles

Literate Stakeholders	Educated Stakeholders	Intelligence Practitioners
• Achieve a basic understanding of the four threat actor categories introduced in the threat framework • Be proficient with the threat framework lexicon	• Understand the threat framework • Be able to recognize which threat actor categories and collectives present the greatest threat to one's organization	• Master the threat framework taxonomy and associated lexicon • Be consistent in use of terminology across all products • Be prepared to update and/or refine the framework as required

Context

This is the first of three chapters designed to promote a common taxonomy and lexicon that cyber intelligence stakeholders can employ both for discussing cyber threats and for planning cyber intelligence operations designed to address those threats. This chapter establishes a working taxonomy in the form of a threat framework.

Table 2.1.1 provides a high level view of the threat framework. It presents a two dimensional matrix with four descriptors on the x-axis (who (threat actors), why (motivations), how (threat characterization), and what (effects)), and four threat actors at the category level (state actors, criminals, hacktivists, and insiders) along the y-axis. The matrix provides a consistent approach for cyber intelligence stakeholders to classify and discuss threats and threat actors. The content of Table 2.1.1 is accurate, but it is presented at a generic level for the purposes of this discussion. For example, there are both criminals and hacktivists that can operate at the sophisticated and persistent levels, but vast majority operate at the opportunistic and targeted levels.

Threat Actors	Motivations	Threat Characterization	Effects
State Actors	Intelligence collection and Intellectual Property theft	Persistent and Sophisticated	Espionage/Theft/Destruction
Criminals	Financial Gain	Sophisticated, Targeted, and Opportunistic	Steal/Extort
Hacktivists	Disrupt/Gain Attention	Targeted	Deny/Deface/Embarrass
Insiders	Money/Beliefs/Ignorance	Targeted and Opportunistic	Steal/Embarrass/Data Integrity

Table 2.1.1 – Threat Framework at the Category Level

Figure 2.1.1 offers the third dimension (z-axis), which is a hierarchal classification schema for cataloging the level of detail that organizations need to be concerned with as they build cyber intelligence capabilities to address threat actors.

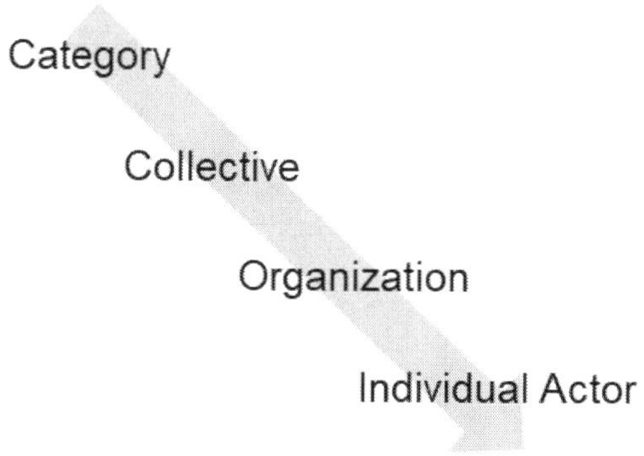

Category

Collective

Organization

Individual Actor

Figure 2.1.1 – Threat Actor Classification Hierarchy

Category: There are four groups of threat actors at the *category level* of this classification schema, and those are the four presented in the threat framework (state actors, criminals, hacktivists, and insiders.) Discussions at the *category level* contribute to macro and theoretical level threat discussions, but in most cases, informed application of cyber intelligence begins at the *collective level*.

Collective: Threat actor analysis at the *collective level* provides cyber intelligence and IT security teams with a sufficient level of detail to be able to characterize likely threat actor tactics, techniques, procedures, and tools (TTPTs) and to develop operations to address those threats. Cyber intelligence teams whose organizations are targeted by state actors and criminals will need to become proficient at developing threat understanding at the *collective level*. The threat actor discussion in this chapter develops detailed characterizations for 11 threat actor collectives. Table 2.1.2 bins the 11 threat actor collectives under their specific threat actor categories.

State Actors	Criminals	Hacktivists	Insiders
State-to-State Espionage	Organized	Publicity	Malicious
State Theft from Non-State Actors	Entrepreneurs	Damage	Negligent
Misrepresentation Attacks	Market Enabled		
	Industrial Espionage		

Table 2.1.2 – Threat Actor Categories and Associated Collectives

Organization: Only a subset of private sector enterprises will derive value from employing cyber intelligence to track state and criminal threat actors at the *organization level*. Two examples are companies in defense industries targeted by reasonably static nation state threat actors and cyber intelligence vendors that need to be able to track threats at this level for clients. Vendors may also choose to work at the *organization level* as a means differentiating themselves from their competitors. Mandiant's APT1 paper[19] in 2013 and Kaspersky Lab's Carbanak paper[20] in 2015 are examples of commercial cyber intelligence vendors publishing threat papers that generated publicity in the mainstream media for the purposes marketing their companies' expertise and brand names.

Individual Actor: Cyber intelligence addressing attribution for personas in the state actor and criminal categories at the *individual actor* level will rarely occur outside of government intelligence and law enforcement agencies, and those agencies protect their sources and methods zealously, and do not publicize their TTPTs or levels of success. Companies in industries frequently targeted by hacktivists will be able to employ intelligence to track threats at the *individual actor level*, because hacktivists have a propensity

---

[19] APT1 – Exposing One of China's Cyber Espionage Units, Mandiant (now FireEye), February 19, 2013.
[20] The Great Bank Robbery: Carbanak cybergang steals $1bn from 100 financial institutions worldwide, Kaspersky Lab, February 16, 2015.

for sharing their beliefs and plans on social media. Not only does this make tracking efforts straight forward, it also justifies the effort, because individual actor communications constitute a primary source of warning of future actions. Insider threat programs also operate at the *individual actor level*, but the role of cyber intelligence support to insider threats is still evolving, and efforts to balance workers' privacy rights and cyber intelligence will take time to get sorted out.

The remainder of this chapter is dedicated to providing readers with a sufficient level of understanding of threat actors and threat characterizations to enable them to apply the framework to their operational needs. The threat actor section provides detailed discussion of threat actors down to the *collective level*. The threat characterization discussion defines the four descriptors used in the threat framework matrix in a manner designed to help readers apply them to support predictive analysis.

Threat Actors

State Actors

It is important for readers to understand that all governments today are leveraging the power of the Internet to enhance their ability to conduct tasks associated with traditional statecraft like diplomacy, information/propaganda, and research/intelligence collection. Much of the activity is being conducted in plain sight without any effort to obscure attribution, and people conducting that work are engaged performing traditional tasks albeit faster, cheaper, more efficiently, and unaffected by physical geography. In other words, the evolution of a cyber domain (to use the military terminology) has not changed the nature of governments, it has only empowered them to be more effective, and the evolution of the cyber domain has leveled the playing field for smaller states. All countries engage in espionage and try to influence the perceptions of other states and their citizens, and much of that soft power statecraft is being wielded online today.

Countries with a history of controlling information available to their populations are continuing to exercise that control by limiting their populations' Internet access while leveraging the Internet to disseminate their propaganda. Countries with large state owned industries have historically blurred their definition of espionage to include theft of intellectual property useful to state-owned enterprises, and much of that theft today is being conducted in the cyber domain. Pariah states that have historically employed organized criminal activities and surrogate groups to generate hard currency to bypass economic sanctions are now conducting state sponsored cybercrime.

Threat actors from countries with highly developed cyber skills are often referred to as advanced persistent threat (APT) actors. APT actors value undetected network presence over quick actions on objective. APT actors will engage in actions designed to regain network access if they are detected (e.g. backdoors) and will avoid behaviors that will trigger anomaly detection. This taxonomy develops three subcategories of state actors at the *collective level* to support threat understanding:

(a) **State-to-State Espionage**:

Countries have spied on one another throughout history, but the characterization of espionage activities has evolved with technology. State sponsored espionage agencies have shifted their TTPTs in response to their targets embracing technologic progress. As data moved from paper to electronic files and transmission evolved from mail and analog telephone conversations to email and voice over Internet protocol (VOIP) communications, spy agencies have evolved their collection capabilities to respond to those changes. Media reporting in recent years has covered stories involving discoveries of indications of foreign intelligence services hacking various government networks. The biggest news story in the US throughout 2017 and 2018 involved the role of the Russian state in trying to shape the outcome of the 2016 US presidential election, and many of the accusations center on cyber capabilities. Russia is also the leading suspect in network intrusions at the US Departments of State and Defense in the 2014-2016 timeframes, and China is the leading suspect in the theft of personal data on more than 20 million people with security clearances from the US Office of Personnel Management in 2015.

(b) State Theft from Non-State Actors:

Groups in this collective are state run intelligence organizations engaged in targeting non-state actors for reasons other than national security. Many nations are suspected of employing their intelligence collection capabilities to steal intellectual property from private sector businesses to reduce research and development costs for state owned industries or to help important national industries. The Chinese government, with a long history of disregarding the traditional western concept of intellectual property rights, have engaged in aggressive targeting of businesses with technology they wanted, and until a couple of years ago, they did not even go to any great effort to hide what they were doing. North Korea is the prime suspect in the theft of more than $80 million from Bangladesh Bank in February 2016, and post-event analysis found evidence of the TTPT and malware employed in the attack being used in at least five other attempted thefts.

(c) Misrepresentation Attacks:

While almost all actors engaged in cyber-attacks will make some effort to obscure attribution efforts, there are instances in which state actors will generate fictitious organizations as a core component of their efforts to complicate attribution and/or to promote the idea that there is some kind of broad popular support for the state's political, ideological, or social agenda outside of the government. In 2012, Iran created a phony hacktivist group that they called "Izz ad-Din al-Qassam Cyber Fighter," and conducted a series of distributed denial of service (DDoS) campaigns against major US banks. The attacks were planned and executed by Iran's Revolutionary Guard Corps pretending to be a hacktivist organization and were designed to coerce the Obama Administration into making concessions in negotiations involving Iran's nuclear program.[21] North Korea attacked Sony Pictures in 2014 in response to their planned release of a comedy in which a central plot element was the assassination the North Korean leader. This was a punitive attack designed not only to coerce Sony into not releasing the movie, but also to send a message to other businesses who might be tempted to embarrass North Korea or its leaders. The attackers transmitted communications calling themselves "The Guardians of Peace," and they both stole and destroyed massive quantities of data. They also released privileged communications of executives designed to embarrass both the individuals and the company.[22]

Criminals

Cybercriminals, malicious actors employing cyber skills to make money illegally, are the most numerous, diverse, and eclectic group discussed in this chapter. Cybercriminals make money in one of three primary ways: they steal money directly; they steal something that has monetary value and sell it to someone who wants it; or they extort money from victims who are willing to pay the criminals either to do something (or not to do something.) The taxonomy in this section is organized around a hierarchy of actor capability.

(a) Organized:

At the top of the cybercriminal food chain are organized criminal groups that are sometimes called criminal APT actors because

---

[21] Department of Justice, Seven Iranians Working for Islamic Revolutionary Guard Corps-Affiliated Entities Charged for Conducting Coordinated Campaign of Cyber Attacks Against U.S. Financial Sector, March 24, 2016.
[22] Pockett-lint.com, Sony Pictures Hack Here's Everything We Know About the Massive Attack So Far, February 5, 2015.

they employ many of the same practices as their state sponsored counterparts. Organized cybercriminal groups possess all of the critical skills they need to execute end-to-end operations without having to commission any external help. This does not mean that they never interact with other criminals in cybercrime marketplaces, rather it means they are not dependent on others for anything. Their ability to operate as a self-contained organization allows them to practice high levels of operational security and to maintain their anonymity. The Carbanak Group referenced in the introduction is the best known actor in this category.

(b) Entrepreneurs:

Some of the most notorious cybercrime groups are entrepreneurs who operate cybercrime-as-a-service business models. Actors in this collective focus on developing products and infrastructure that they can sell to other criminals. Their business models vary, but their primary source of income is fees from other criminals. Two infamous groups that have been exposed by law enforcement in recent years are the GameOver Zeus and Dridex groups. The GameOver Zeus criminal infrastructure was taken over by a coalition of international law enforcement agencies and security companies in June 2014. The group is assessed to have made hundreds of millions of dollars both from employing their own products and selling/leasing their products and services to others. They also distributed the first commercially successful crypto ransomware product (CryptoLocker) and protected themselves by doing pro-bono work for the Russian government.[23] The Dridex group came into prominence in the wake of the demise of GameOver Zeus in late 2014. In late summer 2015, a kingpin in the Dridex group was arrested in Cyprus. Several governments announced that their law enforcement agencies had successfully shutdown Dridex operations in October 2015, but those reports were overly optimistic, and Dridex customers employed the

---

[23] Fox IT, GameOver Zeus – Backgrounds on the Badguys and the Backends, August 2015.

unaffected infrastructure to engage in a series of massive campaigns to infect users with Dridex credential stealing malware and Locky ransomware beginning that same month.[24]

(c) Market Enabled:

One of the key enablers of cybercrime is the existence of robust underground marketplaces/forums in which cybercriminals can buy and sell goods and services in transactions designed to benefit all participants. There are many different underground criminal marketplaces around the world, each catering to the needs, languages, and cultures of their respective clients. They lower entry barriers to criminal actors by giving inexperienced and marginally skilled people opportunities to gain experience and improve their skills. In fact, some underground markets actually sell vocational training for cybercriminals. Enterprising cybercrime entrepreneurs will market their services at multiple levels. For example, some ransomware-as-a-service vendors offer menus of options for the level of service a client might choose, and the percentage of the take that the vendor keeps is based on the level of service provided. Underground markets play a critical role in monetizing theft. Stolen account logons and payment card credentials are monetized by fraud activities that require far different skill sets than those used to steal the credentials and payment card track data.

(d) Industrial Espionage:

This is an area of cybercrime that does not get much attention, due in large part to the fact that neither the criminals nor their victims benefit from attacks being made public. Industrial espionage primarily involves cybercriminals stealing specific intellectual property for a client. Groups commissioning industrial espionage likely include both governments and private sector competitors. As industry becomes increasingly reliant on industrial control

---

[24] HelpNet Security, Dridex botnet alive and well, now also spreading ransomware, February 17, 2016.

systems for a growing range of processes, industrial espionage will likely become a major growth area for cybercriminals, and it will likely evolve to include extortion related crimes. For example, cybercriminals might plant ransomware on industrial controls to shut down an operation or gain access to robotic devices used in manufacturing processes and cause them to produce flawed products that would open the manufacturer to massive litigation.

Hacktivists

The hacktivist category is unique in that the *collective level* of the taxonomy is less significant than the other three, and most useful analysis occurs at the organization *and individual actor levels*. Because hacktivists tend to promote their activities in social media, intelligence analysts have the ability to develop an understanding of different hacktivist movements and prominent individual actors, which is not the case in the other three categories.

The challenges in developing a useful taxonomy at the *collective level* is that hacktivist actors are so diverse in motivations, skill levels, and desired outcomes, and most actors will support more than one cause. A search of open source articles on hacktivist movements reveals a tendency to identify groups using labels addressing motivation, political affiliation, and social causes. Unfortunately, these descriptor do not work well for describing a threat taxonomy, because the line between political and social is quite often blurry or invisible.

Anonymous campaigns in recent years offer clear examples of this challenge. Anonymous has been among the most prominent hacktivist collectives for much of the last decade, but it is a movement, not a group, and hacktivists often affiliate with multiple campaigns being promoted by other Anonymous members. Social media analysis of Twitter activity during different phases of a 2016 anti-banking campaign (#OpIcarus) demonstrated this phenomena well. Groups representing different (sometimes conflicting) political causes joined in for support on a campaign targeting central banks. One group used the campaign as an opportunity to demonstrate its ability to execute large scale DDoS attacks. They would knock a webpage offline and send screen shots proving their target was offline to publicize their work, but campaign organizers wanted to take sites down for an entire business day and they openly criticized their partner for using the campaign for their own benefit.

Given the importance of intelligence at the *organization and individual actor levels*, the most useful way to differentiate hacktivist threats at the *collective level* is to differentiate between intended targeting effects. Traditionally, hacktivists have primarily sought publicity for themselves and their causes, but in a world of evolving and escalating threats, one should anticipate that zealots will up the ante to more punitive attacks in the future.

(a) Publicity:

The primary purpose of most hacktivist attacks is to generate publicity for the group conducting the attack and/or the cause(s) they support. Common forms of hacktivist attacks include DDoS and defacement. DDoS attacks are designed to inconvenience the victim organization and its customers in a manner that communicates the hacktivists have power over their victims. Defacements enable hacktivists to communicate their message on their victims' webpages, and like DDoS, defacements are also intended to communicate that the hacktivists are smarter than their victims and are in control. In the short-term, getting publicity is more important than whether the attack actually created problems for the target, but in the longer term, groups that develop a track record for successfully taking targets offline, acquire the ability to generate publicity just by talking about future attacks.

(b) Damage:

The Syrian Electronic Army or SEA is a hacktivist group that conducts attacks to punish organizations for their opposition to the Assad regime. The SEA blurs the line between traditional hacktivists and state actors conducting misrepresentation attacks pretending to be hacktivists. In April 2013, the SEA hacked the Associated Press' Twitter account and transmitted a false news story claiming the Whitehouse had been attacked and President Obama was injured, which led to panicked trading on the floor of the New York Stock Exchange in which $136 billion were pulled from the market in just three minutes.[25] This attack represented evolutionary increases in effectiveness for hacktivists. One should not be surprised to see hacktivists using ransomware to deny users access to critical information or releasing sensitive stolen data to dump sites to damage reputations.

Insiders

In its simplest form, insider threat can be divided into two groups: malicious actors, and negligent employees. Malicious actors can be motivated by anger or greed, and they use their privileged position and account access to act on their specific motivation. Negligent employees are people who expose the organization's data or IT system access to malicious actors through ignorance, carelessness, or laziness.

Accurate empirical data on costs imposed by insider threats do not exist. Most of the commonly cited work by companies in the security industry relies on survey data from surveys conducted by companies with a monetary stake in the perception of increased insider threat. That said insider threats are real, and most surveys tend to support the notion that costs imposed by negligent employees are higher than those imposed by malicious actors.

It is also worth mentioning that in a large percentage of state sponsored and criminal attacks, malicious actors target and acquire legitimate credentials, and once they have those credentials, their actions leading to their desired actions on

---

[25] Max Fisher, "Syrian hackers claim AP hack that tipped stock market by $136 billion. Is it terrorism?." The Washington Post, April 23, 2013.

objective are often indistinguishable from malicious insiders. Insider threat programs are the best hope for detecting actions by these actors late in the kill-chain. Some published security papers include misuse of account credentials by external actors as a form of insider threat.

(a) **Malicious Actors**:

Any employee who uses their position of trust, insider knowledge, and/or network accesses to do harm to the organization that gave them network access is a malicious actor. Motivations and actions vary significantly, which makes it difficult to develop prevention and detection. Disaffected employees whose employment is being terminated, who have been passed by for a promotion, or who are in conflict with their boss or coworkers may feel motivated to take sensitive information with them when they leave, to delete/destroy work they did for the organization, or to engage in harmful activity targeting a boss or coworker. Employees with severe financial difficulties or lifestyles beyond their paycheck may choose to steal business sensitive information or coworker account accesses to sell for monetary gain. Regardless of the specific motivation, these malicious actors can do great harm, and they are very difficult to detect.

(b) **Negligent**:

Negligent actors are employees who facilitate malicious actions by engaging in a range of dangerous behaviors like: poor password security, visiting dangerous websites, opening suspicious emails (and clicking on links), not locking screens when they leave their desk, and ignoring social engineering threats. Negligent actors enable actions by malicious actors in all of the other threat categories. Seven of the nine case studies presented in Chapter 2.2 cite negligent employee behavior is an enabler of success for the attacker, and it cannot be ruled out as a factor in the other two.

Threat Characterization

The threat framework matrix (Table 2.1.1) uses the term threat characterization to describe the level of sophistication of various threat actors. This section defines the four threat characterizations from that matrix to support consistent usage of the terms in future discussions. The order of presentation in this discussion ranges from the least to the most sophisticated threat characterization.

Opportunistic

Actors in this category leverage opportunities rather than targeting specific individuals or organizations. Opportunistic actors tend to be one or two trick ponies. They have a spam list and/or have gained access to a website and have added a malicious link. They don't care who opens their spam attachment or clicks on their link; any infected endpoint or stolen credential is equally desirable, so success is measured in sheer numbers of clicks.

Targeted

Actors conducting targeted attacks tend to me more sophisticated and more effective than their counterparts conducting opportunistic attacks. Actors at this level know who they are attacking and why. They can engage in spear phishing attacks on specific groups of users, which will allow them to tailor their message in a manner that will increase the likelihood a recipient will execute the desired action of opening an attachment or clicking on a link. While volume is still a desirable outcome, the success metric for a targeted attack is first and foremost measured by whether the attack generated the specific outcome it was designed to produce.

Sophisticated

A good analogy for understanding the difference between the skill levels of actors at this level and the targeted level is to think of targeted attacks as dropping a bomb and sophisticated attacks as employing a precision guided weapon. To actors at this level, access to a specific network is the beginning of the process, not the end; they are looking to gain access to something specific on the network, and in most instances steal it. This is the first threat level at which actors will conduct extensive intelligence on intended targets. Actors need to understand the network design, what devices are on the network, who is on the network, and how people on the network communicate with one another. Sophisticated actors may need to have access to networks for extended periods of time but once they have executed their action on objective, they do not need to continue to maintain access.

Persistent

As the name implies, threat actors operating at this level possess the skills to not only gain access to their targets but to execute their operations in a manner that they create few opportunities to be detected. Persistent threat actors represent the most sophisticated and skilled actors/groups in this threat characterization, and their membership includes some national intelligence services, a small subset of cybercriminal organizations, and a finite number of highly skilled individuals. Given that persistent actors are defined by not being detected, there are many unknowns about the range of capabilities they possess. Intelligence, much of it gained from post-event analysis of known attacks, suggests that there are a number of attributes common to persistent threat actors:

- They conduct intelligence operations against targets to identify network defenses so that they can avoid detection and, where possible, exploit those defenses to hide their attacks and monitor their actions from the defenders' perspective.

- There is evidence of use of web shells and backdoors to facilitate regaining access if they lose it.
- They will move laterally across networks and escalate privileges to move between networks.
- They will also leverage escalated privileges to create new accounts to gain additional accesses.
- If their actions require malware, they will employ unique, tailored malware that will not trigger commercial anti-virus programs.
- They are constantly improving their intelligence once they are on their targeted network.
- They will conduct data exfiltration actions employing practices that reduce their exposure to behavioral analytics, i.e. they will avoid sending unusually large files, and they will exfiltrate data during the victim organization's normal business hours.

Chapter 2.2
Applied Threat Understanding

Key Points

- Case studies provide real world examples of the cyber threats presented in Chapter 2.1.
- The nine cases presented in this chapter represent a subset of successful cyber-attacks, but each is illustrative of an attack by a different class of threat actor and each provides unique perspectives and potential lessons learned.
- Common themes across nine very different cases include:
    - None of the victim organizations were ready for the attack.
    - Most damaged their own credibility by downplaying the seriousness of the attacks in the media, only to look foolish later.
    - In the private sector, leaders are held accountable when their organizations' networks are breached and their customers' data is stolen.
    - Brand reputations and stock prices are both negatively impacted, but to date, those impacts have only proven to be temporary.
- Given enough time and resources, talented threat actors can gain access to even the best defended networks.
- Early reports are generally misleading and lack depth; leaders who have an appreciation for the challenges associated with characterizing the impacts of ongoing events can avoid making statements that create additional harm.

Stakeholder Roles

Literate Stakeholders	Educated Stakeholders	Intelligence Practitioners
• Learn from the mistakes of others • Be prepared for being attacked • Recognize how to avoid compounding problems by doing and saying the wrong things	• Be able apply the key elements of the case studies for the threats of greatest concern to your organization • Apply lessons learned to preplanned responses	• Recognize the common themes present in the case studies • Employ case study methodologies to drive planning and to add richness to awareness programs

Context

Table 2.2.1 provides an index for the nine case studies reviewed in this chapter. The cases are organized by threat actor type and presented in same order as the threat actor discussion in the previous chapter. The purpose of presenting these case studies is two-fold: (1) to demonstrate the applicability of the threat framework from the previous chapter by applying it to real world events, and (2) to highlight some useful perspectives by presenting the actual details of real-world events to help readers to learn from the misfortune of others.

Case Studies

Each case study is presented in four parts: overview, after action, relevance, and takeaways. The overview section summarizes the key points of the case as presented in the media when the cyber-attack was first discovered. The after action section offers additional details of what occurred that came to light after victim organizations and security companies had the opportunity to study forensic evidence. Relevance provides a summary of what cyber intelligence stakeholders need to understand about the case. Takeaways provide a mixture of lessons learned and thoughtful considerations the case added to the collective understanding of what threat actors do and what organizations can do to be better prepared for cyber-attacks.

Threat Actor Category	Threat Actor Collective	Case Study	Desired Effect	Impact
State Actors	State-to-state Espionage	Office of Personnel Management	Steal Personal Identification Information	> 20M Records Stolen
	State Theft from Non-State Actors	Bangladesh Bank	Steal Money	$81M Stolen
	Misrepresentation Attacks	Sony Entertainment Pictures	Damage Company/ Embarrass Leaders	Estimated $35M Costs in First Year
Criminals	Organized	Target Corporation	Financial/ Information Theft	40M Cards/70M Records Stolen –Costs >$250M
	Targeted	Business E-Mail Compromise	Financial/ Information Theft	Estimated $12.5B losses since 2013
Hacktivists	Publicity	The Hacking Team	Political Statement	Loss of Proprietary Information/ Unwanted Attention
	Damage	Ashley Madison	Disrupt Operations/ Damage Company	37M Customers Impacted
Insiders	Malicious	US National Security Agency	Ideology/Ego	Embarrass/ Expose Sources and Methods
	Negligent	Fazio Mechanical	Gain Access to Target Network	Facilitated Attack on Target

Table 2.2.1 – Index of Nine Cyber-Attacks used in Case Studies

State Actor Case Studies

Case Study 1 – State-to-State Espionage – Office of Personnel Management

Overview: In June 2015 the US Office of Personnel Management (OPM) announced that they had been the victims of a large scale data breach involving the loss of personal information on 5.6 million people with security clearances. Over the next month the level of damage was adjusted in an upward direction several times before being set at more than 21 million people. Initial reports could not agree when the data theft began, but some sources indicated the perpetrators may have been on the network for a year before being detected. Reports also indicated that the perpetrators gained legitimate network accesses and employed malware to establish backdoors on the network. The OPM attack was assessed to be the work of the Chinese government whose goal was to have detailed information on the personal lives of people with US government security clearances.

After Action: The OPM breach devolved into a political issue, which slowed efforts to investigate what actually occurred. The US House Oversight and Government Reform Committee finally released a 241 page report in September 2016 that outlined their findings. That report documented lax security practices within OPM and by OPM contractors to whom investigative work was outsourced. The committee found that the US Computer Emergency Response Team had notified OPM in March 2014 that they had detected suspicious activity but that OPM leadership was slow to respond.[26]

Relevance: The OPM attack had all the earmarks of a state sponsored APT cyber-attack. Threat actors gained and

---

[26] Committee on Oversight and Government Reform U.S. House of Representatives, "*The OPM Data Breach: How the Government Jeopardized Our National Security for More than a Generation,*" Sep 7, 2016, p vii.

maintained unfettered access to the OPM network for over a year, and they escalated privileges and moved across the network to execute their actions on objective. They took advantage of seams in the network created by OPM's security architecture and user privileges granted to third party contract employees. OPM leadership and OPM IT leadership failed to establish cultures that valued IT security; they allowed their organization to operate IT networks that were not in compliance with government mandated operating standards and were therefore not accredited for processing and storing sensitive information. Leaders were not fired, but after some delay, most were forced to resign.

Takeaways:

1. Organizational culture matters. Organizations led by people who do not hold themselves or their direct reports accountable for complying with security rules create an environment in which nobody takes security seriously.
2. Bad news does not get better with time. OPM slow rolled their breach notification and repeatedly attempted to downplay impacts and to place blame on others. As a result, OPM leadership ceased being trusted early in the process.
3. Sensitive data needs to be protected by multifactor authentication.
4. Where there is one malicious actor, there may be more. OPM and DHS removed an intruder's network access in May 2014 and thought they had thwarted the attack.
5. Organizations should monitor domain registration activities and watch for domains being registered using the organization's name or a common misspelling of the name in it. Attackers registered a phony domain called "opmlearning.org" to facilitate the exfiltration of stolen data. Had OPM identified the domain and monitored communications from their network to that domain, they would have detected the attack nine months earlier than they did.

Case Study 2 – State Theft from Non-state Actors – Bangladesh Bank

Overview: The central bank for the nation of Bangladesh (Bangladesh Bank) lost $81 million in a theft in February 2016 in which the perpetrators used bank codes and network access to transfer funds held by the Federal Reserve Bank of New York (FRBNY) to banks in Asia. Forensic analysis of the Bangladesh Bank network revealed that attackers used malicious code that security analysts associated with previous attacks by North Korean intelligence operatives that security firms refer to as the "Lazarus Group." The wire transfers were conducted on the Society for Worldwide Interbank Financial Telecommunication (SWIFT) network, which is the most respected and widely used international network for secure transfers. The attackers compromised the software Bangladesh Bank used to generate wire transfers but did not compromise the SWIFT network. The transfers were sent on the Thursday night prior to the Chinese New Year holiday; Bangladesh Bank was closed on Friday (Islamic day of worship) and Monday (Chinese New Year) and the FRBNY was closed on Saturday and Sunday.[27]

After Action: Reports indicate that the Bangladesh Bank network had a number of security shortfalls that both aided the Lazarus Group's ability to compromise it and to remove evidence of their activity when the theft was completed. All reports are second hand, because the Bangladeshi government has not made the results of their investigation public. The actions of the FRBNY have also come under some criticism. The bank first rejected 35 wire transfers because they contained errors, but after telling the bank robbers how to fix their mistakes, they acted on the first five of 35 corrected wire transfers before becoming suspicious and deciding to stop processing additional requests. They transferred $101 million, but an alert bank official in Sri Lanka did not act on a $20 million request because of a misspelling, so the losses from

---

[27] https://www.reuters.com/investigates/special-report/cyber-heist-federal

an attack designed to steal $951 million were limited to $81 million. In May 2016 reports surfaced claiming that there were 11 other efforts to rob banks using similar TTPT, but only five of those were supported by good evidence, and of those five, only the Ecuadoran Banco Austro, which reportedly lost between $9-12 million in early 2015, appears to have lost money.[28]

Relevance: This theft represents a major departure from traditional thefts perpetrated by state actors. Intelligence services have historically focused on stealing intellectual property, but in this case, North Korea's goal was to generate hard currency that could not be traced back to them. The stolen money could be used by front companies to bypass embargoed technology or to run additional clandestine intelligence operations. Eastern European organized cybercrime groups have been conducting similar robberies for years, so North Korea did not break any new ground in terms of tactics. Their employment of SWIFT as the means to transmit their wire transfers created some significant second order effects among SWIFT users. There is evidence to suggest that the FRBNY's trust in the absolute security of the SWIFT network contributed to their slow response in acting on the series of phony wire transfers. The people running the SWIFT Alliance responded to the theft by providing their members with new standards for securing their systems used to communicate over SWIFT to make copycat crimes more difficult.[29]

Takeaways:

1. Poor security practices made both detection and event reconstruction more difficult. Bangladesh Bank had cheap network devices that could not log activity; their transaction verification involved a printer that was unreliable; they were not monitoring for outgoing transmissions during periods when the

---

[28] https://securityaffairs.co/wordpress/47532/cyber-crime/swift-thord-cyber-heist.html
[29] https://www.nytimes.com/interactive/2018/05/03/magazine/money-issue-bangladesh-billion-dollar-bank-heist.html

bank was closed; and they did not know how to communicate with the FRBNY during non-business hours. In the other reported attacks, banks with better IT security were able to detect the illicit activity and block outgoing wire transfers.
2. In a system of systems, the whole network is only as secure as the least secure subsystem.
3. Fraud rules employing behavioral analytics, multifactor authentication, and process ownership could have easily prevented loss of funds.

Case Study 3 – Misrepresentation Attack – Sony Pictures Entertainment

Overview: On November 24, 2014, employees logging onto the Sony Pictures Entertainment network were confronted with a red screen with a message from a group calling itself "Guardians of Peace" (GOP) that stated Sony had been hacked and that the attack was just beginning. Reports indicate that the Sony network was down for a period of time although some reports suggest that Sony took the network down to avoid further damage. That same day the GOP leaked confidential data stolen from Sony Pictures Entertainment that included employee personal information, internal e-mails, executive salaries, and copies of unreleased movies. About three weeks later, the GOP threaten violent attacks at theaters showing the movie *The Interview* (a comedy about a plot to assassinate North Korean leader Kim Jong-un) if Sony did not pull the movie from theatrical distribution. The FBI assessed that the GOP was the North Korean intelligence service using the powers of the state to attack a private company that was engaged in an action perceived to be disrespectful to North Korea and its leader.[30]

After Action: Sony pulled *The Interview* from theatrical release but made it available to customers of streaming services. North Korea denied any involvement in the attack, and no post-event

---

[30] https://www.businessinsider.com/sony-cyber-hack-timeline-2014-12

analysis of tactics or malware was released to the public. While the GOP claimed to have more than 100 terabytes of stolen data, they did not dump any additional stolen data after December 2014. The GOP and the Lazarus Group are likely the same organization.

Relevance: With each new state sponsored cyber-attack on a non-state target, the definition for what is acceptable behavior for a state is being redefined. The absence of a broad international consensus for what actions constitute cyber warfare versus espionage versus criminal activity complicate the formulation of consistent response options. The US government imposed punitive actions when Russian state sponsored actors were accused of stealing internal emails from the US Democratic Party and releasing embarrassing material on WikiLeaks in 2016, but it only made angry statements in response to this attack and to Iranian sponsored actors attacked US banks in 2012/13. To be fair, the US government's range of soft power options were limited in the cases involving North Korea and Iran by the absence of formal diplomatic relations with either country and the fact that severe economic sanctions were already in place for both. The US government also recognized that attribution efforts are imperfect; the case against North Korea was strong but it was primarily based on circumstantial evidence. An attack on JP Morgan Chase early that same year demonstrates the complex challenges involved in threat actor attribution. In that case, malicious actors stole data from 83 million accounts, and media reports quoted FBI sources as saying the Russian government was behind that theft, and there were even calls for punitive sanctions to be imposed. Attribution was based on Russian language in malware coding, but it was later determined that the attack was conducted by an organized cybercrime group led by US and Israeli citizens who outsourced some of their hacking operations to Russian coders.[31]

---

[31] https://www.nytimes.com/2015/07/22/business/dealbook/4-arrested-in-schemes-said-to-be-tied-to-jpmorgan-chase-breach.html

Takeaways:

1. States run by leaders who do not conform to the niceties of normal international behavior are increasingly using malicious cyber activity as an international policy tool, and private sector businesses are used as surrogate targets to keep actions on objective below the threshold of a state-to-state attack that might be more easily classified as an act of war. Companies that pick sides in international disputes or criticize nations or leaders of nations that do not play by the rules might pay a price for their actions.
2. Never put anything in an email that you would be uncomfortable with your customers and stockholders reading on the front page of the *Wall Street Journal*. Among the released emails were executive conversations involving President Obama's taste in movies that perpetrated racial stereotypes.
3. When there is evidence of destructive malware; shut down your network (Sony gets an A for that one.)

Criminal Case Study

Case Study 4 – Organized Cybercrime – Target Corporation

Overview: An unidentified criminal group was able to install point-of-sale (POS) malware on the network of Target Corporation and steal the magnetic track data from 40 million payment cards used in transactions at Target stores between November 27 and December 15, 2013. The perpetrators also stole personal information on an additional 70 million Target customers. In the aftermath of the reported breach, Target lost trust and market share in the retail sector; its stock price was negatively impacted, and many senior leaders, including the CEO, lost their jobs.[32]

After Action: Post-event analysis in the weeks following the discovery of the breach provided detailed information on the random access memory scraping POS malware. It also offered some insights into how the criminals collected stolen card data from the Target network, and how they accessed and exfiltrated the data without being detected. Reports also indicated that Target's security tools did detect and alert on some of the criminals' activities on the network, but the security team did not recognize the alerts as genuine threats. About a year after the breach, reports began surfacing that the criminals had gained access to the Target network through the vendor portal after stealing credentials from a vendor with poor network security practices. This portion of the case study is covered in detail in case study nine.

Relevance: The Target breach was neither the first nor the biggest retail breach in history, but the breach represents a tipping point for US businesses directly (and many non-US businesses by extension) where public opinion, fueled by the media and consumer advocate groups, began demanding greater accountability from corporate leaders for how they protect customers' personal data. In the aftermath of this attack, CEOs, COOs and corporate boards started being held to a higher level of accountability for their roles in IT security. In the US, regulatory bodies in Executive Branch also began exercising increasingly intrusive oversight roles when US companies were attacked, often imposing large fines on the victims of criminal attacks for perceived negligence.[33]

---

[32] Xiaokui Shu, Ke Tian*, Andrew Ciambrone* and Danfeng (Daphne) Yao, Breaking the Target: An Analysis of Target Data Breach and Lessons Learned, https://arxiv.org/pdf/1701.04940.pdf, pp1-10.
[33] https://www.zdnet.com/article/anatomy-of-the-target-data-breach-missed-opportunities-and-lessons-learned

Takeaways:

1. Leaders will be held accountable when cyber-attacks on their organizations impact their customers and/or stockholders.
2. Tools without sufficient training are not much good.
3. Third parties' IT security practices must be thoroughly vetted prior to those parties being granted network access, and their accesses should be limited to a narrow range of specific actions directly related to their role.
4. Extrusion monitoring/logging can detect data flowing off one's network to unknown/suspicious addresses, but analysts need to be trained to distinguish between unusual and malicious.
5. Too many alerts will inhibit detection of malicious activity; this is an area where quality should be valued over quantity.

Case Study 5 – Targeted Cybercrime – Business Email Compromise

Overview: The business email compromise (BEC) naming convention addresses a family of frauds characterized by targeting people with the authority to execute wire transfers in private sector businesses. BEC frauds employ social engineering and a wide range of deceptive approaches to convince people to execute wire transfers to accounts controlled by criminals. Early variations of the fraud employed phony emails sent from compromised senior executives' email accounts that requested funds be wired quickly and outside of normal processes. Over time, BEC frauds have diversified to include communications that appear to come from legitimate vendors requesting that their payments go to a new account and executives requesting they be sent employee personally identifiable information (PII) or wage/tax information. In all cases, the frauds are supported by research on the targeted organization, and many show evidence of extensive intelligence collection efforts, to include understanding of company processes, executives' travel schedules, and intra-office communication styles. The FBI reported in July 2018 that BEC frauds have resulted in more than $12.5B in losses worldwide ($2.9B in the US) since they were first detected in October 2013.[34]

After Action: The BEC is unique among the nine case studies because it is a family of crimes being committed by an undermined number of criminal concerns, and it is still ongoing. It has multiple manifestations, and criminals are constantly developing new variations and focusing on different industries.

Relevance: The BEC is important to understand because it serves as a good example of how the cybercrime ecosystem responds to a successful idea, and it offers some interesting observations regarding how difficult it is for organizations to adjust their processes to combat threats after they have been identified. The FBI has been running an aggressive BEC awareness program since early in 2014, yet despite their efforts and widespread media reporting on BEC and how to detect it, 55% of all reported BEC losses in the US ($1.6B out of $2.9B) have occurred between June 2016 and May 2018.[35]

Takeaways:

1. The BEC demonstrates the consequences of not getting threat information and cyber intelligence to the people being targeted by threat actors.
2. It is an excellent example for the dynamic nature of the cybercrime ecosystem and how quickly participants will leverage new ideas and develop new variations.
3. Human beings constitute one of the greatest vulnerabilities in any network, and cyber threat actors frequently target people to help them bypass security.

---

[34] https://www.ic3.gov/media/2018/180712.aspx
[35] IBID.

Hacktivists Case Studies

Case Study 6 – Publicity – The Hacking Team

Overview: During the summer of 2015, the Hacking Team, an Italian security company that develops and sells intrusive cyber surveillance tools, suffered the indignity of having its security defeated and having more than 400 gigabytes of its internal data, including source code for its tools and internal communications, stolen and dumped on a publicly accessible dump site. The company had a long history of selling surveillance tools to governments with poor human rights records, which its leaders consistently denied. By publishing internal communications, the attacker publicly exposed who the Hacking Team was selling to and what each client bought. [36]

After Action: About nine months after the attack, a hacker using the name Phineas Fisher published a full account of the attack. Fisher executed a complex attack that took advantage of weaknesses in both network and database design. He claimed to have gained persistent access by engineering a zero-day exploit to take advantage of a vulnerability in the firmware of a network device. [37]

Relevance: In the aftermath of the attack, the Hacking Team lost clients who could not afford to be associated with the company; their TTPTs were exposed, making it easier for potential targets to detect and defeat their products. They also suffered undesired publicity and government scrutiny. While details regarding costs of the attack have never been published, the attack significantly impacted the company's profits.

---

[36] https://arstechnica.com/information-technology/2016/04/how-hacking-team-got-hacked-phineas-phisher
[37] https://www.csoonline.com/article/3057200/security/hacker-who-hacked-hacking-team-published-diy-how-to-guide.html

Takeaways:

1. A single highly skilled individual with time and motivation can sometimes be enough to defeat the security of a network protected by sophisticated security.
2. The attack was greatly facilitated by a wide range of known password weaknesses, e.g. passwords being saved in plain text, noncomplex passwords, and password reuse.
3. Analysis of Phineas Fisher's attack suggests that intrusion detection system/ intrusion protection system logging was poor and alerting was also weak.
4. Humility is in order when one has been breached; a Hacking Team spokesman responded to reports of the attack by releasing false information and taunting the attacker, only to have the attacker use the spokesman's own emails against him.
5. Zero-day exploits and code for surveillance tools dumped by Phineas Fisher to damage the Hacking Team were exploited and repurposed by a wide range of malicious actors.

Case Study 7 – Damage – Ashley Madison

Overview: In July 2015, a group calling itself the Impact Team stole the user database of adult hook-up site Ashely Madison and threatened the company that they would release the database and shame the more than 30 million customers by releasing their details in public if the company did not change its policy of charging former customers to have their personal information deleted. Ashley Madison's parent company, Avid Life Media, assured customers that their data was protected and refused to comply with the Impact Team's demands. The Impact Team made good on their threats and released customers' personal details.[38]

After Action: No after action reporting has been published to shed light on how the data was stolen.

---

[38] https://digitalguardian.com/blog/timeline-ashley-madison-hack

Relevance: This is an unusual case, and it primary relevance is as a real-world example of a hacktivist attack designed to damage the target. One could argue that the attack failed. Ashley Madison is still in business, and they claim to have added more than a million new customers. The company agreed to pay a $1.65 million settlement to plaintiffs in a suit joined by 13 US states, but that settlement represents only about 10% of what the plaintiffs sought in damages. The real victims were Ashley Madison's customers whose identities company executives failed to protect.

Takeaways:

1. Humility again. Business leaders whose networks are owned by hacktivists should not call the hacktivists liars in the media; it angers them and increases their desire to do harm and inflict pain.
2. If protecting customer data is a core component of your business model, you need to protect it, and if you fail, you should at least behave like you are sorry.
3. If you engage in deceptive practices, you are more likely to draw the attention of hacktivists than you would be if you were honest.

Insider Case Studies

Case Study 8 – Malicious Insider – The US National Security Agency (NSA)

Overview: This case is better known as the Snowden case. Edward Snowden, a contractor with highly privileged access to NSA computers systems in an NSA facility in Hawaii, used his position to steal as many as 2 million classified files from the NSA. Snowden fled the US in May 2013, and within a few weeks, newspapers began publishing the content of documents he stole.

Snowden claimed his actions were that of a conscientious whistle blower trying to report on the NSA engaging in illegal collection activities against private citizens, and those claims combined with pervasive anti-NSA sentiments in the media and popular culture made him a folk hero in some circles.

After Action: NSA has been less than forthcoming about the specifics of the case, and neither Snowden nor his enablers in the media are credible or objective sources. From what has been published, it appears likely that Snowden used his position of trust to gain increased user privileges and his broad job scope to mask his activities. Previous NSA security breaches have shown a pattern of over-reliance on personnel vetting over security monitoring, which may have been a contributing factor as well. Regardless of the root causes, it is clear that a trusted insider used his inside knowledge and the latitude accorded him as a super user to download large volumes of classified material on an illegal removable storage device and walk that device out past physical security.[39]

Relevance: The Snowden case is a classic malicious insider threat case; an employee who unilaterally decides that his world views no longer aligns with his employer's and uses his/her position of trust to steal and release large volumes of sensitive information belonging to the employer in order to cause embarrassment and publicize his/her disagreement. This case is made all the more interesting by the fact that it occurred at a government intelligence agency that has one of the most extensive personnel security clearance programs in existence. There is also anecdotal reporting that suggests Snowden's co-workers did not report suspicious behaviors, which if true, suggests other problems with the NSA's security culture at that point in history. [40]

---

[39] https://www.venafi.com/blog/deciphering-how-edward-snowden-breached-the-nsa
[40] https://www.infoplease.com/current-events/nsa-edward-snowden-and-surveillance

Takeaways:

1. Actions undertaken by highly privileged users, like systems administrators, need to be subjected to auditable review. In many cases, actions should require some form of two person integrity to be executed.
2. Organizations need to have mandatory reporting for practices dangerous to security, like when a highly privileged user asks other users for account information to which he/she is not entitled.
3. Organizations need to have mechanisms in place to detect disgruntled employees in positions of trust that do not violate employee rights or that might be construed as acts of retribution.

Case Study 9 – Negligent Insider – Fazio Mechanical

Overview: The Fazio Mechanical is the least known and documented of the nine case studies, but it is included because it is an excellent example of the consequences negligent insiders can impose. Fazio Mechanical was a critical enabler for the criminals who attacked Target Corporation in 2013. As a trusted Target Corporation supplier, Fazio Mechanical had access to Target's vendor portal, which the criminals planning the attack determined to be an excellent attack vector for gaining initial access to the Target network. Media and security industry reports have suggested that the criminals gained access to the Fazio Mechanical network after stealing one or more employee(s) logon credentials. Reports also state that the credentials were stolen from employees who had infected their computers with the Citadel Trojan by clicking on a phish. Although Citadel was a well-known piece of malware at the time, the reports claim that Fazio Mechanical was using a free anti-virus program that either did not have Citadel detection signatures or that did not provide real time alerting.[41]

After Action: The knowledge of Fazio Mechanical's link to Target was a byproduct of after action reporting of the Target breach 14 months after the attack, and no additional reporting has been made public since the initial report in February 2015.

Relevance: This is a classic example of how the chain is only as strong as the weakest link. At the moment that Target granted Fazio Mechanical access to their network, Target Corporation's network baseline was lowered to that of Fazio Mechanical's. It would appear that Target Corporation failed to do the due diligence of vetting Fazio's network security prior to granting them access to their network, and they did not have controls in place to monitor activities Fazio account holders were conducting on the Target network. These oversights proved to be costly.

Takeaways:

1. Businesses must vet third parties' IT security prior to giving them network access of any kind.
2. Network security design should employ segmentation practices that isolate business critical data from users whose jobs do not require them to have access to that data.
3. Vendor/third party accesses should be limited to specific applications or network segments, and their activity should be logged and monitored.

---

[41] https://krebsonsecurity.com/2014/02/email-attack-on-vendor-set-up-breach-at-target

Chapter 2.3
Future Threats

Key Points

- New threats are constantly being introduced, but new threats are additive; existing threats never really go away.
- Threat actors will continue to steal ideas from one another; consequently, there is a blurring in TTPTs between threat actors from different threat categories.
- Attacks designed to extort money or compel behaviors will continued to rise.
- The flip-side of technological advances is that they often create new vulnerabilities and opportunities for malicious actors. Future threats are being defined by the technology being adopted today.

Stakeholder Roles

Literate Stakeholders	Educated Stakeholders	Intelligence Practitioners
• Maintain a healthy skepticism of technology that does not have a clear role • Be able to talk about the attack surface your organization presents and how to reduce it	• Understand the strengths and weaknesses of the two analytic approaches presented in this chapter • Hold cyber intelligence team accountable for addressing future threats	• Learn to engage in future threat analysis • Maintain awareness of evolving threat trends • View technology acquisition as an end-to-end process, and know all the interdependencies

Context

Among the greatest challenges facing private sector IT security teams is that they are not facing a static threat. Threat actors are constantly evolving their TTPTs, often in anticipation of, rather than in response to actions by IT security professionals. One can make a case that among the attributes that differentiate the most capable threat actors from the pack are pragmatism and agility. Successful threat actors are constantly monitoring the environment and learning from others, and if they see something they think they can use, they use it. Threat actors do not suffer from the "not invented here" mentality that permeates many security teams, and they do not have to respect the property rights of others.

Unfortunately, as new threats emerge, old ones do not disappear, so threats continue to expand and diversify. This chapter presents some predictions of future cyber threats generated from two analytic approaches that cyber intelligence teams should learn to apply. The first approach is trend extrapolation, which applies contemporary understanding of how specific threats are evolving and projects those trends forward in a linear fashion to predict future cyber threats. The second approach is a technological approach, which involves analyzing how evolving technology will likely alter the attack surface one's organization presents to potential attackers as a basis for predicting how those actors will likely evolve their TTPTs.

Trend Extrapolation

Linear trend extrapolation is a notoriously unreliable way to predict future threats when it is applied to micro-level problems, like what a given individual actor will do in the futures, but it will tend to be more reliable when applied to macro-level trends like how different classes of threat actors are likely to evolve in response to new business or security practices. Because trend extrapolation has a better track record with larger problem sets, the predictions offered in this section all address macro-level trends.

What's Old is New Again: One of the most important perspectives that any reader can take from this discussion of future threats is that new threat TTPTs are additive to, not replacements for, existing TTPTs. Organizations will need to develop new intelligence and security approaches to address threats that malicious actors will develop in the coming years, but they cannot stop doing the things they are currently doing to detect and defeat existing threats. Cyber threat actors spend as much time stealing from each other as they do from their victims. If one actor invents something clever, many others will try to copy that success. From credential stealing banking malware, to the malware-as-a-services business model, to exploit kits, to crypto ransomware, every successful new idea has been copied, and every one of them is still being employed today. Back in 2016, Checkpoint Security published a monthly list of top ten malware types they detected each month, and the Conflicker worm, first introduced in 2008 held the number one spot for the year. Sality malware, which can be traced back to 2003 was also on the list throughout the year, often in the number two spot. Other older malware like Zeus, Tinba, and Cutwail were also fixtures on the list.[42]

It is important to remember that one of the primary targets of all malicious cyber actors is the human user. People can be manipulated into bypassing security for attackers, and skillful social engineering is and will continue to play a critical role in most attacks. Social engineering techniques are applied to various means of communication (e.g. spear phishing emails, text messages, and phone calls) with the goal of getting the recipient to provide some information, open an attachment, or click on a link.

Blurring: One of the clear trends among the case studies covered in the previous chapter is a blurring in the distinction between actions by threat actors in different threat categories. State actors are increasingly employing hacktivist TTPTs as a means of influencing favorable outcomes without expending traditional political capital. North Korea stands accused of executing the largest bank robbery in history. Highly capable organized criminal groups engage in long duration persistent attacks employing state

---

[42] Checkpoint Security, http://blog.checkpoint.com/, Top 10 "Most Wanted" Malware article January-December 2016.

intelligence service TTPTs, while less capable cybercriminals engage in a range of extortion activities involving denial of service techniques pioneered by hacktivists.

This trend will continue for the foreseeable future. Threat actors have a number of incentives to steal each other's ideas; blurring complicates attribution, and it reduces both cost and time associated with developing new TTPTs. Threat actors are studying each other's actions, so IT security and intelligence professionals must do likewise.

Extortion Crimes: Extortion crimes are among the oldest and most practiced crimes in the age of the Internet, but they have evolved from the days when script kiddies locked people's keyboards to extort money for video games into a multi-billion dollar criminal industry. A catalyst for the recent explosion in extortion crimes was the introduction of crypto ransomware in late 2013. Crypto ransomware encrypts the files on an infected computer, and the only way for the victim to recover his/her data is to pay the criminals for the decryption key. Ransomware is broadly employed by criminal actors in cybercrime collectives, and it has become a mainstay for entrepreneurs, who have evolved lucrative ransomware-as-a-service business models. Both criminals and hacktivists have long used DDoS as a tool to impose costs on targets, but in recent years, criminals have evolved both the use of and the threat of the use of DDoS to extort money. Data release attacks are also employed by both criminals and hacktivists. Threat actors first steal data valued by or potentially embarrassing to the victim, then they threaten to make it public if the victim does not comply with a demand to take a specific action or if they do not make an extortion payment.

Extortion crimes will continue for the foreseeable future, and new variants will likely emerge. One should expect to see increasing use of the threat of destructive malware in the future; some variants of ransomware already employ file destruction as an incentive for victims to pay ransoms quickly. It is likely that hardcore hacktivist will embrace the use of ransomware and destructive malware as a means of coercing behavior or causing major damage to individuals and organizations they are targeting. Increased use of highly targeted DDoS attacks that require fewer resources but impose significant costs on targets will become more common place. One should not be surprised if hacktivists also expand the use of data release attacks. State actors have traditionally used extortion as a component of their espionage programs, so while open source examples are few, it is ongoing, and business leaders seeking to do business in or who compete with businesses from nations with predatory intelligence services, should expect to be targets of those intelligence services.

Exploiting Organizational Policies: Organizational security policies, both actions taken and not taken, help to define the attack surface that organizations present to malicious actors. Organizations make risk-based decisions every day to maintain legacy systems, continue using applications written in vulnerable programming languages, extend administrator privileges to users, allow remote network access protected only by a password, and allow employee owned mobile devices to access the network. Smart organizations minimize the number of self-inflicted risks they accept and identify ways to mitigate those risks. At the other extreme, some organizations have such restrictive policies that they have created incentives for employees to develop and use shadow IT infrastructure. Servers and endpoints operated outside of the asset and vulnerability management programs create opportunities for threat actors. As market leaders in security increase the use of encryption, smart threat actors have begun to encrypt stolen data and exfiltrate it in a manner that defeats existing extrusion detection systems.

Capable threat actors recognize they are targeting the human vulnerabilities involved in network design, security policies, and user behaviors when they conduct network reconnaissance to support attack planning. Security leaders should expect that threat actors will increasingly seek to gain network access using legitimate user credentials and that they will, to the greatest extent possible, behave like legitimate users.

We're from the Government, and We're here to Help You: Ironically, some of the gravest threats to private sector organizations' IT security practices in the coming years will likely be driven by well-intentioned government actions (both laws and policies.) National governments and international bodies are increasingly generating policies addressing where data must be physically stored and what data employers can and cannot collect on their employees or transmit on their networks. Oppressive regimes like China and Iran go to great lengths to control the Internet in their counties and the data generated in and transmitted out of their physical borders, but as public awareness of cyber threats has increased, western governments have felt increasingly compelled to take actions to protect their citizens and their national treasure, and some of those actions create costs and erect barriers.

It is bad enough that increased regulation has spiked compliance and audit costs, but in many cases, regulatory requirements are also creating network security architecture challenges and are preventing security teams from taking specific actions. Threat actors will seek to take advantage of all vulnerabilities, regardless of who creates them, so until governments begin working with the organizations they regulate to develop more enlightened approaches, they will be a source for vulnerability creation.

Technology Driven Trends

One of the constants in the behavior of malicious actors is that they will continuously evolve their threat TTPTs to increase their ability to target networks and the data residing on or transiting over them. Less capable actors will tend to evolve existing tools to attack new technologies to do the same things they have always done, while more capable actors will develop new TTPTs and seek to leverage the new technology as a means of increasing their own effectiveness. Given this disparity, the threat predictions presented in this section will address a range of potential actions.

Cloud Services: The growth of cloud services and the rate at which organizations are embracing the advantages they offer have been increasing steadily in recent years. The simplest way to think about the cloud is to focus on two primary service offerings most organizations are purchasing: mass data storage, and flexible IT surge capacity.

Threat actors who target organizational data to achieve their ends, will continue to evolve their capabilities to gain access to data in various cloud environments, and they will continue to steal, release, deny, and extort much as they have in the past. There is evidence to suggest all of those activities, including ransomware attacks, have been executed targeting cloud services.

Attacking the business processes in the cloud will be more complex, but malicious actors are already refining TTPTs to take major cloud service providers offline completely or to disrupt their ability to provide customers with services. The distributed nature of cloud services offer considerable resiliency, but service providers will always need to have central command and control nodes, and those nodes represent lucrative potential future targets for both state actors or highly capable organized cybercrime groups. A ransomware attack targeting critical command and control software could have catastrophic consequences, and it would command a very large ransom.

Internet of Things (IoT)/Industrial Internet/Next Generation Manufacturing: Much like the cloud, threats to the IoT have been a fixture on just about every threat prediction published in the last half dozen years. There have been a steady series of reports regarding botnets created from IoT devices for several years. Everything from refrigerators sending spam to security cameras supporting DDoS attacks have been reported. The hijacking of unprotected or poorly protected network devices to support criminal botnets is a predictable evolutionary development that surprises no one in the IT security field. The trend will almost certainly continue until device manufacturers address security in their design process, and users recognize and act on the need to apply good security practices to their employment of IoT devices.

Sophisticated threat actors will likely focus more on the data being collected and transmitted on IoT devices than on the devices themselves. Manufacturers are embedding devices into their products for a variety of reasons, but one of the main reasons is to collect actual performance data from their products in the field. Sometimes this data will help them to identify design/performance problems to assist in future product design, while in other cases it may provide warning prior to a component failing. This data has great value, and clever people will make efforts to steal it and monetize the theft.

In other cases, IoT devices are used to monitor equipment performance in infrastructure or in manufacturing processes. These devices enable a wide range of cyber-to-physical attacks in which physical processes can be shut down or can be used in destructive ways. Media reporting on threats posed by state actors targeting critical infrastructure are instructive. The IoT revolution is upon us, and the people benefiting from it are rarely the people who will face the consequences of attacks exploiting weakness in their devices' security, so there is asymmetry in the cost/benefit proposition. As the number of end-to-end physical processes tied to network access increases, so does the attack surface available to state, criminal, and hacktivist actors. New application concepts will drive new types of cyber-attacks.

Supply Chains: Supply chains offer a wide range of opportunities for malicious actors to steal and/or disrupt business operations. As supply chains become ever more reliant on technology, that technology is introducing new vulnerabilities into associated processes. There are a wide range of actions malicious actors can take to disrupt operations by denying access to or manipulating data related to in-transit visibility. As drones and driverless vehicles are introduced, cyber hijacking of both the vehicles and the physical goods they carry will become crimes.

Closing Thoughts

In today's environment, properly integrated technology is a great enabler of success regardless of the field in which one operates. Technology can reduce both labor and production costs; it can monitor quality and productivity; and it can accelerate and provide total visibility into one's supply chain. Technology is also a double-edged sword; however, and every process connected to the Internet represents a vulnerability that must be addressed via security and risk management.

Organizations will not be able to remain competitive if they do not leverage new technology, but prudent leaders will increasingly learn to play a devil's advocate role when presented with proposals for acquiring new technology or automating existing processes. Technology that is value-added to core processes or that presents real opportunities to reduce costs should be acquired, but that acquisition should also include a threat assessment that strives to define how the new technology impacts the organization's attack surface and alters threat dynamics. When the case for a new technology is less compelling, acquisition decisions should be based on a risk versus gain calculus that accounts for potential vulnerabilities created by the new technology and how those vulnerabilities are likely to impact threat dynamics.

Appendix B presents a five generation threat model designed to provide context for the existing cyber-threat ecosystem that has created a demand for cyber intelligence. The discussion in that appendix concludes with some thoughts on the technologies that will likely be the greatest drivers of a future sixth generation of threats. That discussion dovetails nicely with the content of this chapter.

Section Three
Understand Your Needs

This section provides content designed to help cyber intelligence stakeholders to develop practices that will enable them to define and prioritize what they need cyber intelligence to deliver. The content addresses the *"understand your needs"* side of the cyber intelligence fire triangle, and it introduces approaches that people establishing new or improving immature cyber intelligence practices can use. Analytic and process models presented in this section offer people charged with applying cyber intelligence capabilities to their organization with proven approaches for refining their intelligence needs at different points in the establishment process, defining what stakeholder inputs are needed to plan for effective capabilities, and for weighing the pros and cons of different establishment strategies. The content is organized as follows:

Chapter 3.1 – *Cyber Intelligence Economics* presents a cost versus proficiency model that organizations can reference in their cyber intelligence planning and implementation processes. The purpose of the chapter is to provide organizations with a framework for considering return on investment and for thinking about cyber intelligence acquisition in realistic terms that address how much capability one's organization can employ at any given point in its maturation.

Chapter 3.2 – *Cyber Intelligence Establishment Planning Process* presents a three-step process (operational design, establishment planning, and selection/refinement) intended to identify expectations for cyber intelligence within the context of organizational culture and to translate those expectations into planning guidance to direct the development of an executable cyber intelligence plan. The chapter focuses on establishing cyber intelligence capabilities where none are present. In the larger context of the book, however, this establishment planning is iteration zero of a larger recurring iterative planning process designed to refine stakeholders' needs and to drive continuous process improvement for cyber intelligence operations. [See *Chapter 5.2.*]

Chapter 3.3 – Application Considerations presents three philosophical approaches to establishing/improving cyber intelligence capabilities designed to address adopting organizations' most important intelligence needs. The discussion for each approach addresses strengths, challenges, in-sourcing/outsourcing tradeoffs, and organizational considerations, and each includes two theoretical application case studies that present challenges of establishing a new capability versus refining an existing capability.

For Your Consideration

In most instances, the decision to invest in a cyber intelligence capability is precipitated by a stimulating event (or series of events) or by an externally driven mandate. Stimulating events includes things like: detecting malicious actors on one's network; suffering a data breach; or seeing successful attacks on peer organizations. The most common type of externally driven mandates are government regulations, but there are cases where senior executives have been exposed to cyber intelligence and have decided to direct their IT leaders to build a capability. Both stimulating events and externally driven mandates will define the macro-level problems for cyber intelligence to address, and acquisition/establishment planning will then break those problems into smaller constituent parts to identify practices against which cyber intelligence can be applied.

People engaged in efforts to establish cyber intelligence practices must not only develop an acquisition strategy that is optimized to meet their organizational requirements, they must also recognize that cyber intelligence skills (both producing and consuming) are subject to experience-based learning. The need to develop a unique approach for cyber intelligence in each organization creates an imperative for people charged with establishing those capabilities to engage in a deliberate self-assessment effort designed to identify and articulate a range of issues like: what functions cyber intelligence will be employed to support; how cyber intelligence will contribute to improving those functions; why the organization is adding cyber intelligence; and what the organization's priorities (generally expressed for a defined period of time) for cyber intelligence are. It is important that the people engaged in the self-assessment process factor in the contributions experience-based learning will make over time and that they create review mechanisms to challenge their initial plan once it is in execution and performance data is available.

People charged with establishing/improving cyber intelligence practices designed to support organizational security needs have a great deal of latitude in how they go about assessing their cyber intelligence requirements, but experience teaches that the range of relevant design elements they need to identify in the self-assessment is actually quite small. Most organizations will be able to identify their key design elements if they address the issues covered in the following twenty sample questions:

1. What data and information constitute the crown jewels of our organization?
2. What legal/regulatory requirements regarding data and information must we comply with?
3. Where is that data and information stored?
4. Who has access to it?
5. Who determines what users will have access?
6. What controls are in place to protect it?
7. Who monitors compliance, and how do they do it?
8. What existing IT security functions contribute to protecting critical data and information?
9. Which of those functions will benefit from cyber intelligence?

10. How will cyber intelligence contribute to improving the performance of those functions?
11. Do we have the people, systems, and processes in place to be able to employ cyber intelligence or to act on the threat information it generates?
12. If not, what do is needed; how long will it take us to get it; and do we have the budget to acquire it?
13. Who will be accountable for the performance of cyber intelligence operations?
14. Who has budget authority?
15. Who is the responsible authority for approving intelligence requirements and establishing priorities among competing demands?
16. Who are the primary customers for routine situational awareness products?
17. Which educated stakeholders will be given responsibilities for consulting and informing literate stakeholders regarding emerging threats?
18. Does the organization benefit from hiring intelligence professionals to run cyber intelligence operations, or can it get what it needs by purchasing products and services from vendors?
19. What do we expect cyber intelligence to provide in six months? One year? Five years?
20. How will we define success?

People charged with conducting the self-assessment need to recognize the importance of both content and process in establishing conditions for planning for future cyber intelligence success. Content is self-explanatory. The questions in the self-assessment should be designed to define what problems cyber intelligence is being acquired to address and how it will contribute value to existing functions and processes that are already addressing those problems. The process employed in conducting the self-assessment can go a long way in contributing to an environment characterized by strong stakeholder buy-in. A self-assessment process in which stakeholders are made to be accountable for defining the organization's cyber intelligence priorities and their own roles in future cyber intelligence operations will contribute to establishing a culture in which stakeholder commitment to future success is more likely. Because cyber intelligence is a support function and stakeholders define success criteria, a culture of stakeholder commitment is a precondition for successful cyber intelligence operations.

The output of the self-assessment will help people to manage the tradeoffs between cost and proficiency presented in Chapter 3.1, and it can contribute a degree of rigor to the cyber intelligence operational design process presented in Chapter 3.2.

Chapter 3.1
Cyber Intelligence Economics

Key Points

- The relationship between cost and proficiency in cyber intelligence is not a straight line with a constant slope; it is a curve with four distinct performance zones that represent proficiency bands.
- Proficiency bands provide a useful basis for defining performance targets in both implementation planning and long-term performance measurement.

Stakeholder Roles

Literate Stakeholders	Educated Stakeholders	Intelligence Practitioners
• Understand the basic model and where the knees in the curve exist • Recognize that the laws of diminishing return govern all investment decisions beyond proficiency band three	• Be able to apply the model as a management tool • Recognize the costs (both financial and human capital) necessary to elevate given intelligence competencies from one proficiency band to the next	• Be able to apply the cost versus proficiency model • Be able to define specific capabilities associated with your organization's targeted proficiency band for all phases of cyber intelligence operations

Context

The processes associated with establishing and refining cyber intelligence capabilities are iterative in nature. As plans and planning assumptions come into contact with the real world, they will almost always encounter unanticipated variables and produce unexpected outcomes. Analysis of real-world outcomes produce understanding that can support efforts to refine planning assumptions and to produce a better plan; however, once that plan is placed into execution, it will initiate new lessons learned that will create the need to start the cycle over again.

This chapter develops a cost versus proficiency model to help planners to understand the relationship between those two key variables at different points in any cyber intelligence capability development process. The model identifies four defined proficiency zones. These zones support the development of a proficiency band concept that lends itself for application in implementation strategies, metrics development, and maturity models.

Cost Versus Proficiency Model

Figure 3.1.1 provides a visual model for the impact of spending on acquiring/developing cyber intelligence capabilities. Given that there are no fixed units of measure for proficiency and that proficiency measurements will be fluid both between organizations and over time as organizations mature, the curve in Figure 3.1.1 is an experience-based model and is not plotted on empirical data. The key take away from the model is that the relationship between investment and proficiency is not a straight line with a fixed slope and that it goes through four distinct phases referred to as zones in this model. Figure 3.1.1 represents a generic case for an organization with a functioning IT security team, supported by basic security tools/systems.

Zone 1 is the startup zone and is dominated by small proficiency improvements relative to initial investments (i.e. the slope of a tangent line at any point in this zone will be low.) This phenomenon reflects the fact that intelligence performs poorly as an aftermarket add on, so long-term cyber intelligence success requires intelligence capabilities to be integrated into supported functions. In addition, many of the startup costs associated with establishing a cyber intelligence capability are related to elevating the maturity of one's IT security capabilities, so in addition to adding intelligence staff or entering into intelligence contracts, most organizations will also need to upgrade some IT security tools (e.g. logging capabilities, network sensor upgrades, detection tools) to be able to apply cyber intelligence efficiently to their IT security functions.

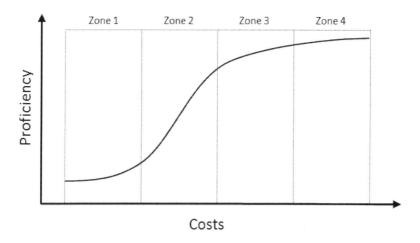

Figure 3.1.1 – Cyber Intelligence Cost vs Proficiency Model

Zone 2 is characterized by rapid growth generated by a relatively high rate of return on additional spending beyond startup costs. Organizations in this zone can expect additional direct investment in cyber intelligence capabilities like adding new analytic capacity, technical tools, and/or threat data sources will have relatively higher marginal return than at any other point in the model.

Zone 3 is the targeted operating zone. Most organizations engaged in executing cyber intelligence will want to execute the preponderance of those operations in Zone 3. Zone 3 encompasses a theoretical knee in the curve where the slope of the curve begins to flatten. There are still opportunities to improve intelligence capabilities with targeted investments, but economic incentives are beginning to shift away from additional investments in new capabilities and toward process improvements like: better refined intelligence requirements, more agile collection tasking capabilities, greater integration of cyber intelligence into supported function, and higher quality performance feedback.

Zone 4 represents a zone of diminishing return on additional investment. The slope of curve is very flat, and it approaches zero as intelligence operations reach a theoretical limit of proficiency (i.e. Law One – omniscience is unattainable at any price.) Organizations operating in the high capability proficiency band in Zone 4 will be rare, and in most cases, operating in Zone 4 will reflect a risk-based decision to achieve that high level of proficiency in only a small number of critical intelligence tasks.

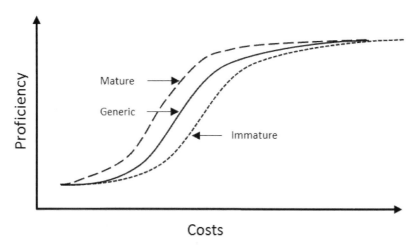

Figure 3.1.2 – Impacts of Organizational Maturity on Model

Figure 3.1.2 provides a visualization for how IT security maturity shifts the cyber intelligence cost versus proficiency curve from Figure 3.1.1. The curve labeled generic is the curve presented in Figure 3.1.1. The curve labeled mature provides a visualization of how adding cyber intelligence to an established IT security capability can provide proficiency gains for lower additional investment. Additional sources of threat data and new analytic capacity can be employed more rapidly because the security tools and a capable workforce are already in place, and the organization can move into Zone 2 at a lower level of investment than the other two models. The curve labeled immature portrays the opposite case. Organizations lacking basic tools and functioning security teams will have to invest in those areas before they can begin to realize meaningful return from investment in cyber intelligence.

Proficiency Bands

Proficiency bands are a construct designed to help organizations develop proficiency targets for intelligence tasks as they engage in iterative planning. The planning models developed in the next chapter will use the same four proficiency bands: baseline, developing, safe to operate, and highly capable. Figure 3.1.3 provides a visualization for how each of the four bands aligns to a range of proficiency levels that one would expect to encounter at the center point of the four corresponding zones outlined in the previous section.

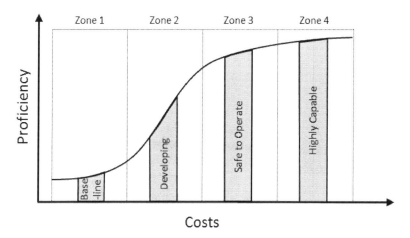

Figure 3.1.3 – Proficiency Bands

The **baseline band** corresponds to Zone 1, and proficiencies in this area are very limited. Organizations in the baseline band have some awareness of what cyber intelligence is and what capabilities it can provide, but they have few resources invested and have not begun documenting processes or doing much original analysis.

The **developing band** corresponds to Zone 2, and because that zone is characterized by rapid growth, proficiency attributes in this band demonstrate a greater range of capabilities than those in the baseline band. Organizations operating in the developing band have generally begun creating and documenting processes, and rapid learning is taking place, so processes are evolving. Many actions are being performed by people who will not be doing them in a more mature organization.

The **safe to operate band** corresponds to Zone 3, and it is characterized by a high degree of standardization, developed and documented processes, and mature relationships and professional networks both inside and outside the organization. This is the first proficiency band in which leaders have sufficient visibility into cyber intelligence operations to be able to have a real-time impact on execution decisions during periods of increased levels of threat activity.

The **highly capable band** corresponds to Zone 4, and intelligence operations in this band produce best in class performance but are characterized by high costs. Most organization that choose to operate in this band will only operate at this level for a small number of very important intelligence tasks for finite periods of time.

Proficiency bands provide a useful construct for developing implementation plans and measuring proficiency bands in maturity models. Employed in this manner, they allow stakeholders to identify the attributes for intelligence core competencies within each of the four proficiency bands and to develop a roadmap for getting to their desired proficiency level for each competency.

As a general rule, most organizations are going to want to perform their identified intelligence core competencies at the safe to operate (Zone 3) level, but that is not always the case and this framework provides a basis for making reasoned tradeoffs. For example, an organization that outsources most of its network monitoring to a vendor might still want the cyber intelligence team to be able to write deployable automation rules, but since the vendor is capable of this as well, the team might target this capability as a proficiency band 2 task, freeing resources and human capital to perform tasks not covered in the contract.

Readers who want to gain an understanding of how their organization might apply this model are encouraged to read Section 5.5.4, which presents the concept of proficiency matrices. The discussion supporting that concept develops three approaches for applying proficiency bands as maturity models and planning tools, and it develops detailed examples for how organizations can define performance standards for each proficiency band. The section concludes with a presentation of "time-phased proficiency implementation matrices," which offers cyber intelligence planners a mechanism for designing a roadmap get to a desired level of cyber intelligence capabilities in a manner that allows them the flexibility to prioritize the development of one capability over another.

Chapter 3.2
Cyber Intelligence Establishment Planning Process

Key Points

- The common denominator in all successful intelligence operations is a shared understanding between intelligence customers and producers regarding what customers expect intelligence to provide and what intelligence can provide.
- Organizations establishing cyber intelligence practices need to conduct establishment planning to align expectations with actual capabilities.
- Cyber intelligence planning is an iterative and continuous process that will be ongoing throughout the lifecycle of a cyber intelligence practice, and its foundation is the establishment planning process.
- This chapter presents a three step process for establishing cyber intelligence capabilities in an orderly, auditable, and transparent manner:
    - An operational design process by which leaders develop and communicate planning guidance involving five critical planning variables.
    - An establishment planning process that translates planning guidance into multiple distinct, actionable courses of action (COAs) in response to the initial planning guidance.
    - A COA selection and refinement process that chooses the COA the organization will execute and refines the content, socializes it among stakeholders, and converts it into an establishment execution plan.

Stakeholder Roles

Literate Stakeholders	Educated Stakeholders	Intelligence Practitioners
• Understand the value of process participation • Participate in course of action refinement process	• Understand roles and responsibilities for planning • Recognized the importance of documenting all guidance and assumptions • Be attuned to how personalities can bias outcomes	• Actions defined in this chapter will occur prior to any cyber intelligence practitioners being hired

Context

This chapter presents a cyber intelligence establishment planning process that is designed to capture and refine stakeholder needs and expectations and apply them as the foundation upon which organizations can build relevant and responsive cyber intelligence processes. Figure 3.2.1 provides a visualization of the three step planning process presented in this chapter. The establishment planning process constitutes iteration zero of a continuous planning/refinement cycle designed to drive improved proficiency and responsiveness in cyber intelligence practices over time. Readers in organizations with functioning cyber intelligence capabilities may find value in reviewing the self-improvement process presented in Chapter 5.1 after reading this chapter.

The establishment process presented in this chapter is kept at a fairly generic level out of respect for the broad diversity in intelligence needs and performance standards that different organizations seeking to establish a cyber intelligence capability will have. The process packages proven intelligence planning best practices, some of which are drawn from military doctrine. Consistent with the philosophy of military doctrine, the intent of the proposed process is to provide planners, regardless of experience, industry, or geographic location, a common approach and descriptive vocabulary aligned to proven best practices. <u>Nothing in this proposed process is intended to limit the creativity or sources of input for any user</u>. In fact readers are highly encouraged to apply additional planning considerations based on their understanding of their organizations' unique needs and decision-making cultures.

People charged with the responsibility of establishing a cyber intelligence capability will need to invest a considerable portion of their planning time to refining planning guidance that accurately reflects priorities among competing demands for cyber intelligence. They must also enter into the process understanding that intelligence planning is an iterative process and that the most important output of the first few iterations of any intelligence planning effort may well be the learning engendered by doing. The second most important output is a set of performance standards against which cyber intelligence operations can be measured.

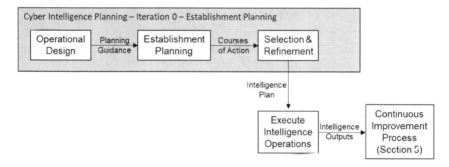

Figure 3.2.1 – The Cyber Intelligence Establishment Planning Process

Operational Design

The term operational design is used as a naming convention to describe a range of leadership inputs aimed at defining the prioritized roles and desired outputs for cyber intelligence operations within the context of the establishment planning discussion. The design elements produced by the operational design process provide planners with concrete planning guidance they can employ to align their efforts to leadership priorities. The process' structure has the added benefit of creating an initial set of performance standards that can be used to measure execution performance against the plan's design parameters.

Operational design takes its name from a somewhat esoteric, graduate-level concept in military doctrine of the same name. Doctrinal operational design describes actions employed to define planning parameters for complex problems with large numbers of unknowns. In application, it is more art than science, and it demands creative thinking about the nature of the problems one is trying to solve. Operational design is normally applied in advance of, or in concert with, the initiation of a new planning process, and it employs tools (design elements) to develop and refine guidance to direct planning. Planning initiated by properly conducted operational design will consistently generate better developed performance measures that can be employed in follow on work than planning processes that do not apply operational design principles.

Step One: Identify Design Elements

Applying the concept of operational design to the task of developing a plan to establish a cyber intelligence capability is pretty straight forward. Stakeholders charged with overseeing the process begin by defining a list of design elements to guide the process going forward. Organizations can create their own list of design elements, but there are at least five design elements that should be used as a starting point: (1) expectations/priorities, (2) organizational alignment, (3) risk tolerance, (4) performance timelines, and (5) available resources.

(1) Expectations/Priorities:

This design element provides the context for the other four, and it creates the basis for measuring process performance as a means of driving process refinement and improvement. Expectations need to address what the organization believes cyber intelligence can reasonably provide and to what level of fidelity. Performance standards created by an external source (regulator, contract vehicle, insurance policy, etc.) also need to be enumerated, and the source of that external requirement needs to be cited. The three intelligence roles developed in Chapter 1.2 offer a good framework for articulating performance expectations. The output of this review is a prioritized list of actions that stakeholders engaged in the planning process believe cyber intelligence should be able to perform. Initial process outputs need not be at execution-level detail, but they must be clear enough to be actionable. For example, the guidance might be, "priority two is predictive threat warning tailored to provide corporate officers and board members with threat trends impacting our industry and the geographies in which we operate to coincide with quarterly board meetings." This statement levies and expectation for a regularly scheduled strategic-level intelligence product without stipulating specific content, sources of input, format, means of delivery or whether it needs to be produced organically or can be provided by an external source.

(2) Organizational Alignment:

A key decision all organizations must address is where to align cyber intelligence capabilities into their existing org chart. Factors in this decision include how the cyber intelligence capability is constituted and who in the organization realizes the greatest return from adding intelligence capabilities. Four logical approaches for constituting a cyber intelligence capability are creating a distinguishable cyber intelligence team, adding intelligence reporting requirements to existing security positions, acquiring specific threat data and/or finished intelligence from external sources, and hybrid solutions combining two or more of the approaches. There are both opportunities and costs associated with creating a designated intelligence leader position and with where that position is placed in the organization. Smaller organizations focused on detection and prevention may choose to make intelligence a function of their detection or security operations teams, whereas a large multi-national holding company involved in frequent mergers and acquisitions might position their intelligence leader as a direct report to the CISO. The bottom line is that organizational alignment needs to be driven by stakeholder expectations and organizational culture. Alignment matters because cyber intelligence operations will evolve to meet the needs of the most engaged stakeholders and to support the person to whom intelligence leader reports.

(3) **Risk Tolerance:**

Actions within this design element address the recognition that in the real world, regardless of available resources, there will always be gaps in available intelligence that will represent risk to the organization, and managing that risk is a leadership function. Design elements addressing risk tolerance should begin by addressing the classes of data that need to be most protected (e.g. personally identifiable information and proprietary data) and software applications critical to continuity of operations (e.g. financial management or control systems) where the organization can least afford to accept risk. Once these high level concerns are identified, planners need to step through a process of articulating progressively less sensitive but important network functions and data that can guide/prioritize cyber intelligence efforts to develop threat understanding in support of risk mitigation through improved security.

(4) **Performance Timelines:**

This design element should be included as a critical data field for all capabilities identified in the expectations/priorities development process. Timelines need to be driven by the established priorities, and initial inputs can be in the form of a no later than date. Organizational alignment and risk tolerance should frequently have timeline requirements as well, and those timelines should reflect leadership expectations related to performance improvements.

(5) Available Resources:

This design element defines the art of the possible. Resource demand increases with the number and complexity of identified expectations, decreases in risk tolerance, and shortened timelines. Successful cyber intelligence operations tend to generate demand signals for more intelligence capabilities, while unsuccessful operations tend to be blamed on insufficient resources, which can also generate a demand signal for more spending. Technical cyber intelligence operations performed under the rubric of "support to security operations" can be limited by the proficiency of the existing security disciplines they are designated to support. Cyber intelligence can therefore drive addition investment in non-intelligence functions. This phenomenon is explains the shallow slope on the curve in Zone 1 of the cost versus proficiency curve covered in Chapter 3.1.

Step Two: Apply Design Elements to Produce Planning Guidance

The mechanics of generating the initial design elements require some consideration in advance of initiating any actions. In a perfect world the CIO or CISO would take ownership of this process and would have sufficient understanding of cyber intelligence to know what they were doing; sufficient knowledge of all aspects of the full range of organizational operations to make informed judgements on how cyber intelligence might reduce risk, and sufficient access to key leaders to get their feedback on the proposed design elements. In the real world, CIOs and CISOs are extremely busy people who only have a portion of the operational picture, and in most cases, they will choose to create a team of trusted professionals to take on the task of defining the design elements.

Future intelligence success is not predicated on creating a perfect first plan, but quality will accelerate the organization's ability to move up the proficiency scale. Regardless of who is assigned responsibility for this process, that person should consider bringing in a facilitator from a firm with cyber intelligence experience to help the team produce a quality initial input; they should commit to an aggressive review process designed to put decisions under stress early for the purposes of accelerating learning, and they should create opportunities to socialize their decisions with leaders outside of the IT field to acquire broader organizational perspectives.

The design elements collectively constitute the input for the planning guidance that will drive establishment planning. There is no prescribed format for planning guidance, but it must be documented in a manner that all stakeholders have a common frame of reference for planning, execution, and performance evaluation. Table 3.2.1 provides a sample planning guidance matrix organizations can use to help them get started. The level of detail is actionable, but it does not limit the ability of planners to examine multiple options for addressing the guidance.

Expectation	Priority	Alignment	Risk Tolerance	Timeline			
				3 months	6 month	1 year	3 years
Reduce endpoint malware infections by 90%	4	Security Operations	Medium	No action	Plan Developed	Reduced 50%	Achieved
Provide advanced warning of cyber-attacks	1	CISO	Low	Plan Developed	Capability in place	Achieved	Achieved
Protect proprietary data	2	Security Operations	Low	Plan Developed	Capability in place	Achieved	Achieved
Identify threat trends to support threat-driven IT security operations	3	CISO	Medium	No action	Plan Developed	Capability in place	Achieved
Present quarterly strategic-level threats to leadership	5	CISO	High	No action	Plan Developed	Capability in place	Achieved
Resources Year One - $1.0 million – 80% allocation to priorities 1 and 2 Year Two - $1.2 million – allocation to be refined by learning within plan execution Year Three - $1.5 million – allocation to be refined by learning within plan execution							

Table 3.2.1 – Sample Planning Guidance

Establishment Planning Process

The term "establishment planning" refers to actions taken to convert planning guidance into actionable COAs that can be submitted to leaders for COA selection and process approval. In most cases, the CISO will want to oversee this process but will want to delegate the actual execution to a subset of his/her direct reports. The CISO's management challenge will be to keep the process on track without imposing limits on planning options.

The team charged with conducting establishment planning should produce between three and five proposed COAs for achieving planning guidance. There should always be three distinctly different actionable COAs. The intent is to provide a range of options involving how guidance can be met to include organizational alignment, intelligence team constitution, functional outsourcing, etc. If the team has sufficient time, they should also develop COAs for what they would recommend if they had either 20% more and 20% less budget. These COAs will provide leaders with some very useful insights into how key stakeholders value potential cyber intelligence contributions.

Viable COAs must not only address all elements of the planning guidance, they must also fit the culture of organization. The establishment planning process outlined in this section has four steps (1) project analysis and documentation; (2) external research; (3) assess organizational cultural aptitude for cyber intelligence; and (4) COA development.

(1) Project Analysis and Documentation

The purpose of a project analysis is to transition planning guidance into the planning process and to document the planners' interpretation of that guidance. A best practice is to begin with the desired end-state defined in the planning guidance and to work backward to the earliest task delineated in the guidance. The project analysis should include seven components:

Delineate Directed Tasks: This is the simplest, most straight forward actions, and it is also the most important. Planners need to step through the planning guidance and make a list of everything that guidance specifically tasks them to do. Using the example in Table 3.2.1, the five expectations combined with their timeline targets constitute the five directed tasks of the planning guidance.

Document Implied Tasks: Implied tasks represent the enabling capabilities the organization will need have in place to perform the directed tasks. Identifying implied tasks requires some analysis, but it is critical for planners identify as many as possible early in the process, because failure to do so creates inefficiencies and gaps later. Implied tasks derived from the planning guidance in Table 3.2.1 might include: developing network visibility to know where proprietary data is stored, and having specific security software loaded on all endpoints.

Identify Available Resources: Resources begin with the budget in the planning guidance, but they include much more than money. Resources include all existing programs and capabilities that might enhance the ability for the cyber intelligence team to do their job. Examples include: user training programs to combat social engineering, a 24/7 security operations center, a mail guard program, programmable detection sensors, membership to an industry information sharing and analysis center (ISAC), etc.

Document Constraints: Constraints include policies, practices, and laws that impose limits on actions available to the organization. Examples of constrains might include: a privacy law that prohibits information sharing, differing reporting laws in different countries in which the organization operates that inhibit or prevent uniform approaches to intelligence; regulator imposed challenges, etc.

List Gaps and Assumptions: All planning guidance will create questions. Sometimes those questions can be answered with a little research, but in many cases they do not have answers.

These unknowns constitute knowledge gaps in the planning process, and they are best handled by developing planning assumptions to address them. Assumptions should always be reasonable; people who try to assume away problems by making overly optimistic assumptions generally pay a high price for their intellectual corner cutting. Assumptions must also be stated in every plan, because the minute that one encounters evidence that an assumption is invalid, the credibility of the rest of the plan comes into question. Referring back to the planning assumptions in Table 3.2.1, the term cyber-attack is not defined in the priority one expectation, so how can planners develop a plan to address it? Rather than go back to the CISO and ask what he/she meant by the term cyber-attack, it is reasonable for planners to define a specific threshold or range of actions that would be sufficient to be classified as a cyber-attack that should then trigger a warning to be communicated. That output should be stated as a planning assumption.

Identify Obstacles to Success: An obstacle is anything that threatens the successful accomplishment of achieving the planning guidance. It can take the form of the presence of something that will prevent cyber intelligence from conducting a required action or the absence of a capability that cyber intelligence will need to be successful. Using priority 2 (protect proprietary data) in Table 3.2.1 as an example, the absence of a written information security policy that defines what proprietary data is and how it should be handled (i.e. controls like classification markings or restrictions on how it is transmitted) would be an obstacle to developing cyber intelligence processes to protect proprietary data. Cyber intelligence cannot develop processes to detect threats to undefined, unidentified, or uncontrolled information.

Develop Recommended Intelligence and Information Requirements: The primary means by which customers direct intelligence operations is by articulating intelligence requirements. [*The intelligence requirements process is presented in Chapter 4.2.*] The act of analyzing intelligence tasks creates insights into what leaders need cyber intelligence to provide to the organization, and those insights should form the basis of the initial set of intelligence requirements. The project analysis process also provides some valuable insights into what organizational information and data cyber intelligence practitioners will need to possess to be able to execute cyber intelligence operations. These insights form the basis of information management practices for identifying categories of critical organizational data and information (CODI), i.e. what has to be protected, and what has to be shared to ensure that intelligence outputs are relevant and are disseminated to the people who most need the intelligence.

(2) External Research

No organization is limited to in-house intelligence knowledge in their planning process. There are a wide range of resources available. Government agencies, non-profit organizations, academia, professional organizations, industry ISACs, business partners, and IT security/cyber intelligence vendors are all potential resources for any organization willing to take the time to do external research.

Government agencies, particularly law enforcement organizations, are increasingly seeking to work with private sector organizations on cyber threats. Nonprofits like the National Cyber Forensics and Training Alliance (NCFTA) and industry ISACs can provide access to useful threat data, archived analytic studies, professional forums, and they provide safe places to ask questions. They can help the team doing the project analysis to build a professional network that might provide useful insights and lessons learned from partners with existing cyber intelligence experience.

While many people will go to great lengths to avoid taking sales calls, it is hard to beat the education one can acquire from talking to sales representatives from a few top cyber intelligence firms. Each company goes to market with a slightly different set of offerings, and they are smart creative people whose firms have solutions to threats most people have never thought about. They also package their offerings in a variety of ways, which can provide food for thought for planning options in the next step. If one's organization has a research budget, one can hire external experts to survey capabilities, identify needs, and make recommendations for COA development.

(3) Assess Organizational Cultural Aptitude for Cyber Intelligence

One of the key drivers for a phased implementation approach for cyber intelligence is the ability of the organization to provide inputs to and act on outputs from cyber intelligence. Organizational cultures with a high aptitude for assimilating a complex interdependent process like cyber intelligence will simplify COA development. Planners should conduct an organizational cultural self-assessment and identify potential barriers/points of friction that need to be addressed in their COAs. Three elements of organizational cultural aptitude that should be assessed are:

Leadership Commitment: Among the key takeaways readers should have from Section One of this book is an understanding that intelligence is a customer-driven capability and that there is a direct correlation between customer engagement and customer satisfaction. Anybody who has ever been in a leadership position knows that their scarcest commodity is time, and most leaders operate at or near the limits of their sustainable capacity at all times. The decision to establish a cyber intelligence capability represents additional time demands on people with little to no additional capacity; therefore, a critical planning factor needs to be sorting out which leaders will have ownership responsibilities and whether they can commit the time necessary to achieve success. Without leadership commitment, it will be extraordinarily difficult to align cyber intelligence capabilities to the organization's most critical threats.

Technical Competence: Organizations that monitor and log outgoing network traffic, monitor and log activities of Internet facing devices, and have security information and event management (SIEM) systems that can alert security operation teams to unusual or unauthorized activities and that are searchable have the prerequisites for establishing technical intelligence capabilities. Cyber intelligence analysis will have the data necessary to identify and analyze threats and to support security team partners' ability to detect, prevent, and defeat those threats. Companies with strong asset management programs can provide cyber intelligence analysts with the information they need to understand the attack surface malicious actors can target, which will enable analysts to focus their energies on threats that matter. Conversely, organization lacking these capabilities lack the foundation for successful cyber intelligence operations and will have to address security deficiencies as a component of their cyber intelligence establishment planning efforts.

Cultural Readiness: This category encompasses a broad range of issues that can impose significant friction on intelligence operations, or stop them completely. A list of key cultural barriers that need to be factored into planning include:

> **Legal environment** – Risk adverse lawyers, i.e. those who calculate risk in terms of personal professional risk rather than institutional risk, can negatively impact intelligence operations. The performance of contemporary intelligence operations can be significantly improved by participation in two way sharing relationships with a broad range of partners. These relationships are defined by a range of sharing, membership, and non-disclosure agreements. Anybody working in the cyber intelligence field has stories of individual lawyers unilaterally invalidating sharing agreements or forbidding employees from sharing intelligence without cumbersome reviews and documentation that slow the process down and greatly diminishes the value of the intelligence to recipients. These actions also siphon off valuable analytic capacity to

perform self-generated bureaucratic actions. Companies that have a lawyer assigned to the CIO and/or CISO whose performance review standards are written to reflect their impact in enabling IT and IT security operations will likely have greater success in developing sustainable cyber intelligence agreements than those that do not.

Internal teaming environment – Successful cyber intelligence operations will require that the intelligence leader and team have the ability to work directly with leaders and peers outside the IT security organization (e.g. people assigned to the Chief Technology Officer and the Chief Digital Officer.) Organizational cultures in which executives and officers limit the ability of their people to develop relationships with people outside their team or that seek to control external communications will struggle to leverage the full value of their investment in cyber intelligence. Conversely, organizational cultures that value and reward employees who build extensive professional networks and see value in seeking new partnerships will constantly find new uses for cyber intelligence.

Resistance to change – Cyber intelligence will drive change, and cultures that are change adverse will seek to limit cyber intelligence operations as a means to maintain status quo. Resistance to change is a particularly insidious attribute in that in most cases, those practicing it do not even realize they are doing so. Resulting actions are often passive-aggressive and create long-term barriers to success. Planners need to make an honest effort to account for the portions of their organization that are most likely to resist efforts to implement cyber intelligence in each of their COAs.

Organizational complexity – One of the major challenges confronting cyber intelligence teams is knowing whether a newly discovered threat is relevant to their organization. If there are not resources available to determine whether a given threat is applicable, intelligence will either over report non-relevant threats or under report relevant ones. The former behavior damages credibility and imposes costs, and the latter leaves the organization vulnerable to known threats. Two real-world examples of friction imposed by complexity are: (1) a company that spent four month trying to identify all of the point-of-sale devices on the network in the wake of the Target breach, and (2) a company whose cyber intelligence team waited more than a year to get a list of employees in their own company who were authorized to execute financial transactions so the team could provide tailored awareness training on the business email compromise scam that used social engineering to elicit fraudulent wire transfers.

(4) COA Development

Most people are probably familiar with a variant of the old adage regarding acquiring a new capability; everyone wants it to be good, quick, and cheap, but they can never have more than two of the three conditions met. People engaged in developing plans for establishing a cyber intelligence practice in an organization without existing intelligence experience will find themselves impacted by the tradeoffs between quality, speed, and cost described in the old adage, and those tradeoffs are a useful mechanism for creating unique COAs.

The four common approaches to building a cyber intelligence capability introduced in the organizational alignment discussion provide a good starting point exploring COAs aligned with planning guidance. Each of the four brings strengths to leverage and challenges to be addressed:

(a) Identifiable cyber intelligence team organic to the organization:

Strengths: Intelligence operations are most effective when they are integrated into the functions they are charged with supporting, and the best way to integrate a strong cyber intelligence capability into IT security operations is establish cyber intelligence as a core function of the CISO team. The presence of a cadre of intelligence professionals provides the CISO and his/her directs with the benefit having people who can: advise them on how to minimize their exposure to threats; respond to emergent intelligence questions; process intelligence from external sources; and provide tailored multi-source intelligence that can highlight meaningful threat information while reducing the amount of time people need to spend reading and researching on their own.

Challenges: Building a team takes time and obligates the organization to long-term recurring costs. The absence of existing intelligence experience makes creating positions descriptions difficult. The people charged with the task of creating the positions often do not know what attributes or experiences are important, or what capabilities they need to prioritize. Once people are hired and in place, there can be a significant learning curve for all stakeholders.

(b) Assign intelligence roles to existing security team members:

Strengths: This approach emphasizes speed and organizational stability, and leverages people who are already in place and who already have an understanding of the core IT security functions that one is trying to strengthen by applying intelligence. Existing expertise means that people have sufficient process understanding of supported functions to be able to develop intelligence requirements to guide their efforts.
Challenges: This approach is subject to zero-sum game theory, i.e. IT security professionals performing cyber intelligence roles are not performing IT security functions. Few organizations have

sufficient numbers of IT security professionals, and this approach will further tax existing shortfalls. Intelligence and security are very different professional disciplines, and they require very different mindsets. Security places a premium on not allowing defined events to take place, whereas intelligence deals with understanding how potential adversaries think, and how they might react to different stimuli. Security professionals tend to view threat intelligence through the lens of their specific security programs which provides fertile ground for being susceptible to confirmation biases. The absence of experienced intelligence professionals will have a greater impact over time, and will likely establish a lower ceiling for potential cyber intelligence proficiency in a mature organization.

(c) Acquire specific threat data/finished intelligence from external sources:

Strengths: This approach maximizes speed and simplicity over all other factors. The range and quality of professional cyber intelligence services available to organizations seeking to outsource all, or elements of, their cyber intelligence needs has improved considerably in recent years. Organizations have the option of contracting for a range of turnkey operations performed by professionals. They can also leverage professional services to aid them in refining how to organize their cyber intelligence operations as a component of an existing IT security construct. Industry leaders in the cyber intelligence sector have years of archived products and technical data (signatures, hashes, detection rules, etc.) that can jumpstart threat-driven security operations.

Challenges: The primary challenge with this approach is that the value one can derive from this approach is directly related to customer proficiency. Most professional cyber intelligence service companies are highly capable of filtering their intelligence feeds to meet their customers' needs, but if the organization purchasing the services lacks people with the skills to tailor those feeds to their actual needs, then the organization can find itself inundated with unusable threat data and paying for finished intelligence that nobody consumes.

(d) Hybrid solutions:

Strengths: Hybrid solutions provide users to trade off strengths and weakness from multiple approaches to develop approaches aligned to planning guidance.

Challenges: Hybrid solutions present challenges in how to mix and match elements of other solution sets, and they force planners to develop a time-phased approach that may bias the long-term cyber intelligence capability toward being dominated by whichever approach they implement first.

Proposed COAs need to align the potential strengths of the various approaches to the time-phased requirements established in the planning guidance, while being mindful of cost tradeoffs. While it is always helpful to work from the three year "end-state" back to the present, most planning guidance will tend to be pretty vague outside of the first year to 18 months, so the greatest level of effort should be focused where the guidance has the most depth.

There are no prescribed formats for presenting COAs, but one should make every effort to highlight the specific actions proposed in the COA and to provide specific time-phased considerations. Figure 3.2.2 provides an example of a potentially valid COA consistent with planning guidance provided in Table 3.2.1. Other COAs might include a variation in which the technical intelligence capabilities are performed organically and strategic intelligence products are outsourced to vendors, or a variation in which a small cyber intelligence team is established to train IT security professionals how to do their own intelligence analysis and to provide quality assurance on their outputs.

COA 1: Two Track Hybrid Approach

Actions:

(1) Execute a cyber intelligence contract with a respected vendor with the capability to produce intelligence that responds to all directed and implied tasks identified in the project analysis process.
(2) Hire an experienced cyber intelligence leader to perform the following roles:
    (a) to act as the primary advisor to the CISO for plan refinement/implementation and additional hiring actions,
    (b) to develop recommended top level intelligence requirements,
    (c) to develop cyber intelligence analysis and production plans and to build an intelligence dissemination architecture, and
    (d) to be responsible for ensuring that vendor provided intelligence is tailored to the organizations prioritized needs.

Time phasing:

(1) First six months: Pursue actions associated with identifying a vendor and hiring an intelligence leader concurrently. If possible, get the cyber intelligence leader in place to participate in the final source selection process, but the contract must be in place within six months.
(2) Second six months: Add 2-4 additional intelligence subject matter experts to be integrated to drive positive customer outcomes for security operations, policy development, vulnerability management, IT security risk, security architecture, the CTO, and the Chief Data Officer.
(3) Years two and three: Refine performance metrics for primary cyber intelligence lines of business and develop business case for future COA 1 refinement or replacement.

Strengths: Meets all planning guidance and establishes a solid foundation that does not limit future options as organizational learning occurs and threats evolve.

Weaknesses: Places a heavy reliance on a yet to be hired cyber intelligence leader and provides no real resiliency if a strong performer cannot be found (and people with the requisite skills are scarce) or if the vendor proves incapable of flexing to evolving organizational needs.

Figure 3.2.2 – Sample Course of Action

COA Selection and Refinement

Once at least three distinctly different executable COAs have been developed, they will be submitted to the leaders who provided the planning guidance for COA selection. In most cases, leaders will select one COA outright; select one contingent upon additional refinements they need to see; select two COAs and ask that they be merged into a new COA or that they are refined in a manner that reduces commonalities; or reject all submitted COAs and direct that the process be reworked based on new guidance.

Once a single COA is selected, it is further refined into a plan of action where specific tasks, associated dates, and responsible parties are assigned. This is also an opportune point for socializing the process outputs with future cyber intelligence stakeholders who have not been included in the establishment planning effort. Literate stakeholders might have expectations of their own once they see something concrete, and the sooner the team becomes aware of those expectations, the more likely they will be to be able to adjust the plan to address them. This is also a great time to commission competing or alternative analyses to capture ideas from people who were not part of the COA development effort. Done correctly, this work will identify weak assumptions and call out confirmation biases if they are present.

Once socialization and refinement are completed, the organization will have the first iteration of an actionable intelligence plan, and it is time to put that plan in execution. The act of executing the plan transitions the cyber intelligence planning process out of the establishment process and moves it into the continuous improvement and self-learning process, which is covered in Chapter 5.1.

Chapter 3.3
Application Considerations

Key Points

- There are three application approaches for establish/improving cyber intelligence tailored to meet any organization's prioritized intelligence needs:
    - Grow customer and practitioner proficiencies simultaneously
    - Prioritize customer proficiency development first and refine cyber intelligence needs before making any long-term investments in acquiring and developing cyber intelligence proficiencies
    - Prioritized acquisition of critical cyber intelligence as the driver for shaping customer understanding of how to employ cyber intelligence to create threat-driven IT security operations

Stakeholder Roles

Literate Stakeholders	Educated Stakeholders	Intelligence Practitioners
• Provide inputs if requested	• Evaluate all three approaches • Determine which best fits the organization's culture and which works best with the establishment plan derived in the previous chapter	• Understand your roles • Seek to understand and provide the feedback needed by educated stakeholders

Context

This chapter develops three unique application approaches for establishing cyber intelligence capabilities. The three approaches represent different philosophies for moving from a position where there is little to no capability to direct, produce, or consume cyber intelligence to a place where all three actions are competencies.

Each of three approaches offers unique strengths and challenges, and each can be helped considerably by prudent employment of external resources and proper recognition of factors involving organizational culture. In other words, all three approaches have merit, but none is perfect, and it is important for people involved in efforts to either establish or improve cyber intelligence service offerings to be able to both understand the relationship between customer and practitioner proficiencies and to assess their organization's proficiency in both areas. To drive home this point, the discussions of each approach include two short theoretical case studies that illustrate how that approach shapes the establishment and improvement efforts.

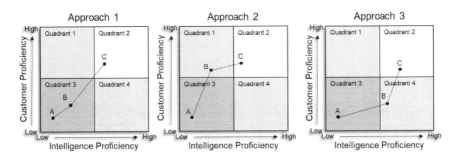

Figure 3.3.1 – Application Approaches

Figure 3.3.1 provides a side-by-side visualization of the three approaches. Each case study employs the assumption that the organization in the case has no existing cyber intelligence capability, so all three begin in quadrant three (low proficiency for both customers and practitioners.) Organizations with existing cyber intelligence capabilities that are seeking to apply the content of this chapter to understand options available to them to improve outcomes are likely to have a starting point either higher up or farther right than those in Figure 3.3.1, but the principles will be the same.

Application Approach One: Neutral Growth Strategy

Application Approach One models an organization in which customer and intelligence practitioner proficiencies grow at similar rates and reinforce one another. It represents a common evolutionary path followed by a high percentage of organizations that have already established cyber intelligence capabilities. Organizations in this case start with limited proficiency for both customers and intelligence practitioners (point A); they acquire some intelligence capability that drives greater customer understanding (point B), and that greater understanding drives more focused intelligence requirements resulting in improved proficiency for all stakeholders (point C).

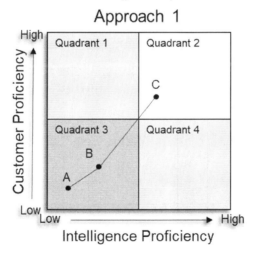

Figure 3.3.2 – Neutral Growth Approach

Strengths

The neutral grow strategy creates an environment in which customers and practitioners increase their proficiencies by working and learning together. This balanced approach offers organizations great latitude in establishing development priorities driven by real-world need. For example, an organization that has specific capability requirements imposed by a regulator can focus on developing those first.

This approach also helps to establish/reinforce the interdependencies that participants will share once cyber intelligence capabilities have reached a higher level of maturity. It promotes mutual respect and encourages the development of communication and feedback processes that will accelerate growth and promote process improvement as a core value for cyber intelligence practitioners.

Challenges

The primary challenges in making this approach work and driving process maturity generally involve identifying key process participants to drive the process forward. People defined as cyber intelligence customers in this model had full-time roles prior to the addition of cyber intelligence, so any time spent on cyber intelligence is additive to their existing workload and represents an opportunity cost. Employees hired to perform cyber intelligence roles will require some amount of time to get oriented to their new organization and to adapt to its culture. Organizations following this neutral growth strategy frequently get bogged down at point B in the model, because once some cyber intelligence capability is in place and threat analysis is being produced and disseminated, many customers will seek to revert to their old roles and assume that the practitioners can drive the process forward. Practitioners can improve efficiency and quality in their assignments but will frequently lack the organizational understanding to drive evolutionary growth.

Another common challenge that most organizations using this approach will face is assessing participants' proficiency levels at different points in the maturation process. Most participants understand they are in quadrant 3 at point A, but at point B, there will be a tendency for customers to assess that they are operating in quadrant 1 and for intelligence practitioners to assess that they are operating in quadrant 4. Organizations that cannot accurately assess their proficiency levels can get stuck in quadrant 3 indefinitely.

In-sourcing/Outsourcing Considerations

This approach is largely agnostic to in-sourcing/outsourcing solutions. Some organizations will place great importance on being able to perform specific cyber intelligence functions organically, while others will be happy to purchase those capabilities from external sources. Outsourcing offers organizations options for accelerating access to specific types of intelligence and for limiting costs associated with hiring full-time employees until decision-makers have some experience with cyber intelligence. Outsourcing is not a panacea, however, and organizations that do not have people actively engaged in consuming products, refining requirements, and shaping outcomes will seldom derive a full return on the money dedicated to outsourced solutions.

Organizational Considerations

The size of an organization's IT staff in general, and its IT security staff in particular, are important factors in developing options to mitigate challenges, manage onboarding of intelligence staff, and manage intelligence contracts. Larger teams allow for greater specialization, which is helpful for implementing this approach. Organizations that have sufficient depth to assign IT security professionals with specific cyber intelligence establishment roles will find it easier to maintain momentum than organizations in which establishment actions are shared across the team. Smaller teams have to develop checks and balances to keep establishment actions on track and to identify/elevate issues of concern.

Organizations must also guard against the tendency for cyber intelligence focus to be hijacked by the most active customers. Correctly conducted cyber intelligence operations address customer requirements, so if requirements are being disproportionately produced by a subset of users, it is highly likely that cyber intelligence outputs will respond to that imbalance. The CISO and his/her directs must work with cyber intelligence leaders to maintain visibility into the allocation of scarce intelligence analytic resources and to seek to ensure it is applied in a balanced manner across the customer base.

Neutral Growth Theoretical Case Study: Establishing Case

Scenario: A large company in a highly regulated industry is directed by their government regulator that they need to establish the capability to share and deploy threat signatures across their industry employing a designated set of standardized tools. The company is told that it will be subjected to a compliance visit by the regulator in 18 months. The company has no dedicated cyber intelligence team but many people on the IT security team read open source threat products, and there is a high degree of awareness of what cyber intelligence is and what it can do.

Self-Assessment Results: A CISO directed self-assessment effort identifies deficiencies in equipment, personnel, and processes that will need to be addressed and determines that a phased implementation for hiring cyber intelligence analysts to coincide with equipment acquisition is the best approach to meet the standards established in the externally driven mandate.

Plan: The CISO is designated as accountable for bringing the company into compliance with regulatory standards. She assigns responsibility to her security operations director and authorizes him to hire an experienced cyber intelligence professional to assist him in hiring and training analysts, process development and documentation, and cyber intelligence integration into designated IT security functions. The CISO establishes six month and one year capability targets in consultation with her team and schedules the company's IT audit team to review compliance at those points.

Execution: The security operations director is unable to find a qualified candidate for his cyber intelligence leader until month nine. Working through his industry ISAC, he is able to get helpful inputs from peer organizations to refine the position descriptions for his hiring actions and becomes aware of two vendors who have expertise in fielding and training users to operate the systems designated by the regulator for intelligence sharing. Internal audits find that intelligence proficiency is behind targeted standards at both of the review gates, which requires the CISO to refine her plan and to allocate additional resources to mitigation strategies.

Outcome: The team sent by the regulatory agency at 18 months finds that all technical standards have been met but proficiency levels for both intelligence customers and providers need work.

Neutral Growth Theoretical Case Study: Refinement Case

Scenario: This case uses the same scenario as the establishment case, but in this case study the company has already established a small cyber intelligence team under the CISO that is primarily focused on providing threat awareness products.

Self-Assessment Results: A CISO directed self-assessment effort identifies deficiencies in equipment, personnel, and processes that will need to be addressed to meet the standards established in the externally driven mandate.

Plan: Consistent with the previous case, CISO is designated as accountable for bringing the company into compliance with regulatory standards, but because he has some cyber intelligence expertise organic to the team and senior staff with experience tasking and consuming cyber intelligence products, his starting point is in the upper right portion of quadrant three. The CISO breaks the capability refinement task into three component parts and delegates responsibility for each part to a different leader on the team with the goal of being able to integrate the efforts at the one year point to have six months of experience/learning prior to the regulator's announced review. The security operations director is assigned the task of working with the CTO to acquire and integrate all required IT systems. The security policy and cyber intelligence leaders are tasked to develop and document standardized cyber intelligence processes in concert with the process owners for supported IT security functions. The cyber intelligence leaders is assigned the role of developing the manpower and training plans to enable the hiring and training of required cyber intelligence staff.

Execution: The equipping piece comes together in less than six months, which allows the security operations center team to experiment with different ways to use it and to gain experience sharing data with other industry partners. This early win and associated experience accelerates the development of standardized processes through experimentation, which provides valuable inputs to inform the development of position descriptions and training plans. Through a series of milestone reviews, the CISO recognizes that his preexisting cyber intelligence team lacks sufficient technical competence to perform their new roles and embarks on an effort to convert technically competent security specialists into cyber intelligence analysts.

Outcome: By the time the 18 month regulatory review takes place, the company is performing at a level that puts them among industry leaders, and it is able provide documented plans for employing cyber intelligence to improve the signal to noise ratio for the data classes being shared to meet the regulator's mandate.

Application Approach Two: Focus on Customer Proficiency

Application Approach Two provides a model for organizations that decide to execute a strategy that places it primary focus at the outset of the cyber intelligence establishment process on developing customer proficiency. Although this approach is uncommon, it is a logical developmental tactic, particularly for organizations that are too small to allow for people to do a great deal of specialization. This approach leverages two factors: (1) the primary cyber intelligence customers are already in place in the organization at the point that the decision is made to acquire cyber intelligence capabilities; and (2) cyber intelligence is a customer-driven discipline. Combined, the two factors create an opportunity for organizations to refine their cyber intelligence needs prior to making any long-term investments in either people or equipment. Properly executed, this approach offers potential for creating cost saving efficiencies.

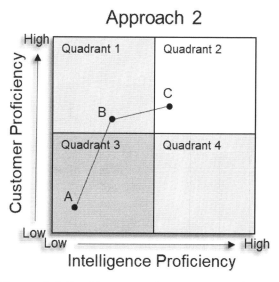

Figure 3.3.3 – Focus on Customer Proficiency

Analyzing the model in Figure 3.3.3, point A is the common starting point for all three cases, and the placement of point B in quadrant 1 represents the focus on customer proficiency as the initial development vector. Point B is a tipping point at which key cyber intelligence customers, like the CISO, assess that they have gained a sufficient understanding of what cyber intelligence must be able to provide that they can shift their focus to the acquisition of intelligence capabilities they need to achieve their goals. Once cyber intelligence proficiency requirements are defined, the organization can build a cyber intelligence capability organic to the CISO's domain, invest in new tools, improve security practices in ways they can take advantage of additional intelligence, and contract for additional intelligence products and services. Done correctly this additional intelligence capability will drive improvements in organizational performance to a point C in quadrant 2.

Strengths

The primary strength of this approach is that it focuses on improving the performance of capabilities already resident in the organization before building out new capabilities. This approach offers the potential to create better defined goals for cyber intelligence than the other two approaches, thus it will theoretically provide clearer planning objectives and reduce the chances of spending money on capabilities or manpower that will not be needed as capabilities mature.

Challenges

The primary challenge will be in acquiring the expertise necessary to increase cyber intelligence customer proficiency in an environment in which cyber intelligence expertise is either limited or not present. If one does not understand the threats to one's networks and data or what a capable cyber intelligence practice can provide, then how does one identify what one wants or needs?

There are also likely to be a wide range of secondary challenges as well, and two that worth calling out in particular are external biases and opportunistic behaviors.

External Biases: Most organizations will likely employ external parties to provide subject matter expertise to kick-start their development process. This is a logical approach, but even the most honest and capable providers will bring their biases into the process, so leaders will need to become skeptical consumers and to learn how to distinguish what those biases are and how they are likely to skew outcomes.

Opportunistic Behaviors: People working in security functions that will be supported by cyber intelligence will generally find themselves competing with other supported functions for the limited resources that will be made available to upgrade tools and add staff. Decision-makers will need to ensure that decisions involving the application of limited financial resources align to actual needs rather than to the effectiveness of different staff elements to compete for resources.

In-sourcing/Outsourcing Considerations

Outsourcing will play a key role in enabling organizations employing this approach to succeed. Third party vendors offer the full range of services organizations will need to make this approach work. They can perform capability assessments or assist in self-assessments. They can train individuals and teams. They can design a full range of intelligence operations, and they can provide tailored cyber intelligence support both during the developmental process and once capabilities are in place.

Organizational Considerations

Customer proficiency is not limited to the readiness of one's workforce to engage in the full range of actions required to build and sustain a capable and evolving cyber intelligence practice. It also deals with organizational attributes upon which cyber intelligence will be built. Examples include whether the IT security team has tools that can employ cyber intelligence, the skill level of security practitioners at their assigned security tasks, the maturity of policy and training programs, and the organization's culture regarding following rules, asking questions, and accepting/ integrating change.

Most organizations will need to make additional investments in their networks and security tools before they will be able to make full use of cyber intelligence. This requirement is captured in the Zone 1 discussion in the cost versus proficiency model in Chapter 3.1.

Customer Proficiency Focused Theoretical Case Study: Establishing Case

Scenario: A small nonprofit organization engaged in public sector policy development and advocacy experiences a network breach that results in the selective release of internal email conversations by hacktivists seeking to put the organization in a bad light and suggest biases and intellectual dishonesty among its leadership. The organization has a CISO aligned under the CIO, but the CISO only has five people on her team and many security functions have been outsourced to vendors.

Self-Assessment Results: The CISO's self-assessment is centered on identifying how the organization's network was attacked and the data exfiltrated without being detected. The results of that effort suggests that the organization and several of its most prolific thought leaders are being targeted regularly by political activists and state actors and that the threat vector employed in those attack is basic social engineering. It also reveals weaknesses in the mail guard application, shortfalls in extrusion monitoring, and the absence of a capability to identify and block suspicious domains.

Plan: The CISO assigns herself the role of developing a threat awareness and social engineering training programs and assigns the task of improving the mail guard to her security architect and the other two functions to her security operations lead. She directs that they all work with partners to identify cyber intelligence capabilities they should acquire to enhance the performance of security improvements and establishes several milestones for reviewing performance and consolidating cyber intelligence needs into an enterprise-level effort.

Execution: The security architect and operations leaders develop security process improvements and system/tool upgrades but neither develop needs for intelligence inputs. The CISO executes a contract with a cyber security firm that specializes in providing executive-level strategic thought products to produce a monthly product that identifies actors with agendas hostile to her organization and the tactics they employ. The CISO expands the contract to provide improved threat indicators for the mail guard and to update suspicious domains to be deployed to block outgoing traffic in the company's proxy servers. A series of small wins cause the CISO's direct reports to identify technical analysis and hunting capabilities they could employ.

Outcome: Improved threat awareness and social engineering detection training leads to increased detections of suspicious activity consistent with reconnaissance of the network. As the security team becomes more comfortable with how threat awareness improves their ability to identify suspicious activity, they become increasingly active participants in the cyber intelligence requirements process.

Customer Proficiency Focused Theoretical Case Study: Refinement Case

Scenario: This case uses the same scenario as the establishment case, but in this case study the company CISO has already had one of her staff publishing a weekly threat awareness product that is delivered via email to a defined subset of employees.

Self-Assessment Results: Just as in the previous case study, the CISO recognizes that none of the existing vendor solutions are employing threat directed methodologies, and while there is broad awareness of the existence of cyber-threats to the organization, the existing product is too general and needs to be improved. The other key finding is that the organization's employees lack sufficient threat awareness to be able to recognize social engineering activities.

Plan: The CSIO develops planning options to address three shortfalls identified in the self-assessment. First, she implements a focused monthly team meeting to focus on cyber-threats and to improve her staff's proficiency in identify what they need and how to ask for it. Second, she identifies and contracts with a cyber intelligence firm that has a service offering that has a strong reputation for engaged client interaction and allocates funds for two key staff members to attend vendor orientation training. Third, she contracts with a firm that specializes in email security, domain protection, and social engineering training.

Execution: The CISO replaces the locally produced threat awareness product with a vendor produced cyber intelligence product designed to increase workforce understanding of classes of threat actors most likely to target the organization and hires a cyber intelligence analyst to drive vendor alignment with organizational requirements and to manage dissemination and integration processes. She assigns her newly trained staff to work with the cyber intelligence analyst to conduct alternative analysis of a subset of the vendor's analysis and to employ the vendor's RFI process to generate deeper understanding. She implements an aggressive workforce phishing and spam awareness program to harden the network against the attack vector employed in the breach.

Outcome: Improved threat awareness and social engineering detection training lead to improved IT security and increased demands for new cyber intelligence products. Investments in IT staff proficiency training generates a culture in which questioning threat reporting is common, and threat reporting is consistently driving IT security decisions.

Application Approach Three: Focus on Practitioner Proficiency

Application Approach Three represents the mirror image of Application Approach Two. Organizations following this approach will have made the determination that the best way to develop a capable cyber intelligence team to support the organization's most pressing needs is to acquire cyber intelligence expertise that can be used as a catalyst for driving the organizational changes necessary to execute highly effective cyber intelligence operations. This approach relies on intelligence professionals to teach IT security professionals how to be effective cyber intelligence customers.

Approach 3 offers a representative case for organizations that choose to invest in an internal cyber intelligence service offering as their primary strategy for establishing a cyber intelligence capability. In this case, Point B is the tipping point at which the cyber intelligence team has reached a level of proficiency that it can actively market its capabilities and products to primary customers in a manner that they can inform and empower those customers to begin driving intelligence priorities more effectively. Point C represent the evolutionary improvement resulting from informed customer participation.

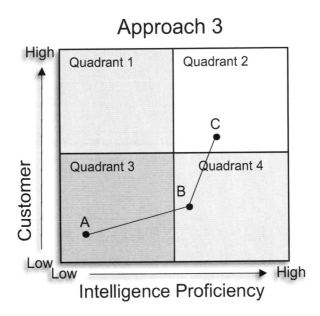

Figure 3.3.4 – Practitioner Focused Approach

Strengths

This approach offers clear lines of responsibility and accountability that are missing in the other two cases. One or more individuals are charged with working with key stakeholders to elevate their understanding of both cyber-threats and cyber intelligence capabilities and to translate that understanding into actionable cyber intelligence requirements that can be employed to establish a functioning cyber intelligence capability optimized to the organization's needs.

Challenges

Organizations that chose this approach must address two key challenges. First, they have to find one or more people with the full range of skills necessary to perform the advocacy role. Cyber intelligence professionals with both the subject matter expertise and the skill sets to perform the wide range of tasks required are difficult to find and in high demand, and organizations with no in-house cyber intelligence expertise often do not know what they need. Second, even if the organization is able to hire a strong cyber intelligence professional, that person will face a wide range of challenges associated with being new to the organization and will need help in developing a professional network and in acquiring an understanding of organizational culture.

In-sourcing/Outsourcing Considerations

Although it would be possible to contract with an external provider to execute this strategy, in the vast majority of cases, organizations will chose to hire a strong cyber intelligence leader and drive proficiency development from inside the organization. Larger organizations will frequently choose to rebrand some number of technically capable IT security professionals as intelligence analysts to provide the critical mass necessary to drive change.

Organizations desiring to accelerate development might consider using contract support to address specific classes of intelligence products during the period of time that the in-house capabilities are being developed. This approach ensures that cyber intelligence customers are seeing a range of intelligence products and learning how to employ intelligence while refining their skill sets as informed customers. Small in-house cyber intelligence staff can focus the preponderance of their time on operational design, process development, and customer awareness, education, and outreach until they have reached a size that they can begin to become the primary cyber intelligence producer.

Organizational Considerations

This approach will work best in reasonably large organizations with fairly mature IT security practices. There tends to be a correlation between size and process specialization/documentation in the IT security, i.e. large organizations tend to have the critical mass to be more specialized, and they are more likely to document their key processes. Conversely, smaller organizations will tend to value breadth over depth in their IT security teams, because they do not have enough employees to engage in deep specialization, and they also have less capacity to refine and document their processes. Newly added cyber intelligence staff will be able to contribute immediately in organizations in which supported IT security processes are in place and documented, but they will have to work with their IT security team counterparts to establish repeatable processes where none exist before they will be able to develop cyber intelligence support processes.

Another important organizational consideration is having clearly defined lines of responsibility and accountability. Cyber intelligence is a support function and it cannot be more successful that the functions it is supporting. A strong CISO who is accountable to the CIO or COO for establishing the conditions in which cyber intelligence can contribute and who holds his/her directs responsible for ensuring they perform their roles in the context of the performance of the entire IT security team, will be able to apply this approach with a high probability of creating successful outcomes.

Practitioner Proficiency Focused Theoretical Case Study: Establishing Case

Scenario: The leaders of a mid-sized company in the manufacturing sector notice an increase in the number of peer competitors that have suffered losses resulting from a range of cyber-attacks. The scale of the losses and the range of threats stimulate the leaders to do a review of their IT security posture that concludes that the absence of threat understanding is limiting the effectiveness of their risk programs and preventing the CISO from being able to direct focused, threat-driven IT security operations.

Self-Assessment Results: The CISO identifies that the primary barrier to designing threat-driven security operations is an almost complete absence of understanding on the team of what cyber intelligence is, what it can provide, how to task it, and how to apply it.

Plan: The CISO assumes accountability for establishing a functional cyber intelligence capability and determines that the best way to create sufficient awareness of what cyber intelligence is and how it can be employed by her direct reports is to build a functioning cyber intelligence team within her organization. Her plan calls for hiring an intelligence leader who will be charged with hiring people with the skill sets to support four IT security functions: security operations, incident response, vulnerability management, and security architecture. Once cyber intelligence capabilities are established and are driving organizational change in those four key functions, the CISO will implement a phase two that will expand the number of functions supported based on learning from phase one.

Execution: The CISO hires an experienced cyber intelligence professional, who develops cyber intelligence capability options in concert with the leaders of the first four supported functions and translates those options into a draft cyber intelligence support plan and position descriptions to be used to hire additional staff. In addition, the new cyber intelligence leader is directed to produce a weekly awareness and a quarterly predictive threat warning product to help the CISO to begin to create the cadre of literate and educated stakeholders that will be necessary to drive sustainable and successful cyber operations.

Outcome: Plan execution drives a slow but steady adoption of cyber intelligence as a core enabler of improved IT security operations. Employees feeling threatened by cultural changes being driven by cyber intelligence move to other organizations, providing the CISO with opportunities to hire/promote to fill key vacancies with candidates who have greater interest in and understanding of how to become proficient cyber intelligence customers.

Practitioner Proficiency Focused Theoretical Case Study: Refinement Case

Scenario: This case study uses the same scenario as the establishment case, with the one difference being that the CISO already has cyber intelligence capabilities upon which to build.

Self-Assessment Results: A CISO led self-assessment identifies that there is a mismatch in focus of existing cyber intelligence capabilities based on analysis of threat actor capabilities and threat vectors revealed in post event analysis of cyber incidents targeting peer competitors.

Plan: The CISO develops a plan to expand existing cyber intelligence application from its current focus on threats to engineering and proprietary data to also include threats to manufacturing processes, payment/billing systems, personnel/customer sensitive data, and supply chain/logistics databases. The CISO believes that the key to making this shift work is to assign cyber intelligence practitioners to the leaders of the newly supported functions to help them to cultivate their understanding of threats facing their portfolios and to work with them to identify process shortfalls and to develop intelligence requirements. The CISO accepts risks associated with outsourcing cyber intelligence support to the existing IT security function because the people running those functions have a realistic understanding of how to apply cyber intelligence to meet their needs.

Execution: The cyber intelligence team struggles with their new role until they are able to establish relationships that allow them to identify the threats to the newly supported functions. The CISO hires a more experienced cyber intelligence leader to knit together the various efforts, and the new leader's personality and listening skills begin deepening trust and opening lines of communication.

As cyber intelligence products become more relevant, customer interest increases and leaders in the newly supported functions begin reengineering processes to take advantage of their greater understanding of cyber threats and begin moving from point B to point C in the model.

Outcome: Small successes improve customers' outlooks and drive their desire to learn more. A payment clerk recognizes actions associated with her social engineering training and reports the suspicious activity rather than executing a $150K fraud, which increases the demand signal for more frequent and realistic training. The security operations team responds to a cyber intelligence generated alert and discovers an ongoing attempt to infect industrial control systems with malware, and they take several infected endpoints offline to thwart the attack. This event is the catalyst for a company-wide review of patching and alerting practices for control systems that leads to multiple new intelligence requirements.

Section Four
The Simplified Cyber Intelligence Process

This section presents a scalable and sustainable model for organizing and conducting cyber intelligence operations in private sector organizations with little in-house intelligence experience and for which cyber intelligence is a support function and not a core business. The cyber intelligence process presented in this section was developed by identifying the critical tasks in the doctrinal intelligence process [*Chapter 1.3*] and repackaging them into four phases, each of which addresses actions involving three lines of intelligence operation. This simplified or 4E (Establish, Enable, Execute, and Evaluate) intelligence process is presented in a manner that clearly delineates stakeholder roles. Figure IV.1 provides a visual side-by-side comparison of the 4E and doctrinal intelligence processes.

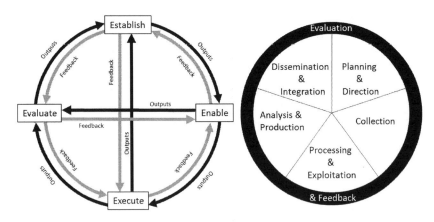

Figure IV.1 – 4E and Doctrinal Intelligence Processes

The linear nature of the model in Figure IV.1 is not intended to suggest that the process itself is linear; the intent is to present the range of actions and the interrelationships between actions in the different phases in a visual manner to promote understanding. Once a cyber intelligence capability is in place and cyber intelligence operations are ongoing, actions associated with all four phases will be occurring concurrently.

The presentation in this section concentrates more on process output than on feedback. Each chapter begins with a table that lists process inputs (which are the outputs of the previous process (counter-clockwise on the 4E diagram)), tasks and supporting subtasks, and outputs. The horizontal and vertical arrows in the 4E diagram in Figure IV.1 are not intended to suggest that the *enable phase* produces an output that bypasses the *execute phase* and goes straight to the *evaluate phase*. Rather, it is meant to show that during the *evaluate phase*, outputs from the *enable phase* are being processed, and where they were particularly effective or fell short of the mark, that assessment should be provided to the people responsible for *enable phase* tasks as direct feedback. A similar relationship also exists between people performing *execute* and *establish phase* tasks. People in the *establish phase* will consume *execute phase* products and will provide feedback in the form of new guidance that will impact operations in the *execute phase*.

The feedback arrows are intended to represent the ideal state, in which all process participants share feedback with other participants. One of the common traits shared among high performing intelligence operations is that they operate in a culture that encourages and values feedback, and in which process participants are encouraged to share their thoughts. That said, acquiring meaningful feedback will always require effort, and the 4E process will generally be more effective in capturing feedback from intelligence practitioners than from literate and educated stakeholders.

Each of the four phases of the simplified cyber intelligence model is presented as an individual chapter:

Chapter 4.1 – *The Establish Phase* is customer focused, and actions in this phase deal with defining and prioritizing intelligence requirements.

Chapter 4.2 – *The Enable Phase* deals with planning intelligence operations designed to address customer requirements levied in the previous phase.

Chapter 4.3 – *The Execute Phase* is exactly that. It is the phase in which threat data acquired from actions directed in the enable phase are processed, exploited, analyzed, produced, disseminated, and integrated.

Chapter 4.4 – *The Evaluate Phase* encompasses actions designed to measure the performance of intelligence operations against requirements developed in the *establish phase*.

For Your Consideration

The doctrinal intelligence process presented in Chapter 1.3 is the byproduct of decades of development that knits together learning from experimentation, wargaming, and real-world experience. Several advantages accrue to organizations that choose to use doctrine as a basis for organizing their cyber intelligence practices. Among these advantages are that the processes and language codified in doctrine are proven to work, stakeholder roles are clearly defined, interrelations and interdependencies between various tasks are developed in detail, and employing recognized standards makes teaming and sharing easier as opportunities arise. Unfortunately, the processes documented in doctrine can be very labor intensive, and consistently successful outcomes are contingent upon the presence of well-informed and highly engaged leaders driving operational focus, consuming intelligence products, and contributing thoughtful feedback. These conditions are difficult to establish and maintain in organizations in which cybersecurity or cyber intelligence are not core business functions.

Private sector organizations seeking to develop cyber intelligence capabilities to address specific threats to their enterprises need to be able to accomplish three tasks:

(1) adopt the discipline and standards of the doctrinal approach;
(2) apply them in a manner that they can be scaled to be executed within manpower and budget constraints; and
(3) sustain associated actions over long periods of fairly routine operations when literate and educated stakeholders have a low sense of urgency regarding cyber-threats and are not inclined to invest much time in updating inputs or offering feedback.

	Principal Actions	Literate Stakeholders	Educated Stakeholders	Intelligence Practitioners
Establish	Concentrates customer-centric activities involving requirements establishment, priority setting, and actioning customer feedback into one phase of the process	Consulted on operational design elements and prioritized intelligence needs and for updates on organizational strategic initiatives that may impact CODI	Accountable for establishing and prioritizing intelligence needs, formulating performance standards, and defining production formats and articulating dissemination strategies	Responsible for consolidating and deconflicting stakeholder inputs, applying feedback and lessons learned, and updating execution planning and performance measurement standards
Enable	Clusters together the range of tasks that involve intelligence planning, applying operational design, and conducting collection management	Informed on process updates that have potential to impact previously established capabilities	Accountable for ensuring that planning inputs from the establish phase are addressed in actions in this phase	Responsible for developing PIRs and collection plans to address them; updating execution planning and tools, and for refining intelligence management processes and measures
Execute	Encompasses the tasks involved in collecting and converting raw data into threat information and finished intelligence and timely delivery of that content to customers in the format most useful to them	Informed when cyber intelligence operations identify indicators related to PIRS; responsible for consuming cyber intelligence products, and providing feedback	Accountable for the effectiveness of cyber intelligence operations measured in relation to requirements and standards generated in earlier phases; and for consuming cyber intelligence products, and providing feedback	Responsible for executing cyber intelligence operations driven by planning from the previous phase; consulting with educated stakeholders when plan is not performing as expected; engaging in customer outreach, collecting/monitoring performance data
Evaluate	Covers cyber intelligence team actions to evaluate both performance and effectiveness of cyber intelligence operations to drive self-learning and continuous improvement	Consulted regarding major performance issues and lessons learned; responsible for providing feedback in the form of updated operational design elements	Accountable for ensuring that intelligence practitioners execute required reviews/assessments and update stakeholders in a manner that allows them to refined requirements and operational design elements	Responsible for assessing performance of the three core lines of intelligence operations and ensuring that learning from real-world execution is captured and applied

Table IV.1 – 4E Process at a Glance

The simplified/4E cyber intelligence process presented in this section was developed to address all three tasks. The 4E process preserves the primary process elements, process flows, and the interdependent relationships between tasks developed in the doctrinal process, but it greatly reduces the demands being placed on stakeholders to participate in standing planning organizations and to contribute to formal input processes. It does this by consolidating most of the primary tasks for literate and educated stakeholders into a single phase, the *establish phase*. Stakeholders are responsible for making inputs to and approving the priority intelligence requirements (PIRs), advising intelligence practitioners when there are changes to critical organizational data and information (CODI) or their intelligence requirements, and consuming cyber intelligence products and providing feedback. Table IV.1 provides a summary of the 4E process and the stakeholder roles for each phase expressed in the language of responsible, accountable, consulted, and informed.

In addition to reducing the number of phases and consolidating primary stakeholder roles, the 4E process also organizes cyber intelligence functions to three core lines of intelligence operations:

1. **Intelligence Information Acquisition and Management (IIAM)** encompasses all actions involving collecting, refining, and prioritizing intelligence and information requirements (customer-driven and internally identified), converting them into formats in which they can be applied to intelligence collection processes, and executing intelligence collection operations.
2. **Planning and Executing Intelligence Operations** involves actions designed to convert data related to threats into threat information and intelligence, packaging that information and intelligence into consumer friendly formats, disseminating it to the people who need it and who can apply it, and integrating it into knowledge management practices.
3. **Intelligence Management** addresses oversight of intelligence operations to ensure that they are being performed efficiently

and that they focus on stakeholder priorities and drive self-learning.

Actions in each phase of the 4E cyber intelligence process contribute to the life-cycle management of the three lines of business. Table IV.2 presents an executive-level wing-to-wing view of the 4E process by mapping the supporting actions in each phase against the three lines of business.

	Intelligence and Information Acquisition Management	Planning and Executing Intelligence Operations	Intelligence Management
Establish	Document what you know and what your customers need to know – consolidate and prioritize	Convert planning guidance, feedback and learning into executable actions – document and assign actions	Evaluate the performance of management processes and refine/ update measures from experience
Enable	Develop the tools and processes needed to acquire the threat data, information, and intelligence identified in the Establish Phase	Refine and document product and dissemination templates, warning problems, and preplanned responses	Produce workforce utilization targets, strategies for managing external partnerships, and metrics for measuring performance
Execute	Collect threat data, respond to alerts, conduct research, and track the performance of published requirements against customer expectations	Process and exploit threat data; analyze and produce intelligence; and disseminate and integrate new intelligence	Manage analyst capacity, production activities, and external relationships; monitory KPIs, and both solicit and provide feedback
Evaluate	Review requirements process to measure performance and the effectiveness existing requirements; review/refine KPIs, and conduct customer outreach	Assess intelligence impact on supported operations and decision-makers; conduct alternative and post event analysis, and update threat assessment products	Evaluate the performance of existing performance measures, external relationships, return on investment, and process feedback; compile/share lessons learned

Table IV.2 – Key Actions Supporting Core Lines of Intelligence Operations by Phase

Chapter 4.1
The Establish Phase

Key Points

- The e*stablish phase* encompasses actions that address collecting stakeholder inputs, consolidating and aligning those inputs into coherent planning actions, and producing prioritized intelligence needs, new execution and planning guidance, and updated performance guidance measures to focus and direct *enable phase* actions.
- *Establish phase* activities are ongoing continuously.
- Developing the cultural norms in which literate and educated stakeholders provide the quality of input necessary to keep cyber intelligence operations focused on the threats of greatest consequence is not easy, and most organizations will be well advised to identify a primary intelligence customer to help the intelligence team to drive intelligence integration and to create greater agility to respond to emerging requirements and conflicting priorities.
- Each of the three core lines of intelligence operation have clearly defined roles in this phase.

Stakeholder Roles

Literate Stakeholders	Educated Stakeholders	Intelligence Practitioners
• Consulted on operational design and prioritized intelligence needs and for updates on organizational strategic initiatives that may impact CODI	• Accountable for establishing and prioritizing intelligence needs, formulating performance standards, and defining production formats and articulating dissemination strategies	• Responsible for consolidating and deconflicting stakeholder inputs, applying feedback and lessons learned, and updating execution planning and performance measurement standards

Context

The e*stablish phase* encompasses actions designed to improve the effectiveness of cyber intelligence operations and to align them to evolving intelligence requirements driven by stakeholder feedback and performance reviews. Stakeholder inputs to this phase are very similar to the inputs required to conduct establishment planning [*outlined in Chapter 3.2.*] The primary difference is that once cyber intelligence operations are ongoing, allocated resources and organizational design should become increasingly stable, and the focus of stakeholder inputs will shift to substantive intelligence needs and expressions of risk tolerance.

Figure 4.1.1 provides an overview of the e*stablish phase* process. It lists process inputs, tasks/subtasks performed, and process outputs. The three primary tasks in this phase are to develop an IIAM strategy, update intelligence operations execution plans, and refine the intelligence operations management process. Outputs include a consolidated and prioritized list of customer intelligence needs, updated cyber intelligence execution guidance, and performance management refinements, and those outputs constitute the inputs to the e*nable phase*.

Inputs
Stakeholder Requirements Review Updated Intelligence Operations Execution Process Guidance Lessons Learned Updated Analyst Threat Databases
Tasks/Subtasks
Develop an Intelligence Information Acquisition and Management (IIAM) Strategy • Consolidate Threat Concerns/Intelligence Needs • Establish Customer Priorities • Collect and Document Critical Organizational Data and Information (CODI) Update Intelligence Operations Execution Plan • Incorporate New Operational Design Elements • Evaluate Impacts of Organizational Change • Process Customer Feedback • Integrate Performance Assessment Outputs Refine Intelligence Operations Management Process
Outputs
Consolidated/Prioritized Customer Intelligence Needs List Updated Cyber Intelligence Execution Performance Management Refinement Update from Experience-Base Learning

Figure 4.1.1 – Establish Phase at a Glance

Establish Phase Inputs

The *establish phase* receives inputs from all three stakeholder groups. Inputs address organizational factors, intelligence needs, and performance issues identified during the execution of actual cyber intelligence operations. The aggregation of updated threat concerns, evolving organizational changes, and feedback/self-learning from previous intelligence operations provide the cyber intelligence leadership team with a solid basis for establishing new performance goals in each of their three core lines of operation.

Given the centrality of customer inputs as a means of defining the parameters of intelligence success, no organization can sustain cyber intelligence operations for any length of time without refining repeatable processes within the e*stablish phase*, yet experience demonstrates that actions in this phase are among the most frequently ignored in the intelligence process. This is especially true in organizations with little to no prior experience executing cyber intelligence operations. The success of actions in this phase hinges on intelligence practitioners' ability to acquire thoughtful inputs from literate and educated stakeholders. This can be difficult in organizations with immature cyber intelligence practices, because those stakeholders will have limited understanding of relevant processes, and many will avoid participating out of fear that their contributions will reveal their lack of depth.

Organizations must overcome senior staff reticence to participate in intelligence requirements development efforts, and one effective way of accomplishing this is to develop cyber intelligence advocates within each stakeholder group. Organizations should initially concentrated on educated stakeholders, and should begin by designating a senior IT professional as the "primary intelligence customer," and assigning that person with the role of facilitating higher quality stakeholder participation in e*stablish phase* tasks. In small organizations, the CISO should probably assume this role, but in larger organizations, deputy CISOs or a designated CISO direct report are good candidates. Once the CISO is comfortable that the educated stakeholder requirements and feedback processes are working, he/she can place greater emphasis on improving the quality of literate stakeholder contributions to the process.

Top performing intelligence operations are defined by their ability to generate actionable customer inputs across all phases of intelligence operations. The ability to create more dynamic and timely feedback and generate substantive updates to intelligence and information requirements should be a goal for all organizations with a cyber intelligence professional practice. As organizations make progress in achieving that goal, e*stablish phase* activities will become evenly distributed across the entire intelligence process.

Task 4.1.1 – Develop an Intelligence Information Acquisition and Management (IIAM) Strategy

This task is concerned with converting inputs involving intelligence needs and threat understanding into an actionable IIAM strategy that can unify efforts across the other three phases. The three primary subtasks address identifying intelligence and information needs, establishing priorities among the needs, and collecting and documenting critical operational data and information. Figure 4.1.2 presents an IIAM requirements flowchart designed to help readers differentiate between different types of requirements.

Subtask 4.1.1.1 – Consolidate Threat Concerns and Intelligence Needs

Consolidated user threat concerns and intelligence needs constitute the primary input to the intelligence requirements development process, and PIRs developed from these concerns (*enable phase*) form the cornerstone for all cyber intelligence operations. Every organization will develop its own unique processes for how it will collect and consolidate inputs, but one common theme across all cyber intelligence operations will be that success in this subtask will require active stakeholder engagement at every opportunity. This means that the cyber intelligence team should be constantly evaluating existing intelligence requirements in the context of real-world operations and determining whether they are providing expected outcomes. Cyber intelligence leaders should engage requirements owners in a continuing dialog regarding the effectiveness articulated requirements in driving desired outputs. Cyber intelligence practitioners play a critical role in developing stakeholder trust and elevating the stakeholders' knowledge of and confidence in their ability to contribute to cyber intelligence processes.

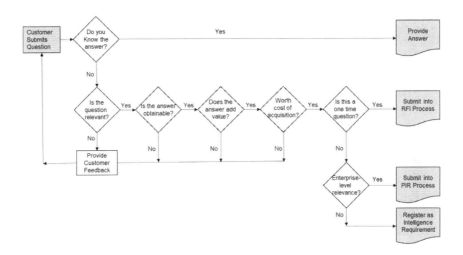

Figure 4.1.2 – IIAM Requirements Identification Process

Threat concerns are relatively undeveloped expressions of a customers' anxiety regarding threats to some element of the organization's operations. They are seldom based on known threats or specific vulnerabilities, which means that they require some refinement before they can be translated into an information or intelligence requirement that can drive collection. The act of refining threat concerns can create opportunities for intelligence practitioners to engage customers in a manner that will allow both parties to gain greater understanding of each other's roles and challenges. As cyber intelligence practitioners gain knowledge of supported functions, they can play an increasingly important role in identifying new threat concerns and intelligence needs that they can share as feedback to their customers. Those customers, however, are still accountable for articulating their own inputs that reflect their equities and understanding.

Intelligence needs can be statements that define a specific output that customers want intelligence to provide or gaps in the intelligence requirements process detected by the cyber intelligence team during the conduct of intelligence operations. In most cases, intelligence needs are sufficiently well formed to lend themselves to being developed into new requirements fairly easily.

Subtask 4.1.1.2 – Establish Customer Priorities

No cyber intelligence operation will have the capacity to do everything that everybody wants done simultaneously. Organizations that can differentiate a "must have" from a "nice to know" will be able to establish priorities that will enable the cyber intelligence management team to focus scarce resources on the threats that matter most. The IIAM process must be able to build a comprehensive list of potential requirements that can be employed to coordinate priorities with key stakeholders. This subtask presents CISOs with an opportunity to align cyber intelligence to their most pressing threat concerns.

Subtask 4.1.1.3 – Collect and Document Critical Organizational Data and Information (CODI)

Most organizations of any size have an information protection program that identifies categories of institutional data and information that must be afforded special protection. A common approach is to generate a data classification schema that defines categories of protected information and establishes policies for how data in each category will be protected. This book uses the naming convention critical organizational data and information (CODI) when referring to data and information about the organization (its operations, products, services, people, and customers) of sufficient sensitivity or value that having it released outside the organization or losing access to it would impose significant consequences and/or costs.

Not all sensitive information is CODI, and not all CODI is equal. Organizations have wide latitude available to them to define the range of information they will designate as CODI, but it is critical for the cyber intelligence team to know what CODI is and when it changes. Proprietary information, information protected via legal agreements, legal data, accounting and risk models, employee and customer personally identifiable information, and privileged correspondence with government regulators are all examples of classes of data and information most firms would designate to be CODI. Executive pay scales, budget discussions, and strategic planning documents are all highly sensitive classes of information that require controls but that some firms might not classify as CODI, because, while their unauthorized release would be undesirable, it would not trigger legal action or empower a competitor.

Cyber intelligence operations guided by a clear understanding of what CODI is and where and how it is being protected can align intelligence levels of effort to address threats of greatest consequence. Because CODI is a dynamic reflection of evolving organizational focus, it is an important component of e*stablish phase* reviews.

Task 4.1.2 – Update Intelligence Operations Execution Plan

Cyber intelligence operations need to evolve both to respond to detected changes in the threat environment and in anticipation of potential shifts in threats driven by organizational changes. The four key subtasks cyber intelligence leaders must perform are: incorporate new operational design elements; evaluate impacts of organizational change, process customer feedback, and integrate performance assessment outputs. As cyber intelligence practices mature and integrate more deeply with supported functions, organizations should see fewer perturbations in execution planning, and process changes identified in planning reviews will tend to become smaller.

Subtask 4.1.2.1 – Incorporate New Operational Design Elements

Operational design elements [*Chapter 3.2*] define the expectations for cyber intelligence operations within the context of the organization's core business, its risk appetite, performance timelines, and the resources available to apply to cyber intelligence. Over time, organizations make decisions that impact operational design elements, and those changes have the potential to impact the focus of and priorities for various aspects of cyber intelligence operations. Leaders need to think of operational design elements as interdependent variables; a change in any variable affects all other variables. They also need to view cyber intelligence operations as a component of their risk mitigation strategy and to recognize cyber intelligence planners must be aware of changes in operational design elements before they can employ intelligence to mitigate risk.

Subtask 4.1.2.2 – Evaluate Impacts of Organizational Change

Many of the variables referred to as organizational change in this task will be classified as components of business development in most organizations. These include: changes in core business operations such as the introduction or elimination of new products or services; business acquisitions, divestitures, and mergers; and decisions to outsource major lines of operation, entering into new partnerships, or embarking in new joint ventures. Organizational change also includes leadership turnover and externally driven changes like new legal regimes and/or regulatory requirements. Organizational changes alter the attack surface presented to malicious actors, and they often generate uncertainty and confusion that create vulnerabilities that clever cyber-threat actors can exploit. Cyber intelligence has the potential to mitigate risks associated with organizational change, but only if planners are fully aware of what the changes are so that they can evolve collection plans and update analyst reference materials.

Subtask 4.1.2.3 – Process Customer Feedback

In a perfect world, cyber intelligence teams would get near continuous, constructive feedback, but in the real world, quality customer feedback is often the byproduct of customer outreach or after action reviews of high stress security events. Regardless of how one gets feedback, it is important to process it carefully and develop approaches to address identified issues. Contrary to the old slogan, the customer is not always right; the content of customer feedback is not always correct, but what the customer is saying always matters. In many instances customer feedback will have a greater impact on shaping relationships than on reshaping intelligence processes, but it is important to remember that the most common form of intelligence failure is unmet expectations. If one dismisses feedback as unrealistic and does not engage the person who provided it, the gap between expectation and reality will grow, and with it, the likelihood of future intelligence failures.

Subtask 4.1.2.4 – Integrate Performance Assessment Outputs

One of the marks of a true intelligence professional is that he/she is always his/her own biggest critic. Professional presentation can cover a multitude of inefficiencies in the intelligence process, so deeply flawed processes can often be transparent to intelligence customers. Three primary sources for conducting performance assessments are: processing metrics, engaging in after action reviews, and evaluating process outputs via alternative analysis. All can be useful approaches for identifying inefficiencies, flaws, and redundancies. Cyber intelligence leaders need to address all lessons learned from previous intelligence execution to drive future execution planning.

Task 4.1.3 – Refine Intelligence Operations Management Process

The third line of operation is intelligence operations management. The e*stablish phase* provides intelligence leaders with an excellent opportunity to review recent cyber intelligence operational performance and to identify areas where performance did not meet expectations. It is also a good time to align intelligence management goals to operational changes driven by stakeholder inputs and new process design decisions. Leaders should identify opportunities to automate collection of critical performance data to enable real-time recognition of processes that are under stress or that are underperforming expectations.

Application Considerations

Readers need to keep in mind that at any given moment, a cyber intelligence practitioner can be multitasking across multiple phases and that there is no point at which all cyber intelligence operations cease so that all stakeholders can focus solely on e*stablish phase* actions. Furthermore, the phase inputs can frequently be in conflict with one another (or with previous inputs), and they are often delivered to the cyber intelligence team randomly and with a fair amount of ambiguity. Agile response to newly articulated priorities is only possible in organizations in which clarification and deconfliction of inputs/feedback can be handled quickly and in a decisive manner.

Organizations with a clearly defined intelligence leader who has unfettered access to the CISO are generally able to recognize and respond with greater agility to shifting, ambiguous and/or conflicting priorities. Conversely, organizations in which no cyber intelligence is designated, or in which that cyber intelligence leader lacks regular access to senior stakeholders will generally struggle in their efforts to respond to shifting priorities.

Chapter 4.2
The Enable Phase

Key Points

- The *enable phase* encompasses actions designed to translate stakeholder needs, guidance, and feedback into actionable plans that can be executed by the intelligence team as an integrated element of IT security operations.
- *Enable phase* activities are ongoing continuously during cyber intelligence operations.
- *Enable phase* subtasks are organized under three major tasks, each of which is aligned to one of the three core lines of intelligence operation:
    - IIAM subtasks address converting intelligence needs into actionable requirements and addressing them in intelligence collection planning;
    - Execution subtasks address updating processes and tools to be employed in the *execute phase* that respond to new guidance and priorities; and
    - Intelligence management subtasks involve establishing allocation targets for scarce intelligence resources and improving the organization's ability to measure key *execute phase* actions.
- *Enable phase* outputs constitute process refinement for the three core lines of operation moving into the *execute phase*.

Stakeholder Roles

Literate Stakeholders	Educated Stakeholders	Intelligence Practitioners
• Informed on process updates that have potential to impact previously established capabilities	• Accountable for ensuring that planning inputs from the establish phase are addressed in actions in this phase	• Responsible for developing PIRs and collection plans to address them; updating execution planning and tools, and for refining intelligence management processes and measures

Context

The purpose of the *enable phase* is to translate customer needs, guidance, and feedback collected and processed in the *establish phase* into actionable plans that can be implemented by the cyber intelligence team during the *execute phase*. While many actions in this phase correlate directly to actions from the *plan and direct* and *collection phases* of doctrinal intelligence operations, the *enable phase* also includes actions designed to integrate cyber intelligence operations into supported IT security operations and to leverage IT security tools for intelligence collection and processing.

Consistent with the presentation order of the previous chapter, *enable phase* tasks and subtasks will be present as components of the three core lines of intelligence operation:

- **Define the Core Components of an IIAM Strategy**: Subtasks aligned under this task involve converting information and intelligence needs refined in the *establish phase* into actionable requirements management and data acquisition/ collection strategies. The three primary task outputs are intelligence requirements, threat information requirements, and a collection tracking matrix. The first two outputs prioritize intelligence actions in *execute phase* operations. The third maps questions formed in the requirements development process against potential sources of collection to be employed during collection operations, and the fourth seeks to automate processes to free up analytic capacity.

Inputs
Consolidated/Prioritized Customer Intelligence Needs List Updated Cyber Intelligence Execution Performance Management Refinement Update from Experience-Base Learning

Tasks/Subtasks	Outputs
Define the Core Components of an IIAM Strategy • Refine Prioritized Intelligence Requirements • Conduct Collection Requirements Management • Leverage Organic Network Sensors • Automate Collection Processes Refine Intelligence Operations Execution Processes • Conduct Threat Research • Establish Predictive Threat Warning Problems • Develop Production Templates (with Dissemination) • Develop Preplanned Responses Update Intelligence Operations Management Tools • Develop Analyst Time Utilization Targets • Develop a Utilization Plan for Leveraging Partnerships • Update Metrics to Reflect New Management Goals	IIIAM Process • Intelligence Requirements • Threat Information Requirements • Collection Tracking Matrix Updated Cyber Intelligence Execution Guidance • Allocate Analysis Capacity • Warning Problems • Production Templates • Dissemination Strategy • Preplanned Responses Management Plan • Analyst Time Utilization Goals • Refined Role for External Intelligence • Updated Key Performance Indicator (KPI) Library

Figure 4.2.1 – Enable Phase at a Glance

- **Refine Intelligence Operations Execution Processes**: Actions conducted in support of this task address making adjustments in future cyber intelligence execution processes based on shifts in the organization's operational focus, newly defined customer intelligence needs, and performance-based self-learning. Associated task outputs include workforce allocation priorities, analytic tools, and production/ dissemination templates.

- **Update Intelligence Operations Management Tools**: This task is focused on establishing performance targets that can be monitored by the leadership team during execution of cyber intelligence operations to assist in recognizing and responding to trends before they become problems. Outputs include time utilization goals for the cyber intelligence workforce, performance expectations for external intelligence providers, and refined metrics.

Task 4.2.1 – Define the Core Components of an IIAM Strategy

IIAM is concerned with the lifecycle management of three categories of intelligence and information: intelligence requirements, information requirements, and critical organizational data and information. Figure 4.2.2 provides simple definitions for each category. Task 4.2.1 is concerned with the portion of the lifecycle that must take place during the *enable phase*. Tasks associated with this phase deal with processing and refining the prioritized intelligence needs input from the *establish phase* into intelligence and information requirements, and a collection plan to drive *execution phase* operations.

The starting point for task 4.2.1 is stakeholder expressions of their perceived threat concerns. The task requires the cyber intelligence team to determine if those expressions are both relevant and realistic. Relevance deals with the question of whether answering the requirement will actually contribute to the organization's security position or provide useful knowledge. For example, questions addressing threat actor attribution or threat actor group targeting processes might yield some interesting insights, but if those insights do not translate into actions that contribute to improved security, they are largely irrelevant to the task at hand. The realistic attribute deals with the art of the possible; in other words, is it likely that intelligence will be able to answer the question? Proposed requirements can be unrealistic for a wide variety of reasons, but among the most common reasons are that the requirement is too broad (in which case one can work with the requestor to refine the input), that collection is physically impossible, or that collection to address the requirement would violate a law.

Intelligence Requirements	Information Requirements	Critical Organizational Data and Information
Intelligence requirements are questions that intelligence operations need to address that are likely to require analysis to answer.	Information requirements within the intelligence process are questions dealing with threats to the organization or its operating environment that can be addressed by exploiting collected threat data	Critical organizational data and information (CODI) refers to a range of sensitive data belonging to the organization that must be controlled or protected.

Figure 4.2.2 – Intelligence, Information, and Critical Organizational Data

The four subtasks supporting task 4.2.1 address converting stakeholder inputs into a form that can be applied to the collection process, prioritizing requirements, shaping the organization's sensor grid to support detection, and automating collection where possible.

One of the most important functions of IIAM is to establish relative priorities among proposed intelligence and information needs that takes into account the art of the possible and factors in the level of effort necessary to satisfy a given requirement developed in the process. A list of intelligence and information requirements containing large numbers of unanswerable questions is of little value to the organization that created it. While all stakeholder generated questions should be logged and maintained, only questions that will contribute to understanding threats, drive security actions, or inform leadership decisions should be developed into intelligence and/or information requirements. A subset of the most significant intelligence requirements should be designated PIRs, and PIRs should play a significant role in driving intelligence operations.

What separates PIRs from other requirements is that they are vetted outputs of a deliberate process with a designated approval authority responsible for signing off on a priority schema and for settling conflicts between stakeholders. Given that cyber intelligence addresses threats to networks and the data that reside on them, the approval authority in most organizations will be the CISO, although there may be organizations in which the CIO might choose to assume the role to ensure that cyber intelligence supports all IT operations and not just IT security operations.

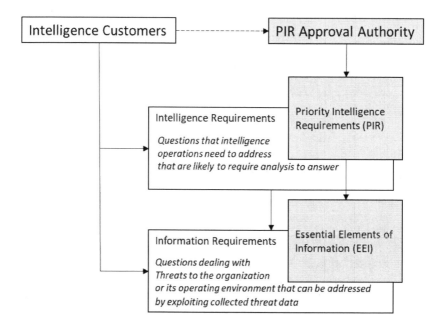

Figure 4.2.3 – Intelligence/Information Requirements Relationships

Subtask 4.2.1.1 – Refine Prioritized Intelligence Requirements (PIRs)

PIRs represent a contract between the PIR owners and the intelligence team. The PIR owners are stating that they have exercised due diligence to identify their most pressing intelligence needs, and the intelligence team is committing to optimize their intelligence operations to address those needs. There are no hard fast rules for what a PIR is or how many PIRs any organization might choose to create; those decisions are left to each individual organization. Most organizations will frame their PIRs as questions to be answered, but a statement works just as well. While there is no magic number, experience suggests that most organizations will want to have at least three and no more than seven PIRs. Organizations with only one or two PIRs probably do not understand the threat environment in which they operate, and organization that cannot organize their threat concerns into seven or fewer PIRs lack sufficient discipline to make the kinds of hard decisions required to run successful cyber intelligence operations.

A good rule of thumb is that a PIR should be of sufficient importance that the PIR approval authority would want to be notified immediately if there was intelligence relevant to answering it. If something can wait until normal business hours, it probably does not belong on this list. Refining that a little further, the answers to PIRs represent threat information that the CISO will either need to share with organizational leaders or that has the potential to trigger immediate actions for people on the IT security team.

It is also important to establish that the PIR approval authority does not have to be the PIR originator. PIR generation is an iterative process, and in almost all cases, new PIRs or recommendations to modify existing PIRs will come from the cyber intelligence leader in organizations that have a designated leader, and from analysts where no leader is designated. Cyber intelligence practitioners will be the first people to be aware of new threats or changes in the existing threat environment. The PIR approval authority's job is to evaluate the merit of cyber intelligence recommendations from the enterprise and leadership perspectives and to determine if the newly identified threat questions meet their established threshold to be a PIR. In other words the PIR process and the intelligence content of PIRs will be unique for each organization, and they should be shaped to reflect the adopting organization's culture.

Most organizations (at least until they have some experience working with PIRs) will find it beneficial to keep their PIRs relatively broad. This helps to eliminate pressures to add new PIRs every time there is a new threat, but it also necessitates that the IT security team spend more time creating and reviewing the essential elements of information (EEIs) that define intelligence collection associated with addressing PIRs. This approach shifts the preponderance of effort onto the cyber intelligence team, which although offering some benefits in terms of speed and agility can also increase the risks of cyber intelligence operations becoming decoupled from critical stakeholder priorities over time. A best practice for ensuring process integrity is for the CISO to create a periodic review process in which the people running IT security disciplines supported by cyber intelligence review EEIs to ensure their equities are addressed.

The most difficult step for most organizations with no experience in developing formal intelligence requirements will be to create some legitimate PIRs to initiate the process. Figure 4.2.4 is provided to help kick-start that process by presenting five generic PIRs that can be used as a point of departure by most organizations. They are presented as both statements and questions so that readers choosing to use them can also choose which form best meets their needs.

Generic Priority Intelligence Requirements in Statement and Question Formats

1. Imminent Attack:
Statement: Indications of changes in the threat environment that increase the likelihood that the organization will be attacked by malicious actors
Question: Are there any indications of near-term or imminent malicious cyber activity targeting our organization, our network, partners, or customers?

2. Changes in the Threat Environment:
Statement: Indications of changes in the threat environment impacting threats to industry, business partners, vendors, or professional organizations
Question: Are we seeing evidence of new threat actors, emerging technologies, or changes in intent by malicious actors that alter the threat calculus to our organization and industry?

3. Indications of Ongoing Malicious activity:
Statement: Evidence of malicious activity on one's network
Question: Have we detected any activity that might suggest that our organization, network, employees, partners, or customers are being impacted by ongoing malicious cyber actions?

4. Organizations Target Profile:
Statement: Changes in how the organization might be viewed in the public domain
Question: Are seeing any changes in how the organization, its senior executives, or our industry are being covered in the media or emerging social, cultural, or political trends that have potential to impact future public perception of our organization?

5. Future Threat Trends:
Statement: Threat trends and technical capabilities that offer potential for changing the future threat environment
Question: What threats/threat trends are being detected that have the potential to impact the cyber-threat landscape of our organization (to include its products and distribution networks and access to financial capital), our partners, customers and employees?

Figure 4.2.4 – Generic PIRs

Subtask 4.2.1.2 – Conduct Collection Requirements Management

Collection requirements management (CRM) addresses identifying what data needs to be collected to answer the questions being posed to cyber intelligence by its stakeholders. Actions conducted within CRM involve converting intelligence and information requirements into intelligence collection requirements, mapping those collection requirements to collection capabilities, and evaluating how well those actions address customer needs.

Doctrinal CRM, particularly tactical military service doctrine, distinguishes between information requirements and intelligence collection requirements, and it develops an entire process for identifying detectable indicators that are then supported by even more refined collection guidance called specific information requirements. A few very large organizations (particularly those working in the defense sector) may want to develop processes to that level, but for the vast majority of organizations adopting cyber intelligence, those processes would not add sufficient value to justify the costs and efforts associated with developing and tracking requirements to that level of detail.

In the vast majority of cases, well-crafted information requirements developed from intelligence requirements will create conditions in which translating information requirements into intelligence collection requirements is relatively straight forward, and over time, cyber intelligence customers can learn to state their needs in ways that assist the cyber intelligence team in identifying actionable collection opportunities. The key in all cases is to develop requirements with collection in mind and to state them in a manner that they can be used to drive collection operations. Figure 4.2.5 provides examples of information requirements that double as intelligence collection requirements.

> **Intelligence Requirement:**
> Indications of Ongoing Malicious activity: Have we detected any activity that might suggest that our organization, network, employees, partners, or customers are being impacted by ongoing malicious cyber actions?
>
> **Information Requirements Identifying Indicators to Task the Collection System:**
>
> a. Are we detecting any new or unusual activity on our network?
> b. Are we detecting anomalous outgoing traffic?
> c. Have we detected any unusual malware infections or increases in callouts to sites associated with malware?
> d. Have we detected any increases in organization employee PII be sold on criminal forums?
> e. Is internal organization information being detected on dump sites?
> f. Are we seeing an increase in organization email account takeovers?
> g. Have customers or partners reported suspicious emails from organization accounts that might indicate email spoofing?
> h. Are employees getting suspicious emails from other employees, particularly from senior executives and organization officers asking them to take actions?
> i. Are there any indications of attempts to register domains that could be used to spoof the organization?
> j. Have any of our suppliers or partners reported data breaches or significant changes in their security posture?
> k. Are we seeing indications of increases in fraud activities using the organization's name or brands?
> l. Have we detected any changes in phishing targeting organization employees?

Figure 4.2.5 – Sample of Information Requirements Supporting Collection of an Intelligence Requirement

The simplified CRM process presented in this task replaces the doctrinal six-step collection management cycle and the concept of a collection management plan with a collection tracking matrix.

The collection tracking matrix ties the requirements and requirement owners to actions taken in the CRM and collection operations management (COM) processes in a manner that ensures collection activities are integrated into the larger cyber intelligence operation, i.e. intelligence produced from data collected in response to a requirement is being disseminated to the designated requirement owner. The collection tracking matrix is an output of the *enable phase*, and a sample collection tracking matrix that identifies the fields CRM must complete is provided in Table 4.2.1.

Four CRM best practices that cyber intelligence practitioners should strive to meet address are:

1. **Create actionable information requirements:** Intelligence requirements tend to be complex questions that address higher level ideas, and as such, they are not in a format that lends itself to being addressed directly by intelligence collection. A proven approach for addressing this challenge is to dissect requirements into a number of narrowly scoped questions, each of which lends itself to being addressed by specific indicators of activity. Once one has a list of indicators, one can develop a collection strategy for detecting activity that would be consistent with triggering identified indicators. Figure 4.2.5 provides an example of the output of this approach. The intelligence requirement used in the example was PIR 3 from Figure 4.2.4, so the information requirements listed are technically EEIs supporting PIR 3.

2. **Identify overlaps and gaps in requirements:** Because requirements gathering is a continuous activity and involves a large number of stakeholders, the process lends itself to some group think fallacies; two common examples are multiple stakeholders asking the same questions, and stakeholders not asking questions because they assume somebody else will ask it. It is not unusual for the intelligence team to discover that an indicator they are collecting to answer one requirement also addresses multiple stated requirements. These overlaps,

once identified, create opportunities to knit together similar requirements and reduce the overall number that the intelligence team has to track. Intelligence teams engaged in CRM actions should analyze whether all logical/known threats have been covered in their customer-driven requirements process, and they should document any gaps they discover and highlight those gaps to stakeholders. All gaps need to be documented and tracked until they are addressed.

3. **Maintain relevant portions of the collection tracking matrix:** CRM is responsible for completing specifically identified fields assigned within the collection tracking matrix. The sample tracking matrix in Table 4.2.1 assigns four fields to CRM.

4. **Design inputs with the Evaluate Phase in mind:** Well-crafted observables based on comprehensive requirements do not guarantee success, so it is critical for the CRM process to establish logical collection metrics that can be used to improve collection system performance, inform customers, and drive requirements refinement. Common metrics should include both absence of collection as well as high false alarm rates.

Supporting Information Requirement	Indicators	Overlaps/Gaps	Evaluation	Collection Sources	Exploitation Plan	Information Dissemination	Future Collection Considerations
CRM Activities				**COM Activities**			
Are we detecting any new or unusual activity on our network?	Pattern and volume analysis; new phishing campaign; malware detections	Shares indicators; current A/V does not log detections when it "cleans virus"	No alerts in the previous 30 days - Need to review definitions and alerting thresholds	Logging from extrusion sensors, mail guard program, A/V, IDS, and IPS	Alert sent to tactical intelligence high interest email collective	Topic for daily threat update call; post updates to intelligence KM tool	Effectiveness of approach will increase as data set is refined and thresholds for defining normal become more precise
Are we detecting anomalous outgoing traffic?	Pattern and volume analysis	Shares indicators with four questions; extrusion sensors at capacity, so not all definitions loaded	High false alarm rate. Need to refine definitions	Logging from extrusion sensors	Alert sent to tactical intelligence high interest email collective	Topic for daily threat update call; post updates to intelligence KM tool	This requirement would benefit from a network hunting research project to better define anomalous events that should be logged and alerted on
Have we detected any unusual malware infections or increases in callouts to sites associated with malware?	Pattern and volume analysis; new phishing campaign; malware detections; review open source reporting	Shares indicators with requirement one. Loading malicious IP updates is still a manual process	Too many malicious emails still being delivered. No efficient way for intelligence to warn users quickly	Sensor logging, mail guard, anti-virus/IDS, open source data, RFIs to external partners	Alerts posted to intelligence dashboard to cue analysts	Update in daily intelligence email; topic for daily threat update call	Intelligence team needs to understand the technical parameters of mail guard program; what is logged, blocked, stripped, and delivered and how to employ capabilities for timely alerting

Table 4.2.1 – Sample Collection Tracking Matrix

Subtask 4.2.1.3 – Leverage Organic Network Sensors

Cyber intelligence operations must be fully integrated with the IT security functions that perform actions that involve network monitoring. The intelligence team needs to understand what sensors are in place, the capability of those sensors, the process by which detection signatures are loaded, the process for nominating changes (adding, deleting, or modifying), where sensor outputs are logged, what outputs generate alerts, who is processing the alerts, and what rules are in place that govern actions/notifications resulting from those alerts.

Although most organizations' organic network sensor grids were designed for specific network defense purposes, they represent a valuable intelligence collection resource. Cyber intelligence operations should be consistently acquiring new atomic indicators (e.g. malicious signatures, IP addresses, and domains) that can be applied to update detection sensors and event logging/alerting rules.

Once the cyber intelligence team has sufficient understanding of detection capabilities (e.g. sensors, mail guards, intrusion detection and prevention systems, and behavioral analytics), and how those to contribute to what events get logged, it can help define what activities should alert in security monitoring consoles to warn the security team of indications of potentially malicious activity. Like many cyber intelligence tasks, establishing alerts is not as straight forward as it might appear to be at first blush. Alerts are only actionable if they are sufficiently unambiguous that the operator processing them knows what they mean and what to do when the alert appears.

Strategies for establishing alerts need to be shaped by a number of variables, to include: how the security team is organized; who will process the alert and what their proficiency level is; whether the organization has an organic 24/7 security operations function; sophistication of the SIEM being employed; and whether there is a cyber intelligence person on the watch or on call to respond to alerts outside of normal working hours. The bottom-line is that cyber intelligence operations need to be integrated into security operations, but they cannot overwhelm or interfere with other security functions. Immature cyber intelligence teams will tend to create too many alerts, and important/potentially actionable warnings will often be buried in large noise fields of interesting but unimportant events.

Subtask 4.2.1.4 – Automate Collection Processes

The ability to automate cyber intelligence processes is critical for a couple of reasons. Cyber threat actors, particularly capable cybercrime and state sponsored actors, constantly change their means of infecting networks and the infrastructure they use to support their attacks (e.g. websites infected with exploit kits and IP addresses for sites supporting malware downloads). Organizations that rely on manual means for searching for intelligence and updating their detection/prevention rules based on that intelligence will expend a good deal of labor to stay hopelessly behind threat actors. In addition, many technical tasks are repetitive and need to be performed with great frequency to be of value. Cyber intelligence practitioners who are adept writing and deploying detection and search rules in their security tools and automatically ingesting critical threat data from trusted sources via tailoring application programming interface tools will not only gain speed, but they will also give their technical analysts more time to do original and creative analysis.

Task 4.2.2 – Refine Intelligence Operations Execution Processes

The combination of stakeholder inputs from the *establish phase* and process performance feedback from the *evaluate phase* will drive changes in execution processes. The four subtasks outlined in this section address actions by the cyber intelligence team that can translate *enable phase* inputs into improved cyber intelligence operations.

Subtask 4.2.2.1 – Conduct Threat Research

In the context of task 4.2.2, threat research describes actions taken to update the organization's understanding of and to broaden the sources of information and intelligence relevant to evolving requirements and CRM actions identified in task 4.2.1. Threat research should inform stakeholders of changes in potential threat actor TTPTs that need to be accounted for in cyber intelligence planning and operational execution.

Threat research may focus on acquiring additional technical indicators or new sources of technical indicators. It can also be applied to strategic analytic problems to provide greater context for perceived threat changes. Sources for threat research include self-driven network hunting, inputs from external partners, intelligence vendors, and open source forums, blogs, and databases. Open source material can be a critical difference maker, but leaders need to be cautious and engage in due diligence before allowing analysts to begin participating in new forums to ensure they know what other organizations are forum participants and what conditions members are expected to meet. Organizations with immature data classification processes or conservative approaches to external data sharing need to vet membership conditions fully before committing to new sharing relationships. Intelligence leaders will also be well advised to ensure that they exercise sufficient oversight in this area, and they should establish standards to ensure research is documented sufficiently that analysts can cite original sources when necessary.

Subtask 4.2.2.2 – Establish Predictive Threat Warning Problems

Predictive threat warning is one of the three primary roles for cyber intelligence, and as organizations mature in their understanding of how to employ cyber intelligence, they will inevitably develop one or more PIRs that will deal with threat warning concerns. A proven old school approach to conduct predictive threat warning intelligence is to create warning problem sets. Each problem set addresses a specific threat and what indicators one might expect to detect if one were being targeted by the threat. Armed with this information, analysts can drive IIAM actions designed to increase the probability of detecting indicators of threat activity.

This approach is applicable to almost any threat that an organization can identify. One can develop both standing and temporary warning problems. For example, the organization might have a standing warning problem designed to provide strategic warning that hacktivists are targeting the organization or its industry, and when that problem identifies a new hacktivist campaign, that discovery might trigger the decision to create a temporary warning problem concerned with that specific campaign. Businesses involved in mergers or acquisitions or nonprofits engaging in operations with unpopular governments or industries might also choose to create temporary warning problems to run for the duration of those relationships.

The key components of a warning problem include:

1. a clear statement of the threat the problem addresses,
2. a summary of what stakeholders are impacted by the problem and who needs to be notified in the event that are there indications of activity,
3. a list of indicators to drive collection operations,
4. a matrix of primary and secondary sources and resources for submitting requests for information (RFI), and
5. a review date.

Table 4.2.2 provides a generic warning problem collection matrix that maps primary (P), secondary (S), and RFI (I) sources to address the individual indicators listed down the left-hand side of the matrix. This kind of approach helps organizations to identify what the organization can provide on its own and where gaps and redundancies in collection capabilities may exist.

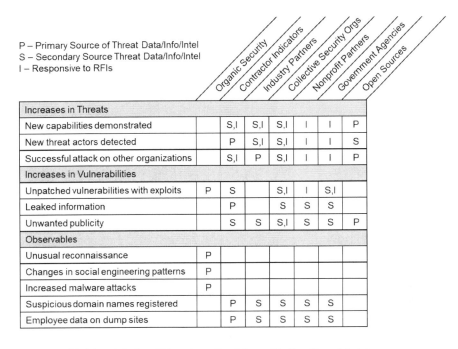

P – Primary Source of Threat Data/Info/Intel S – Secondary Source Threat Data/Info/Intel I – Responsive to RFIs	Organic Security	Contractor Indicators	Industry Partners	Collective Security Orgs	Nonprofit Partners	Government Agencies	Open Sources
Increases in Threats							
New capabilities demonstrated		S,I	S,I	S,I	I	I	P
New threat actors detected		P	S,I	S,I	I	I	S
Successful attack on other organizations		S,I	P	S,I	I	I	P
Increases in Vulnerabilities							
Unpatched vulnerabilities with exploits	P	S		S,I	I	S,I	
Leaked information		P		S	S	S	
Unwanted publicity		S	S	S,I	S	S	P
Observables							
Unusual reconnaissance	P						
Changes in social engineering patterns	P						
Increased malware attacks	P						
Suspicious domain names registered		P	S	S	S	S	
Employee data on dump sites		P	S	S	S	S	

Table 4.2.2 – Warning Problem Collection Matrix

A secondary benefit to this approach for organizations that employ it for a range of problems over a period of time is that it will provide them with some useful return on investment metrics. The matrix in Table 4.2.2 uses generic labels, but suppose an organization has three intelligence contracts and creates a column of each vendor. If vendor A is a primary source for 11 indicators (across five warning problems) and are a unique source on two, vendor B is a primary source on only four indicators and is not a unique source on any, and vendor C is a primary source on seven indicators and a unique source on one, cyber intelligence can cite those numbers in budget discussions.

Subtask 4.2.2.3 – Manage/Update Production Templates (with Dissemination)

Standard product formats benefit both the producer and the consumer. They provide the producer with a checklist of items they must account for in production, which will help guide both the research and analysis processes, and they provide customers with a comfort level based on knowing what to expect when an intelligence product arrives. Product standardization also create efficiencies for the dissemination process as well.

Product formats need to blend form and function. For example, a daily executive awareness product will tend to be brief, high impact, and focused on most likely impact of threats being reported. Conversely, a threat analysis paper written in response to a technical RFI should be more expansive in scope and should address unknowns, alternative hypotheses, and future actions to address unknowns. Formats must also take into account customer preferences, particularly products designed to support decision superiority for a targeted subset of customers.

Periodic Executive	Security Team Update	Strategic/Future Threats
1. Summarize threat in title 2. Threat assessment up front – include context and precedents 3. Summary of threat reported 4. Value-added analysis to include future actions	1. New threat intelligence since last update 2. Impact assessment to team from new intelligence 3. Recommended actions	1. Issue – define threat 2. Background – context 3. Discussion – analysis citing knowns and unknowns 4. Projected impact to organization and actions to mitigate impact
Special Event Reporting	**RFI Responses**	**Analyst Working Tool**
1. The facts – what you know 2. What you do not know and are working to find out 3. Relevance to stakeholders 4. Decisions/Future actions 5. Follow on reporting plan	1. Direct answer to question asked 2. Presentation of supporting evidence 3. Additional considerations 4. Future actions	1. Summary of intelligence 2. Source citations/links 3. Actions taken (include points of contact) 4. Metadata tagging

Figure 4.2.6 – Content Considerations for Six Cyber Intelligence Products Types

Figure 4.2.6 provides suggested key components and presentation order for six classes of intelligence products that most cyber intelligence teams will find themselves producing:

- **Periodic Executive** refers to daily or weekly situational awareness products that most organizations will be tasked to produce. A good rule of thumb is that only a handful of people will do more than read article titles, so headers and titles are important. Executive products need to stress clarity over detail, and products should differentiate between when something is being included for awareness only and when it is being included because it relates to a future action.

- **Security Team Update** addresses a range of updates that cyber intelligence teams will make to their IT security teammates and other IT professionals. Most organizations will have monthly or quarterly all-hands meetings, which provide cyber intelligence leaders with a great opportunity ensure that large subset of their critical customers share a common threat picture.

- **Strategic/Future Threats** address long-term strategic thought products designed to support future planning. These products should be written with senior executives as the primary audience, and they offer an opportunity to go into more detail and to introduce relevant uncertainties. Analysts should define the threat issue and its relevance prior to presenting their analysis and making recommendations. Executive summaries and article abstracts are a key feature of this kind of product.

- **Special Event Reporting** are products designed to notify cyber intelligence customers that a high interest event has occurred or that a significant new threat has been discovered. In many instance, these reports will be tied to either intelligence or information requirements. This type of reporting needs to be very concise. It needs to address what is known, what is unknown, why it is relevant (citing requirements when applicable is a good practice), and what decisions or actions should be considered. It should state how additional intelligence on the subject will be provided (i.e. this is the first in a serial and follow up reporting will be included in periodic executive reporting.)

- **RFI Responses** are a key product for any functioning cyber intelligence operation. The act of communicating threat intelligence should engender stakeholder questions. The key deliverable is always a direct answer to the question that was asked and a summary of how the analyst arrived at that answer. In addition, analysts should also address relevant topics that were not specifically addressed in the RFI but that will contribute to questioners' understanding, and they should consider offering alternative analysis to combat group think. The content of RFI responses should be tailored to the person asking the question, i.e. executive-level responses to senior non-IT questioners and technically detailed for members of the IT staff.

- **Analyst Working Tool** refers to a range of intelligence produced primarily employed to support future cyber intelligence analysis (e.g. intelligence databases and wikis). Analyst working tools need to document intelligence sources and actions, and cyber intelligence leaders need to exercise a high level of oversight to ensure that content being entered is complete and its applicability is sufficiently broad to justify the effort being expended to maintain it.

The intent of developing/refining intelligence products and associated dissemination strategies for each in the *enable phase* is to provide intelligence analysts with plug and play solutions for production and dissemination to give them more time to conduct research and analysis when the team is confronted with stressing events.

Subtask 4.2.2.4 – Develop Preplanned Responses

The worst possible time to begin thinking about how one should respond to a crisis is during a crisis. Anybody who has worked in the cyber intelligence or computer incident response fields knows that at the moment that their organization becomes aware of a potential security related event, the team has two challenges; they must address the source of the security event, and they must deal with well-intentioned (but generally not well-informed) people in their own organizations who will place demands on them that will compete with their ability to address the source of the security event.

Preplanned responses enable the cyber intelligence and incident response teams to reduce the demands being placed on them by their own leadership teams by seizing the initiative and getting in front of the problem. They enable the team to communicate a plan at the outset of the event and to communicate clearly what they know, what they do not know and what they are doing to address unknowns. This kind of communication instills confidence in stakeholders and will generally reduce the number competing demands being placed on the team. In its simplest form, a preplanned response can consist of three templates.

1. The first is an email notification template that is preaddressed and formatted. At a minimum, the format should have headers for the team to populate that will address what is known, what is unknown, what is being done to address unknowns, what the initial assessment of the situation is, who recipients should refer questions to, and when they can expect the next update.

2. The second template is a preformatted intelligence update email. All update messages should begin with a current situation assessment and a summary of what the organization has learned since the previous update. Other useful information includes: a list of all ongoing actions to address unknown information and to remediate known problems (to

include who is responsible for each action); a list of RFIs that are being worked; a breakdown of key points of contact; and a reminder of when the next update will be disseminated.

3. The third template is a problem/solution definition worksheet. This template is designed to be used within the IT security team to focus everybody on the same set of objectives. While one could have a philosophical debate regarding whether this action should belong to the incident manager, CIRT/SOC leader, or cyber intelligence leader, experience indicates that in IT security organizations in which cyber intelligence is fully integrated, the cyber intelligence team is in the best position to drive this interdisciplinary process. The purpose of this template is to give the IT security team a starting point for identifying the problem(s) they need to focus on first and to assist in differentiating between cause and effect.

As cyber intelligence teams mature, they should move from having a single generic preplanned response to developing plans for a range of specific threats deemed to be most likely or most dangerous. Plans should be validated through executive or tabletop war-gaming exercises that include participation by key stakeholders on the IT security team. Beyond looking for gaps in the preplanned responses, teams should employ tabletop exercises to identify the key events and data elements that need to be captured in the execution process and to assist in post-event analysis and lessons learned reviews.

Task 4.2.3 – Update Intelligence Operations Management Tools

The primary focus of activity in this task during this phase involves addressing issues identified in performance assessments and potential adjustments in intelligence asset allocation driven by changes in intelligence and information requirements and stakeholder priorities. The goal is to update tools and processes that can provide leaders with a better understanding of how effectively cyber intelligence operations are being performed in a sufficiently timely manner to allow them to reapportion capabilities as needed to ensure that the most critical functions can be performed.

Subtask 4.2.3.1 – Develop Analyst Time Utilization Targets

Figure 4.2.7 provides a visual breakdown of time allocation across the four primary labor categories for intelligence analysts. The figures represent three theoretical time allocation models for cyber intelligence operations. Real-world intelligence experience consistently demonstrates that organizations that do not actively manage the amount of time analysts spend on production related activities will find that those activities will slowly consume the time available for analysts to perform their other key functions.

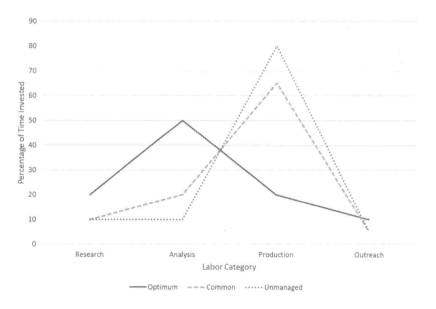

Figure 4.2.7 – Analyst Time Allocation Model

Cyber intelligence leaders need to establish utilization targets and mechanisms for measuring actual performance. Tracking this data can make analysts more self-aware of their own time utilization, and it will provide leaders with the ability to measure analysis and production costs. This costing data will enable the organization to make rational cost-based decisions involving tradeoffs between adding new staff, contracting for specific capabilities, and membership fees to intelligence sharing organizations.

Subtask 4.2.3.2 – Develop a Utilization Plan for Leveraging Partnerships

Once leaders have established a schema for allocating organic intelligence analytic capacity, they should develop utilization plans for leveraging the capabilities of external partnerships. Each of the different intelligence sources listed on the warning problem collection matrix in Table 4.2.2 offers capabilities that can be used to compliment or replace work being done by one's own analytic team. Commercial cyber intelligence vendors generally produce intelligence products, and in cases where those products have significant overlap with one's own products, there are opportunities to federate some production requirements or outsource them altogether. Vendors also provide unique collection capabilities and will respond to RFIs, both of which should be leveraged fully in intelligence planning and execution. Capable cyber intelligence leaders will develop mechanisms to maximize their organization's return on investing in partnerships, and clever leaders will be able to create greater capacity on their own teams by taking full advantage of the work of others.

Subtask 4.2.3.3 – Update Metrics to Reflect New Management Goals

Once new management goals are identified, leaders need to update existing key performance indicators (KPIs) to reflect the changes. They must also eliminate redundant or invalid measures and develop new KPIs as necessary.

Chapter 4.3
The Execute Phase

Key Points

- The execute *phase* encompasses all actions associated with performing collection operations, processing and exploiting collected data, analyzing and producing intelligence, and disseminating and integrating intelligence products.
- *Execute phase* activities are ongoing continuously during cyber intelligence operations.
- The *execute phase* subtasks in this chapter are organized under three tasks, each of which is aligned to one of the three core lines of intelligence operation:
    - IIAM subtasks address collecting threat data to address intelligence and information requirements and measuring IIAM performance in execution;
    - The eight execute intelligence operations subtasks address the full range of intelligence actions needed to acquire threat data, information, and intelligence, provide value-added context, and produce then disseminate outputs to appropriate stakeholders; and
    - Intelligence management subtasks involve the execution of oversight plans developed in the *enable phase* and providing necessary course adjustments to keep cyber intelligence operations on track.

Stakeholder Roles

Literate Stakeholders	Educated Stakeholders	Intelligence Practitioners
• Informed when cyber intelligence operations identify indicators related to PIRS; • Responsible for consuming cyber intelligence products and providing feedback	• Accountable for the effectiveness of cyber intelligence operations measured in relation to requirements and standards generated in earlier phases; • Accountable for consuming cyber intelligence products, and providing feedback	• Responsible for executing cyber intelligence operations driven by planning from the previous phase • Responsible for informing stakeholders when planning assumptions prove false • Responsible for engaging in customer outreach and collecting/monitoring performance data

Context

The *execute phase* encompasses all actions associated with performing collection operations, processing and exploiting collected data, analyzing and producing intelligence, and disseminating and integrating intelligence products. Priorities for actions in this phase are provided by outputs from the *enable phase*. Figure 4.3.1 provides a summary of the inputs, tasks/subtasks, and outputs associated with the *execute phase*. The content of this chapter addresses conduct of the three tasks and the 17 subtasks listed in Figure 4.3.1.

Inputs		
IIIAM Process • Intelligence Requirements • Information Requirements • Collection Tracking Matrix	Management Plan • Analyst Time Utilization Goals • Refined Role for External Intelligence • Updated Key Performance Indicator (KPI) Library	Updated Cyber Intelligence Execution Guidance • Allocate Analysis Capacity • Warning Problems • Production Templates • Dissemination Strategy • Preplanned Responses

Tasks/Subtasks	Outputs
Collect Threat Data • Alert Response • Task Research/Hunting • Track Requirements Satisfaction Execute Intelligence Operations • Process and Exploit Data • Conduct All-Source Analysis • Support IT Security Operations • Provide Threat Warning • Build & Maintain Shared Situational Awareness (SA) • Produce Intelligence • Disseminate Intelligence • Integrate Intelligence Manage Intelligence Operations • Manage Analytic Capacity • Conduct Production Management • Manage External Relationships • Solicit Customer Feedback • Monitor KPIs • Provide Feedback	Updated IIAM Plan • Customer Feedback on Requirements • Refined Requirements • Updated Collection Tracking Matrix Intelligence Products • Updated Detection Signatures • Strategic Intelligence Assessments • Current Intelligence Products • Updated Threat Databases Empirical Performance Data • Analyst Time Utilization Breakdown • Empirical KPI Data • Contribution by External Sources • Customer In-Stream Feedback

Figure 4.3.1 – The Execute Phase at a Glance

Task 4.3.1 – Collect Threat Data

The intelligence discipline charged with executing intelligence collection operations is called collection operations management (COM). COM is concerned with answering the questions developed in the CRM process by (1) identifying data collection from in-house sources and optimizing them to provide desired outputs, (2) finding external sources of threat data and information that can be leveraged and developing mechanisms for acquiring that data and information, and (3) delivering collected threat data where it can be processed and exploited. The sample collection tracking matrix (Table 4.2.1) illustrated the relationship between COM and CRM.

COM execution in cyber intelligence operations is very much an evolving concept; the preponderance of existing COM doctrine is focused on collection operations designed to detect physical attributes in the traditional physical domains in which warfare has been conducted. Much of it deals with planning elements of time and space that are not applicable in the cyber domain, but the core elements of the practice that address knowing one's sensors, time delays in processing sensor outputs, and the architecture involving data flow and the ability to automate various aspects of the detection/threat recognition process all still apply. Every organization executing cyber intelligence operations will have both unique collection requirements and a unique mix of capabilities to address those requirements. COM is a discipline where creative thinking is an important attribute. Clever practitioners will be able to develop multiple sources of data to address most requirements. Leaders should encourage this multisource approach by consistently asking about what additional sources might be available.

Effective COM execution will employ both internal and external sources for threat data and information, and it will seek external sources of finished intelligence. Most COM actions associated with external sources of threat data involve monitoring output from those sources and evaluating what is actually being collected to determine whether the sources are producing what the intelligence team needs, and if not, what actions are available to adjust what is being collected. Internal coordination with teammates on the IT security team should include at least five actions:

- **Update system logging:** COM will ensure that actions on the network that may represent indicators of malicious activity are being logged.

- **Manage detection signatures/site blacklists:** As intelligence operations identify threats and threat actors, they will likely identify TTPTs associated with those threats. Many tools employed by threat actors will have detectable signatures, and in cases involving malware, infrastructure supporting the malware is identifiable. COM will work with the appropriate detection and monitoring teams to ensure that their lists are up to date.

- **Maintain a collection resource list:** People engaged in COM activities should maintain a master list of all internal resources available to them. The list should include the capabilities and limitation, process for tasking/using the resource, how the resource outputs data, and who owns the capability. This resource list supports COM execution by providing practitioners with a comprehensive list of resources and capabilities they can apply to address ever changing collection requirements. It also supports resource conversations by cataloging both redundancies and gaps in capability. Redundancies may offer opportunities to save money, and gaps in areas of critical need become a primary rationale for additional investment.

- **Automate redundant processes:** Where possible, routine/redundant intelligence collection processes should be automated. Proficient COM operations will not only identify good candidate processes for automation, they will also address prioritization and tracking/vetting of automation actions to ensure that they have full visibility into what is being automated, that they can assure that the automation is producing what it was intended to produce, and that associated actions are improving quality not just increasing quantity.

- **Establish alerting criteria:** Once COM has brokered the inclusion of key events to be logged and the inclusion of malicious signatures/sites, the next step is to define reporting thresholds for those indicators. Most security operations have the ability to set alerts to notify operators that something of interest has occurred within the network, but there is an art to establishing alerting thresholds in a manner that cues the security team that something bears additional attention without overwhelming the console operator in the SOC. COM needs to provide that value-added input for cyber-threats.

Subtask 4.3.1.1 – Alert Response

If the IIAM process is conducted properly, alerts generated by the organization's SIEM will constitute indicators of potential malicious activity, and well-run IT security organizations will have mechanisms in place to ensure that cyber intelligence can assess and provide value-added analysis of events triggering alerts in a timely fashion. The two critical challenges for the cyber intelligence team are to control the false alarm rates that plague most rules-based automated detection systems, and to have qualified people on watch or on call who can accurately determine the nature of the alert and what occurred to trigger it. Consistently successful outcomes are a byproduct of planning and training. The cyber intelligence team needs to have plans in place to evaluate what occurred for every alert it puts into any automated system, and in instances when those alerts occur outside of normal business hours, they need to have a coverage plan to deal with those alerts as well.

Subtask 4.3.1.2 – Task Research/Hunting

There is an old adage in intelligence that the first report is always wrong, and like most adages, it represents a viewpoint based on long-term collective experience. A defining attribute of most successful professional intelligence analysts is their ability to maintain a healthy skepticism toward most of the threat reports they encounter. Skeptics tend to be curious and like to prove other people wrong, and in a field like intelligence, those are positive attributes. Research is the pathway to greater understanding and the primary means for acquiring the information necessary to challenge somebody else's analysis. New threat reports, particularly those written with high degrees of uncertainty, should initiate research efforts to validate or dispute analytic findings.

One of the more successful forms of research is network hunting. Hunters can fill the gaps in automated and signature/rules-based approaches. Cyber intelligence teams with hunting capabilities can look for both technical indicators associated with new threat streams and behavioral characteristics associated with threat actors. They can apply their understanding of malicious actors' TTPTs and hunt for evidence that the organization has been targeted based on how those actors behave.

Many organizations have made the choice to build a dedicated hunt team to conduct longer-term, more strategic technical intelligence projects, while others assign technical analysts to conduct hunt-like research projects outside of their daily tactically focused roles. Some organizations have found great value in pooling groups of analysts for short duration, high intensity hunting projects. Regardless of the organizational approach, cyber intelligence teams need to have the ability to employ network tools to conduct intelligence cued research targeting malicious activities, data anomalies, and network irregularities.

Subtask 4.3.1.3 – Track Requirements Satisfaction

With the exception of some higher-level intelligence requirements that are very narrow in scope, most intelligence and information requirements should generate activity. Requirements that the cyber intelligence team can develop collection to address but that do not generate any meaningful threat information or intelligence should be reviewed to determine whether there might be better approaches for addressing the underlying intelligence need. Analysts executing IIAM activities should track which requirements are generating useful returns and which are not. Requirements that generate a good deal of collected data but little in the way of meaningful intelligence should be updated to try to collect data that might support more fruitful analysis. Requirements that generate little or no collection should be reviewed to determine whether the shortfall is the question, the collection strategy, or the fact that the requirement addresses something that has a low probability of occurring.

Task 4.3.2 – Execute Intelligence Operations

Analysis is the central function around which intelligence operations are built, and it is the one discipline within cyber intelligence that is fully dependent upon the quality of one's human capital – analysis cannot be automated. Cyber intelligence teams must balance the need to answer questions posed in the requirements process with the need to understand threats that have potential to impact operations and are not addressed in an articulated requirement. Intelligence analysts must also develop and maintain a firm understanding of both past and present threats to formulate a baseline of threat knowledge that can provide context for predicting future threats.

Many organizations will divide their analysts into tactical and strategic intelligence analytic teams. Tactical analysts require strong technical IT skills and are also called technical analysts in many organizations. They tend to focus at the data exploitation to threat information portion of the intelligence process, and their outputs tend to focus on threat actor capabilities. Strategic analysts will build on the work of their teammates, and they operate at the information to intelligence portion of the intelligence process and will address threat actor intentions and opportunities to apply their capabilities. The combination of capability, intention, and opportunity builds a more realistic view of threats than one has from looking at those qualities individually or in isolation.

Task 4.3.2 involves a range of execution subtasks conducted in the collection, processing and exploitation, analysis and production, and dissemination and integration phases of the doctrinal intelligence process.

Subtask 4.3.2.1 – Process and Exploit Data

Data processing addresses the conversion of threat data into a format that it can be exploited by human technical intelligence analysts. Exploitation represents the application of human cognitive capabilities to seek to identify patterns and changes in collected data. Common activities include organizing and collating new data and comparing new data to historic data to look for patterns or changes in patterns and to identify unique new collection. Analysts will also correlate data seeking to build relationships and understanding within and between data sets.

The output of this task is threat information. Threat information has multiple applications in cyber intelligence, and understanding who needs to see threat information and how it will be consumed are important competencies for technical analysts. The three scenarios below provide examples of threat information being disseminated and applied within an IT security team:

- A new spam campaign is detected, and exploitation of the data sample identifies commonalities that can be used to identify spam emails. Technical analysts provide that information to the team managing email security or they write a detection rule for the mail guard system to quarantine incoming spam.

- Technical analysts conducting research stimulated by a bulletin from a software company notifying users of a newly discovered vulnerability uncover the existence of an exploit for that vulnerability in the wild. The cyber intelligence team provides that threat information to the vulnerability management team so they can make a better informed decision on where patching this new vulnerability fits into their priorities.

- An ISAC sharing partner posts indicators they discovered in analyzing a recent attack. The technical intelligence team runs searches on the indicators provided and discovers that a dozen internal endpoints have connected with the malicious infrastructure identified in the intelligence. Notifications include:
    - the CISO and the broader IT security team for awareness;
    - the response team to isolate the endpoints from the network and run analysis software to determine the impact;
    - the strategic intelligence team so they can do deeper analysis of the threat and provide that intelligence to the leadership team; and
    - the collection management team to ensure they develop collection capabilities to detect additional malicious activity.

Subtask 4.3.2.2 – Conduct All-Source Analysis

One of the hallmarks of good intelligence is that it is the byproduct of an analytic process in which analysts consider all available sources of threat information. The first action that intelligence analysts should take when presented with evidence of potential threat changes is to evaluate the veracity of the evidence. The most reliable way to establish veracity is to examine other intelligence sources. Analysts need to ask the questions like: (1) if this report is correct, what else should we be seeing; (2) who else should be seeing and reporting corroborating evidence; (3) if the report is false, what evidence would support that conclusion and where should we look; and (4) what evidence should we be seeing that we are not seeing?

All-source analysis, the practice of seeking out all available sources of data, information and/or intelligence to build the most complete understanding possible, produces better quality, more reliable intelligence than reports based on a single source. The all-source approach also drives both an analytic mindset and operational practices that elevate the quality of cyber intelligence operations. Some best practices for analysts to follow include:

- Document both the knowns and unknowns before presenting one's analysis;

- Clearly differentiate between analytic judgements (what one thinks), and facts (what one knows);

- Where possible, present alternative hypothesizes;

- Share what actions one is taking to both solidify and challenge one's own analysis;

- Provide context to help customers understand how the new intelligence impacts them and their operations; and

- Be clear about one's level of confidence in one's sources and analysis.

A key challenge for intelligence analysts is being able to put threats into a context that their customers will understand. Media reports concerning new cyber threats and threat actors occur daily, and costly attacks against high profile businesses and/or government agencies are almost as routine. The continuous, unfiltered, and largely unanalyzed flow of threat reporting and bad news tends to produce customers who have either become numb to most reporting and tune it out, or customers who view every report as a harbinger of the end of the world and want to respond to every threat report they read. Cyber intelligence practitioners need to be able to reach people at both extremes. They need to be able to able to convey why a threat or event matters without generating overreactions. Analysts should strive to build context around the nature of the threat to their organization, i.e. "if someone targets us with this threat, could it hurt us," and "what is the likelihood somebody would target us?"

Subtask 4.3.2.3 – Provide Threat Warning

This is the first in a series of three subtasks that address the three intelligence roles defined in Chapter 1.2. The threat warning role focuses on providing intelligence stakeholders with advanced warning that some condition identified as a threat concern and/or expressed in a requirement will likely change. Threat warning intelligence is almost always tied to an EEI within a PIR, and as cyber intelligence organizations mature, the majority of threat warning intelligence will be tied to preplanned responses developed in the *enable phase*.

In the vast majority of instances, threat warning intelligence will be single source, but cyber intelligence analysts should apply the principles of all-source analysis presented in the previous subtask to frame and provide context to the threat being reported. Threat warning intelligence should be communicated by "Special Event Report" products developed in the *enable phase*. Attributes for that product category are described in detail in subtask 4.2.2.3.

Subtask 4.3.2.4 – Build & Maintain Shared Situational Awareness (SA)

Actions associated with developing and maintaining SA (aka current intelligence) support several important analytic and production functions. First, the act of reviewing sources and evaluating the output of others will, over time, provide intelligence analysts with a feel for the speed and patterns of evolving threats, and it will help analysts to learn to evaluate sources. Smart analysts will learn to differentiate between honest well-thought out reporting and hyped threats. Second, it supports team building and provides a basis for developing analytic skills and practices. The scope of material available for review is so vast that intelligence teams will have to establish priorities among competing sources of intelligence. High performing intelligence teams will develop federated approaches for source review, which will serve as a catalyst for building trust between analysts. Third, daily threat review and regular production support relationship building between cyber intelligence analysts and their customers.

Execution of actions that support efforts to maintain SA will vary depending on team size, availability of unique sources, and production demands. Organizations with immature cyber intelligence capabilities must be wary of over investing in current intelligence early in their development cycle, because it can easily consume all of one's resources and arrest cyber intelligence development. The primary contributions of current intelligence are elevated threat SA and context of threats to the organization.

Subtask 4.3.2.5 – Support IT Security Operations

A core function of cyber intelligence is to improve the effectiveness of IT security operations by providing security professionals with an improved understanding of threats that are applicable to each individual security role. Highly effective cyber intelligence operations are only possible in environments in which there is two-way communications flow between IT security and cyber intelligence professionals. IT security leaders who understand how to apply cyber intelligence capabilities can develop more tightly written requirements and will be able to better leverage intelligence analysis. Cyber intelligence analysts who understand the IT security functions they are supporting can engage their customers with potential changes in customer intelligence needs before the customer recognizes their needs have changed. The reverse is also true; IT security professionals who understand how cyber intelligence works will be able to contribute ideas for leveraging their capabilities to assist cyber intelligence collection.

Cyber intelligence should have a healthy relationship with all IT security functions assigned to the CISO, not just detect and respond functions. Cyber intelligence can inform security policy development, user awareness training, network security architecture decisions, risk processes, IAM, and vulnerability management just to name a few capabilities most organizations have in places.

Subtask 4.3.2.6 – Produce Intelligence

The output of intelligence analysis is production. Production is one of the most important parts of an analyst's job, and it is frequently the most time consuming. Cyber intelligence operations will generally have two categories of products, periodic/standing products and event-base reporting.

Periodic/standing production requirements lend themselves to production schedules and enable federated production in which levels of effort can be spread across the intelligence team. With a team approach comes the ability to allow individuals to engage in specialization and to develop deep expertise. It also enables leaders to break up the very time consuming task of screening the large number of open source intelligence sites that need to be reviewed, often multiple times a day.

While team approaches are mostly beneficial, they do present some management challenges that need to be addressed. Not all analysts are equally talented; they do not all share the same work ethic, and they do not all share the same work quality standards. Leaders must also account for the fact that matrixed research assignments require daily oversight to account for people who will not be in the office for the wide range of reasons that employees miss work. Federated production also presents leaders with challenges associated with ensuring consistent product quality and delivery timeliness in an environment in which the production team changes daily. Leaders of immature teams will frequently need to play the role of project manager and executive editor, but as teams add depth and experience, these roles can be delegated to senior analysts.

Event-based reporting is intelligence produced in response to the discovery of unusual activity or the determination that conditions identified in an intelligence or information requirement have been met. Discoveries driving event-based reporting can be urgent and important, urgent and unimportant, not urgent but important, and neither urgent nor important. Cyber intelligence practices need to have planned for each of the four conditions, and they should ensure that they convey their assessment of urgency and importance at the front end of their notifications. Non urgent events can be covered in periodic reporting, although important events may be highlighted to selective customers outside of those channels. Urgent but unimportant events are discoveries of major threats or attacks that do not impact one's organization but that will likely impact customer perceptions. Cyber intelligence teams that can get out ahead of media reporting will spend more time informing and less time responding. Urgent and important events generally involve intelligence indicating evidence of malicious activity targeting one's organization or the discovery of a consequential new threat stream. These events are rare, generally arrive without warning, and are stressful for the workforce. Few cyber intelligence teams consistently perform well in these situations if they have not exercised the due diligence of developing and testing preplanned responses in the *enable phase*.

Subtask 4.3.2.7 – Disseminate Intelligence

Dissemination practices will be driven by the culture of the organization in which intelligence operations are being conducted. Intelligence dissemination strategies will mix the combination of active communication (pushing) with social media and website posting (pulling).

Email is the most common form of pushing intelligence, and it lends itself to employing distribution lists that can be tailored to specific intelligence products. Telephone calls, texting, and briefings are also common methods for pushing intelligence. The key advantage to pushing intelligence is that it gives intelligence producers a means to shape what intelligence customers are seeing. Effective use of subject lines can allow readers to prioritize when (or if) they are going to open an intelligence email as they scan a field of unopened emails. Producers can also prioritize what they believe to be the most important intelligence upfront. The downsides of pushing intelligence is that recipients might find it annoying and any significant efforts to tailor products to different groups of customers can be labor intensive.

The growth of mobile computing and the popularity of social media are transforming opportunities for cyber intelligence analysts to populate popular sites on their organization's intranet with intelligence products. Intelligence customers who enjoy social media and who live on their smart devices may be more likely to read cyber intelligence products and to drill down on embedded links while using their phone than they would be to open an email on their laptop. Allowing users to pull intelligence of greatest interests to them will increase the likelihood they will read it. The downside of pull is that the customer has to decide that he/she wants to read the intelligence and make a dedicated effort to go look for it.

Most organizations should be able to develop hybrid strategies in which they push some products while posting others. Some will post products then send an email with a link to the posting. As more organizations develop internal social media products, there will be many opportunities for leveraging those technologies to customize delivery of cyber intelligence. Customers can choose to follow certain topics or analysts, and they can provide feedback or ask questions using social media tools like they do in their personal lives.

Subtask 4.3.2.8 – Integrate Intelligence

Intelligence integration refers to actions designed to update existing cyber intelligence resources and databases with new intelligence. Intelligence integration involving structured data can be automated, but unstructured data, like textual reports and verbal discussions require that people take the time to update the resources for which they are responsible. For many organizations, intelligence integration will be disciplined by knowledge management practices that drive consistent archiving of intelligence products in a manner that they can be searched. Cyber intelligence organizations that maintain comprehensive analysis tools will find that the integration process can be quite time consuming, and costs associated with keeping tools current need to be tracked. Cyber intelligence teams that have intelligence databases or analyst tools that can be accessed by people not assigned to the cyber intelligence team need to be particularly diligent about keeping those resources updated to prevent customers from making decisions based on old intelligence.

Organizations with effective knowledge management programs and a finite number of well-constructed intelligence requirements will be able to stay on top of integration actions. Intelligence integration is important but it lacks urgency, so many organization allow themselves to be subsumed by the tyranny of urgent demands and fail to update reference material until they are put under stress by a real world incident.

Cyber intelligence leaders need to either own this subtask or assign it to responsible analysts then verify that it is being done. A weekly analytic review with the intelligence team is an excellent way to stay on top of the integration subtask.

Task 4.3.3 – Manage Intelligence Operations

Cyber intelligence operational priorities are governed by variables beyond the control of the cyber intelligence team. Threat actors change constantly as do the TTPTs that they can bring to bear. Organizational leaders are constantly refining operational priorities, budgets, and risk tolerance. These changes impact how the CIO and CISO run networks and associated security practices and drive changes in priorities and requirements for cyber intelligence.

Cyber intelligence leaders must not only be able to track changes imposed on their operations by external factors, they must also be able to respond to them by evolving how they conduct cyber intelligence operations. Rapid recognition of change signals and the agility to respond in a timely fashion require that cyber intelligence leaders maintain active dialogs with key stakeholders and that they have management processes in place to shift cyber intelligence resources within the flow of ongoing operations. Intelligence management actions need to address effective employment of intelligence manpower, solicit and provide feedback on operational performance, and manage external relationships.

Subtask 4.3.3.1 – Manage Analytic Capacity

Analyst capacity is almost always the scarcest commodity in any intelligence operation. At least three factors need to be addressed in managing analytic capacity: total capacity, analytic assignments, and time utilization.

Total capacity expresses the aggregate number of hours available for analytic assignment over a fixed period of time. In a simple model, all hours are equal, but as teams grow and mature, managers will want to consider weighting metrics to reflect the variation in proficiency of individual analysts (e.g. a strong experienced analyst might have a multiple of 1.4 or 1.5 applied to his/her available hours, while a new or less talented analyst my get a multiple of less than 1.0.)

The analytic assignments factor addresses the range of work allotted to the team, accounting for both individual and federated assignments for research, analysis, and production activities. Managing this factor requires leaders to establish relative priorities among assignments so that when total capacity assigned and time utilization are calculated, leaders will be able to determine where each assignment falls relative to the capacity cut line.

Time utilization is the most difficult factor to manage. There is often great variance between what a given analyst claims they are spending their time on and what they are actually doing. Leaders will often need to engage in a level of intrusive management to prioritize analytic efforts and ensure the workforce is focused on tasks of greatest importance to the organization.

Subtask 4.3.3.2 – Conduct Production Management

The output of intelligence analysis is production. Intelligence products are the calling card for cyber intelligence operations, meaning the credibility of cyber intelligence is directly related to product quality. Production can take many forms. Intelligence production encompasses everything from simple phone calls and emails requiring minutes to prepare, all the way up to formal written products and highly polished briefings that may take weeks to produce. Regardless of form, however, every cyber intelligence product imposes costs on the organization producing it. Some costs, like direct labor, are fairly easy to track; whereas, indirect/opportunity costs, like the inability to research a new threat report because production time consumed research time, require more skill to measure and quantify.

Cyber intelligence leaders need to master three production management practices to be able to conduct sustainable and high quality cyber intelligence operations and to provide their leaders with business case analysis for funding future cyber intelligence capabilities. The three management practices are: product management, workforce management, and people management.

- **Product Management:** Creating and delivering quality products is the first and most important production management challenge for cyber intelligence operations. Product management has at least three distinct components:

    o **Product design** deals with whether each specific product has a clear role in the cyber intelligence process and whether the product is designed in a manner that allows customers to find the intelligence of greatest interest to them with the least amount of effort. Considerations include consistency in design across a range of products

that allow customers to anticipate presentation order and ensure that the key facts and analysis are up front.
- o **Product delivery** addresses whether established cyber intelligence products are being produced in accordance with established publishing timelines and whether special products are meeting tasked deadlines.
- o **Content quality assurance** deals with managing the quality of the intelligence in the products. Cyber intelligence operations that consistently report cyber threats multiple production cycles after they were covered in high profile media reports, present confusing, conflicting, or inaccurate accounts, cover threats lacking context, and/or disseminate products that contain grammatical or formatting errors will neither be respected nor trusted.

- **Workforce Management:** Intelligence production activities are conducted by intelligence analysts, meaning that time spent on production is time that will not be available for research, analysis, and customer outreach. As cyber intelligence organizations mature, they will frequently create new production demand signals among customers, and as production demands increase, the time available for analysts to conduct research, analysis, and customer outreach can all be impacted. A healthy balance between these roles is critical for organizations seeking to improve capabilities. Analysts who lack sufficient time to conduct research, attend analytic forums, and participate various forms of learning will stagnate. Intelligence leaders need to maintain a keen awareness of analyst time utilization and be able to communicate production costs effectively to the CISO and CIO. Figure 4.2.9 (in the previous chapter) provided a visualization of three theoretical analyst time utilization cases to demonstrate the zero-sum nature of analyst workforce capacity. The goal of this management process is to create conditions that provide cyber intelligence leaders with sufficient process transparency that they can balance the competing demands being placed on their analyst workforce, and make rational decisions to optimize workforce capacity.

- **People Management:** Once workforce management develops targets for time available within the analyst workforce to conduct production related tasks, cyber intelligence leaders must manage at the level of the individual analyst. Intelligence production is primarily a human activity, and managers need to be attuned to workplace and team dynamics, and the impact of engaging in repetitive tasks over a long-term period. Even the best and most highly motivated professionals will get worn down by repetitive production demands, and they will fall into predictable patterns. This leads to a narrowing of research sources, recycling intelligence themes, less creativity and initiative, and more execution errors. Leaders need to recognize patterns that suggest individual analysts need to be rotated out of the production cycle before product quality suffers too much. In addition, the intelligence profession tends to draw introverts who like structure and order, and who can find great fulfillment in tackling complex problems. Unencumbered by management oversight, most intelligence analysts will build incredibly detailed analytic databases to support future analysis projects and those analyst tools can become so complex that individual analysts can actually expend 100% of their available capacity maintaining their own tool, meaning the tool is maintained but never applied. Cyber intelligence leaders need to ensure that all analysts are contributing to a commonly accessible analytic support repository, and they will need to tamp down on efforts to gold-plate and beautify internal analytic working aids.

Intelligence leaders must own every product their team disseminates, and they are accountable for establishing the quality standard, training their team, and holding analysts accountable for their performance. Managing execution variables involving timeliness and presentation quality can largely be addressed by training to and enforcing standards. Managing product relevance requires customer inputs. Managing production as a sustainable component of the cyber intelligence operation and operating cyber intelligence as a business function will require leaders to identify and measure relevant performance variables and to establish business cases for continuing or eliminating specific products based on accurate cost data.

Subtask 4.3.3.3 – Manage External Relationships

Intelligence sharing relationships with external partners are a necessary component of any successful cyber intelligence program. These relationships can take many forms. Bilateral relationships with partners, sharing agreements with vendors, industry organizations, government agencies, nonprofit/academic organizations, and contracts with security/intelligence providers can all provide increased threat data, information, and intelligence. Each relationship is unique in terms of what it provides and the level of effort required to make it work for one's organization.

All external relationships are governed by one or more documents defining terms of the relationship in a legal form. These documents include user agreements, non-disclosure agreements, and performance contracts that define the relationship and establish the expectations for all parties. While contract execution and formal internal legal review and approval processes are not trivial, they are the easy part of external relationship management.

Once relationships are up and running, organizations need to train their teams to understand those relationships and track compliance where necessary. In relationships involving contracts or membership fees, cyber intelligence leaders need to track return on investment metrics to develop business cases for relationships to support budget decisions on whether to renew contracts at the appropriate time. These business cases can be somewhat complex, because in most relationships, the benefit one derives is directly proportional to the level of effort one puts into the relationship. Organizations with the labor capacity and budget to attend meetings, professional forums, and training accrue advantages that are not available to organizations who passively consume outputs. ISACs and nonprofits will establish priorities based on their understanding of what their members want.

Organizations that attend forums, dial into teleconferences, and who participate by offering inputs can drive agendas will derive greater benefits than those that do not, and organizations that contribute to the sharing process will get more favorable treatment than those who do not make similar commitments.

There are four types of external relationship management that cyber intelligence teams need to practice:

- **Agreement management:** Cyber intelligence needs to maintain a comprehensive database on external relationships, to include relationships with government agencies, industry groups, nonprofit/academic organizations, and vendors. The database needs to include copies of all governing documents approved by the legal department. It should also track all employees who have formal roles in the relationship, dates for relationship reviews, technology considerations, financial costs, and company guidelines for relationship participation.

- **Financial management:** Many relationship have a financial component to them, so managing relationships in a manner that allows for measuring return on investment becomes a critical management function.

- **Intelligence content management:** The primary reason for engaging in external relationships is to gain access to source material or analytic expertise not available or in scares supply in one's own organization. Members of the intelligence team who drive COM process can assess collection gaps and leaders should have a good handle on analytic expertise shortfalls. These collection and analysis gaps should form the critical inputs for prioritizing selection of external partners, particularly in the case of intelligence vendor selection. For example, businesses targeted by market enabled cybercriminals should prioritized finding vendors with proven accesses to underground markets and criminal forums in relevant geographies over other considerations.

- **Technology management:** Most organizations involved in cyber intelligence have the means to support automated data transfers via application programming interfaces (API), and intelligence teams seeking to maximize the benefits of those relationships need to be able to leverage those capabilities to automate data transfers. For the last half dozen years, the US government has been pushing Structured Threat Information Expression (STIX) as a standard for structuring threat information and Trusted Automated Exchange of Indicator Information (TAXII) as the standard transport mechanism for exchanging STIX formatted data. US based organizations that are not already heavily invested in other structured threat databases would likely benefit from adopting these standards, or perhaps other emerging standards, but adoption will require a degree of proficiency and an understanding of how to integrate the new capabilities into existing IT security operations.

Subtask 4.3.3.4 – Solicit Customer Feedback

Like so many of the tasks in this chapter, this is a task that requires intelligence practitioners to understand organizational culture and to have established relationships with the right stakeholders. The only way to get consistent high quality customer feedback is to develop a culture in which intelligence professionals interact with their customers and build trust. Organizations that engage in various forms of internal process reviews present intelligence professionals with opportunities to understand how their customers make decisions and what information might be useful for helping them to make better informed decisions. Intelligence teams that have opportunities to present to customers can leverage those events to acquire feedback. Sometimes that feedback will come in the form of body language or a reluctance to respond to questions concerning performance, and intelligence presenters need to be looking for cues that people have something to say but are reluctant to speak in that forum.

The bottom line is that getting meaningful feedback takes work and requires trust. The best feedback conversations generally spin off from substantive discussions or from proposals by the intelligence team to change a process or a product.

Subtask 4.3.3.5 – Monitor KPIs

Most of the subtasks in this chapter lend themselves to one or more KPIs, and monitoring them is an intelligence management function. KPIs should provide the first indication that something is not going according to plan, and they should provide tactical warning to allow leaders to address potential problems before they become acute.

When KPIs fail to provide designed awareness, they should be modified or eliminated. That also applies to KPIs that provide data that is not actionable. KPIs requiring manual intervention should be automated whenever possible.

Subtask 4.3.3.6 – Provide Feedback

It is easy for intelligence practitioners to focus on trying to acquire feedback from other stakeholders and to forget that they need to provide feedback to improve intelligence processes and inputs from other phases of ongoing intelligence operations. People engaged in executing cyber intelligence operations in the *execute phase* are applying stress to outputs from the *enable phase*, decisions from the *establish phase*, and process adjustments and KPIs produced in the *evaluate phase*.

Analysts exploiting technical threat data are the best source of information on the performance of logging, alerting, and automation actions. They should be the first people to recognize that changes in the COM process have created new work or complicated a process that was working well. Strategic analysts should be a primary source for cuing technical analysts to threat indicators cited by their external sources. People performing COM functions should be generating feedback on the applicability of new PIRs/EEIs in real-world collection operations. Finally, cyber intelligence leaders should be able to provide their workforces with frequent updates on the quality and timeliness of their work and trends being detected with existing management tools. Feedback, both positive and negative, will drive self-learning and continuous improvement.

Chapter 4.4
The Evaluate Phase

Key Points

- The primary purpose of the *evaluate phase* is to drive continuous improvement in cyber intelligence operations at rates that keep pace with or close the gap on the constantly evolving threats facing one's organization.
- *Evaluate phase* actions are ongoing continuously throughout cyber intelligence operations.
- *Evaluate phase* subtasks are organized under three tasks, each of which is aligned to one of the three core lines of intelligence operation:
    - IIAM subtasks address assessing the performance of IIAM processes across the other three phases and determining whether identified threat data is being acquired, and if it is, whether it is answering the questions it is being acquired to address;
    - Execution subtasks address cyber intelligence performance from two perspectives: whether operations are providing stakeholders with the intelligence they need. and how to improve performance going forward; and
    - Intelligence management subtasks involve measuring the performance of KPIs and external relationship, and executing honest feedback and lessons learned processes.

Stakeholder Roles

Literate Stakeholders	Educated Stakeholders	Intelligence Practitioners
• Consulted regarding major performance issues and lessons learned • Responsible for providing feedback in the form of updated operational design elements	• Accountable for ensuring that intelligence practitioners execute required reviews/assessments and update stakeholders in a manner that allows them to refined requirements and operational design elements	• Responsible for assessing performance of the three core lines of intelligence operations and ensuring that learning from real-world execution is captured and applied

Context

The *evaluate phase* of the 4E process aligns with the evaluation and feedback actions of the doctrinal intelligence process. The tasks and contributing subtasks presented in this chapter offer cyber intelligence stakeholders with proven approaches for acquiring and applying relevant stakeholder feedback and documenting/employing experience-based learning from the conduct of cyber intelligence operations. The purpose of the phase is to drive continuous process improvement for cyber intelligence operations in a threat environment characterized by rapidly evolving, self-learning threat actors.

Like the previous three chapters in this section, this one aligns higher level tasks to the three core lines of intelligence operation. Feedback and lessons learned generated in the *evaluate phase* can inform processes in any of the other three phase.

Inputs	Tasks/Subtasks
Updated IIAM Plan • Customer Feedback on Requirements • Refine Requirements • Updated Collection Tracking Matrix Intelligence Products • Updated Detection Signatures • Strategic Intelligence Assessments • Current Intelligence Products • Updated Threat Databases Empirical Performance Data • Analyst Time Utilization Breakdown • Empirical KPI Data • Contribution by External Sources • Customer In-Stream Feedback	Assess Performance of IIAM Process • Review Performance Against Requirements • Review Effectiveness of Answered Requirements • Review IIAM Related KPIs • Conduct Customer Outreach Evaluate Effectiveness of Intelligence Operations • Assess Intelligence Value to Supported Operations • Assess Value of Intelligence to Customers • Perform Alternative Analysis on a Subset of Products • Conduct Post-Event Analysis • Develop an Updated Threat Assessment Refine Intelligence Operations Management Process • Evaluate Effectiveness of KPIs • Evaluate Performance of External Partners • Process Feedback • Compile Lessons Learned
Outputs	
Stakeholder Requirements Review Updated Intelligence Operations Execution Process Guidance Lessons Learned Updated Analyst Threat Databases	

Figure 4.4.1 – Evaluate Phase at a Glance

Task 4.4.1 – Assess Performance of IIAM Process

Actions supporting this task address questions of both efficiency and effectiveness of one's ongoing IIAM efforts. The primary goal of the task is to streamline the elements of IIAM to reduce (and where possible eliminate) intelligence and information requirements that are consuming resources but failing to contribute to positive outcomes. The two primary questions addressed in this task concern whether individual requirements are driving collection, and when collection is successful, whether the collected data contributes to intelligence actions that provide answers to the questions that generated the requirements.

Task execution requires equal parts art and science, and it requires both creativity and skepticism; outputs will rarely provide black and white answers. For example, the performance assessment might identify a dozen collection actions that have not generated any collection. In some cases the absence of collection might indicate that the collection plan is poorly conceived, but it might also mean that indicators in the collection deck have not triggered because no threat actor has attacked the organization. Intelligence leaders will need to develop their own criteria for how to evaluate discoveries in this process.

Subtask 4.4.1.1 – Review Performance Against Requirements

This subtask measures the effectiveness of the collection tasking matrix generated in the CRM process. It reviews the data collected in response to the collection tasking matrix and seeks to understand which collection requirements listed in the matrix are being collected against successfully during the *execute phase*.

This review is primarily focused on whether COM execution actions were able to achieve the IIAM goals generated by CRM planners. The review should begin with the generation of a data set that addresses what collection has been generated by each individual collection requirement over a defined period of time. Once that data set has been built, there are a range of analytic questions reviewers can address.

For requirements that generated large amounts of collection activity, analysis should seek to identify both unique and redundant/overlapping collection sources. Analysis should also identify which sources produced high quality data and which generated ambiguities and/or high false alarm rates.

For requirements that generated little or no collection activity, analysts should seek to understand the root causes for the absence of results. They need to determine whether the absence of collection reflected performance issues with tasked sensors, or whether there was nothing for the sensors to detect. Reviewers need to apply all-source analysis and to seek out alternative data sources and collection capabilities to gain a better understanding of what factors are at play.

The review should also examine collection systems performance at a macro-level. It needs to assess how the collection tasking matrix performed at the level of individual intelligence and information requirements, i.e. are there specific requirements in the matrix that collection operations have not addressed at all? An intelligence requirement supported by multiple collection requirements, none of which are generating useful threat data, is a requirement that one should consider reworking.

Subtask 4.4.1.2 – Review Effectiveness of Answered Requirements

This subtask deals with questions regarding whether process outputs from requirements generated in the IIAM plan contributed to the understanding they were designed to address. In other words, in instances in which the plan worked, and the cyber intelligence team was able to collect the data identified in the CRM process as being critical to addressing specific intelligence and information requirements, were cyber intelligence analysts able to use that data to produce threat information and/or intelligence that actually answered the questions that generated the requirement?

The goal of this subtask is to examine the value of collected data in addressing the questions it was collected to address. Outputs from this review will drive refinements in the collection tracking matrix designed to drive future actions that will generate data and information that is increasingly relevant in answering the questions posed in intelligence and information requirements.

Subtask 4.4.1.3 – Review IIAM Related KPIs

The long-term goal of any IIAM operation should to be able to measure process performance in as close to real-time as possible. IIAM related KPIs are a critical enabler for consistent and timely performance measurement. IIAM related KPIs can be both quantitative and qualitative. Quantitative (those that support subtask 4.4.1.1) are easier to develop, whereas, qualitative (those associated with subtask 4.4.1.2) are more difficult to both develop and keep updated. [*Chapter 5.2 presents an in-depth discussion of KPIs.*]

Subtask 4.4.1.4 – Conduct Customer Outreach

Cyber intelligence operations are customer-driven, so success is not possible without a clear understanding of what customer expectations are and where current operations are meeting and missing those expectations. Customer outreach can take many forms, but its purpose is always the same, to close the gap between what customers expect and what intelligence is delivering. Customer surveys and feedback solicitations on products are among the most common approaches, but experience suggests they are among the least productive in terms of generating participation and quality feedback. Scheduled calls with customers can be effective, but only if the person conducting the meeting is properly prepared and has some understanding of how their customer makes decisions. After action reviews tend to generated good feedback, but one has to be careful to recognize which elements of that feedback only apply to the specific case being discussed and which can be applied more broadly.

Engaging customers to get a better understanding of their expectations can be thought of as engaging in proactive solicitation of feedback that can be actionable for the intelligence team. In many instances, these outreach efforts help to refine customer intelligence requirements, because the differences between what intelligence is reporting and what customers were expecting it to report can often be found in the differences between what questions the customer thought they asked and how intelligence analysts interpreted the words that were actually submitted.

Customer outreach should also seek to understand how key intelligence customers acquire and process information and whether they have strong preferences for product format or overpowering grammatical biases. Here are ten sample questions for cyber intelligence leaders to consider addressing in customer outreach:

1. Do your CISO and CIO read their email?
2. Do they read things as they come in, or do they block time periodically during the day?
3. If they block time for correspondence, do you have access to their calendar so that you can determine when they might see intelligence you sent to them?
4. Do they have rules that bin email into folders, and if so, which folders do they read first and what are the rules?
5. Does flagging something as important make a difference?
6. When they process their inbox, what are the triggers that cause them to open an email?
7. When they open an email, do they read the whole thing, or do they just scan topic headers or read the first sentence of each paragraph?
8. Do they open attachments or click on links?
9. Do they have strong personal dislikes in terms of style or grammar that one needs to avoid?
10. How do they want to be notified when something really matters?

Intelligence professionals who have been in the business for any length of time have all experienced a situation in which timely critical intelligence was properly transmitted but did not get processed by a crucial decision-maker because of one or more of the issues addressed in the questions above. The second day of a major network intrusion is not the time to find out that the boss has an "if it is important, you need to call me" rule.

There are no rules preventing intelligence professionals from applying their analytic skills to their customers. If one has a customer who asks more than one question about an intelligence article that was either answered in the body of the write up or in a linked attachment, that information is feedback, those questions are advising the intelligence team that this customer skims titles but does not read full emails, click on links or open attachments. Do not be afraid to apply that understanding in future interactions. One cannot dictate how one's products will be consumed, but intelligence professionals who seek to understand how their critical customers consume information will have a much higher success rate in communicating critical intelligence than those who do not.

Task 4.4.2 – Evaluate Effectiveness of Intelligence Operations

Organizations conduct cyber intelligence operations to improve the performance of their IT security operations and to lessen risk to the organization's networks and data, and the operations they enable. Consequently, the effectiveness of cyber intelligence operations must be measured in terms of how they impacted supported operations and intelligence customers.

Subtask 4.4.2.1 – Assess Intelligence Value to Supported Operations

There is no one size fits all approach to measuring the contribution of cyber intelligence on supported operations, so there is a good deal of flexibility available for how any given organization or supported function measures value. That said, the ultimate arbiters of value in this subtask are the process owners for processes to which cyber intelligence is applied. Value in most instances will relate to balancing costs imposed by cyber intelligence against cyber intelligence contributions to the supported function. Costs may include expenses associated with adopting/applying cyber intelligence, labor costs associated with participating in cyber intelligence processes or in consuming/integrating intelligence products, or opportunity costs. Contribution measures will also vary considerably, but key factors include improved decision quality and timeliness, cost avoidance, malicious actions prevented, and compliance objectives supported.

Value calculations will vary from one supported function to the next, and it is important that process owner for each supported operation and the cyber intelligence team agree on the measures being applied and how supporting data will be collected. Like many of the processes described in this book, this one is iterative and criteria will change over time based on shifts in operational focus, changes in threats or the threat environment, and personality differences of customers as jobs change hands.

Subtask 4.4.2.2 – Assess Value of Intelligence to Customers

This subtask seeks to quantify the contribution of cyber intelligence to stakeholders not engaged in executing specific supported operations. Actions supporting this subtask will focus primarily on the contribution of intelligence produced in the "provide threat warning" and "build and maintain situational awareness" roles.

Objective and qualitative measures are more difficult to develop than are subjective and quantitative measures, but they provide the critical data required to assess the value associated with cyber intelligence products. Examples of an objective measure might be costs saving resulting from decisions informed by greater threat understanding or savings from fraud prevention resulting from user awareness training in which users were exposed to realistic threat actor techniques. Other measures might be the percentage of PIR/EEI related events that leaders first heard about from their cyber intelligence team versus their own open source reading or from conversations with peers in their professional networks.

Measuring the impact of intelligence on actual decisions and their financial consequences is extremely difficult to do without direct interaction with senior leaders, so most organizations will need to develop surrogate measures. Frequently, the most valid measures are year-over-year trends, and those take time to identify and develop.

Subtask 4.4.2.3 – Perform Alternative Analysis on a Subset of Products

One of the consistent lessons learned from most studies of intelligence performance is that analysts tend to fall into patterns for how they conduct research, and they tend to form biases for and against different intelligence sources. Groups of analysts who work together reinforce one another's points of view over time, leading to groupthink. Intelligence leaders and vocal customers also tend to imprint biases on the process. In extreme cases, analysts may be told what answer a customer wants and may feel pressure to develop an intelligence case that supports the customer's desired answer.

Organizations need to recognize that these behaviors are artifacts of human nature and group dynamics and unless organizations combat them, they will impact the quality and honesty of intelligence analysis. A best practice for combating the behaviors outlined above is to engage in alternative analysis. The simplest and perhaps most effective approach is to assign analysts to play the role of "devil's advocate" on some number of products each week. The devil's advocate's role is to take the position that the analysis presented in the product is wrong and to develop alternative hypotheses employing the same threat data and information. The analyst should look for flaws in the analysis presented and in the sources used to produce it. They should also look for sources not used in the original work and ask questions dealing with what they are seeing that they should not be seeing or what evidence is not present that should be present.

The goal of this approach is not to prove that the original analysis is flawed or to attack the analyst(s) who produced it, it is to identify where it is incomplete or where analytic process can be improved. Actions associated with performing alternative analysis help analysts to develop the discipline to be more self-critical and to identify their individual and group biases.

Subtasks 4.4.2.4 – Conduct Post-Event Analysis

Every security incident provides the cyber intelligence team with opportunities to review team performance and to evaluate whether existing processes contributed to producing desired results when put under stress. Self-learning organizations take advantage of any opportunities they have to develop lessons learned from meaningful real-world experiences, so for cyber intelligence teams, any event that generates an IT security team response represents an opportunity for the cyber intelligence team to review intelligence outcomes from the perspectives of both the intelligence team and its impacted customers. Cyber intelligence teams that institutionalize these reviews into their culture will mature more rapidly and perform at consistently higher levels than teams that do not.

Cyber intelligence leaders should develop and document post-event analysis process standard that identify specific data they will need to conduct event reviews so that they can develop practices for capturing that data during actual events. Email and chat records are uniquely valuable in that they both document actions and carry time stamps to aid in reconstruction. Intelligence team members need to maintain/archive those correspondence threads for reconstruction. Decisions made and directions provided on phone calls or at meetings should also be logged by participants and provided for event reconstruction.

The cyber intelligence team needs to address all aspects of their performance, both as an intelligence team and as an integral part of the IT security team. Addressing the former, they need to question not just the performance of documented processes, but also whether there were gaps or conflicts in those processes. They need to question whether the event could have been detected earlier or prevented all together with better intelligence, and if so, what changes they need to enact. Issues identified in the intelligence review should be shared with other stakeholders in the process to get their perspectives and feedback. For events discovered by something other than intelligence, reviewers need to examine when the cyber intelligence team was brought into the process and what it was asked to do. Answers to these questions provide insights into how others view the cyber intelligence team and what intelligence contributions customers most value.

Once intelligence process issues are identified, the team needs to update its processes to reflect lessons learned, and those updates should be put under stress in a table top wargame or a red team exercise. Once new processes have been reviewed and vetted, they need to be published and their standards trained to.

Issues involving suboptimal or inappropriate tasking of intelligence need to be raised with the other leaders on the IT security team, and process improvement should be worked out prior to the next event.

Subtask 4.4.2.5 – Develop an Updated Threat Assessment

Cyber intelligence teams should maintain a high level threat assessment document and/or briefing that is available for stakeholders to review at any time and that can be used as the foundation for any threat briefing the team might be tasked to provide. Threat assessments need to be living documents, which means in theory that they should be being updated continuously. Few organizations will have the analytic capacity or self-discipline to conduct continuous updates, so the most consistently successful approach is to establish regularly scheduled review sessions. Maintenance of a threat assessment should be most organizations' most important application of intelligence integration, and like other integration tasks, it is helped considerably by people flagging/archiving applicable intelligence updates as they occur so that the updated material is already available for the person or team responsible for performing the periodic update.

Task 4.4.3 – Refine Intelligence Operations Management Process

The subtasks under task 4.4.3 are a bit of a catchall for process improvement. While some specifically address refining/improving intelligence operations management processes, others involve efforts to create a better understanding of stakeholder expectations that can be applied to future management processes.

Subtask 4.4.3.1 – Evaluate Effectiveness of KPIs

KPIs, like intelligence requirements, are a commodity in which quality is more important than quantity. The goal for any metrics program should be to measure process outputs for key processes for the purpose of gaining insights into performance that can be applied to process improvements. KPIs that support measuring costs, product quality, and analyst performance are particularly useful, and in cases where they can be combined to demonstrate interdependencies, they can provide valuable insights for managing ongoing intelligence operations.

Leaders should periodically review their KPIs and ask questions regarding the cost of maintaining any individual KPI versus that KPI's contribution to the management process. If the output of the measure provides no clear cut value, it should be retired. Conversely, if one is being asked performance questions or is seeing wide variance in some element of cyber intelligence performance that are not covered by any KPIs, one should begin developing measures to address those issues.

Subtask 4.4.3.2 – Evaluate Performance of External Partners

External relationships are a critical component for successful cyber intelligence operations. Each external relationship is unique, and leaders need to have a basis for understanding both the benefits derived from and costs associated with maintaining each.

While there are a number of useful approaches for measuring the costs/benefits for any external relationship, four organizations should almost always consider are:

1. **Performance against expectations** – The primary reasons for cyber intelligence practices to enter into a relationship with external partners are to gain access to: threat data, analytic capacity, technical expertise, threat warning, and/or finished intelligence. When evaluating relationship contribution, it therefore makes sense to ask "did we get what we thought we were going to get when we entered into this relationship?" One should follow up that question by identifying if there were contributions the organization accrued from the relationship that were not anticipated, and what those contributions were.
2. **Contribution to threat understanding** – This factor addresses measuring the actual contribution of the intelligence provided to one's cyber intelligence operations. This is another area where quality is much more important than quantity. An automated data feed that shares large numbers of threat indicators is not providing value if those indicators are not useful in supporting security operations, if they are redundant, if they do not represent current threats, or if one has to expend large amounts of analytic capacity to employ them. Conversely, a partner that responds to RFIs with products that can be shared with stakeholders is contributing positively.

3. **Unique contributions** – If one analyzes the intelligence sources employed by one's external partners, one is likely to discover they are getting the same threat data multiple times, and in a manner that makes it difficult to separate unique from redundant reporting. External partners that consistently deliver unique intelligence have a greater value than partners who do not.
4. **Opportunity profits** – An opportunity profit is the opposite of an opportunity cost. External partners who can be counted on to perform specific intelligent tasks in a competent manner create the potential for in-house analysts to be reprogrammed to new work. This freed up analytic capacity represents an opportunity profit.

For one to understand the total cost of any relationship, one needs to look at all costs (direct, indirect, and opportunity.) The most common form of direct costs are contract fees and membership dues. Indirect cost might include things like maintaining additional IT infrastructure to participate in the relationship and the cost of human capital employed in processing data and maintaining the relationship, as well as costs associated with participating in events sponsored by the partner. Opportunity costs are analytic actions not taken because analytic capacity needed to perform the actions was consumed in processing and reformatting partner intelligence inputs to make them usable to the organization.

Subtask 4.4.3.3 – Process Feedback

Intelligence leaders have a responsibility for demonstrating that they take all feedback seriously and that they respect and appreciate customer participation. That said, not all feedback is equally constructive, useful, or actionable, and it is sometimes offered for purposes other than improving intelligence performance. Given these real-world factors, intelligence leaders need to develop practices for processing feedback in a manner that their actions are fully visible to all customers. This transparency reinforces that the intelligence team cares about feedback, and it defines a clear pathway for all stakeholders to submit actionable feedback.

Figure 4.4.2 offers a sample feedback processing flowchart that cyber intelligence leaders can adapt for their use. The key review points of addressing whether the feedback is clear and unambiguous and whether the intelligence team can act on it should be worked out with the person offering feedback. Once those issues are resolved, the next question is whether addressing issues identified in the feedback will require additional resources. Resource requirements must be worked out with the budget authority (in this model the CISO was assumed to be that person.) If resources are not available, the feedback is archived for future action in the next budget cycle. If resources are not an issue, then the next level of review addresses whether actions associated with responding to the feedback will impact intelligence support being provided to another customer. If no conflicts exist, or if conflicts can be worked out, the cyber intelligence team will implement changes to respond to the feedback. If conflicts cannot be resolved, then the action is archived for future review and action.

Feedback is also offered in many forms, and intelligence professionals need to be attuned to statements with phrases like "it would be nice if intelligence," or "I wish somebody could." That kind of input is soft feedback, i.e. it is feedback that is not being submitted in a manner that lends itself to being captured and tracked. Intelligence professionals need to recognize soft feedback when they hear it and seek to refine their understanding of issues during the flow of the conversation. Soft feedback also provides useful conversation starters for customer outreach efforts. Partially formed issues communicated by one intelligence customer might stimulate actionable feedback from another.

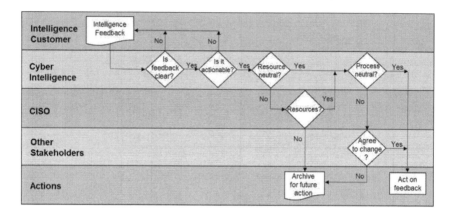

Figure 4.4.2 – Generic Feedback Processing Flowchart

Subtask 4.4.3.4 – Compile Lessons Learned

Lessons learned is a catchall term for all experienced-based self-learning that can be applied to process improvement and improved process management. The byproduct of diligent performance of the aggregate of the *evaluate phase* tasks will be lessons learned, and it is critical that intelligence practitioners recognize them as such and capture/track them in a manner that they can be applied to actions in other phases.

Lessons learned can be both subjective and objective, and organizations should be cautious about applying subjective lessons; in most cases they should be handled as indicators of an issue that requires more research. Lessons learned from actual experience should form the baseline for updating planning and execution processes across all three lines of operation, and those updates should provide the basis for workforce training. Most organizations will find merit in maintaining an archive of lessons learned, even after they have applied them. Over time, the lessons learned one applies in the current day will be challenged by new learning from cyber intelligence operations in the future, and when that happens, it is incredibly useful for the people charged with applying the new lessons to have some understanding of the original intent of the process they are modifying to ensure they do not reinvent a previously documented and solved problem.

Section Five
Sustaining and Improving Cyber Intelligence Capabilities

Cyber intelligence is but a single capability in a dynamic operations and security ecosystem. Variables associated with changes in the business environment (e.g. products, services, acquisitions/ divestitures, partnerships), operational environment (e.g. economic conditions, laws, regulatory oversight), IT environment (e.g. new hardware, software, operating systems, bring your own device policies), and threat environment (e.g. new threat actors, new TTPTs, newly discovered malware) all define the trade space in which cyber intelligence operations are executed. Changes in the business, operational, and IT environments for any organization will alter the collection of vulnerabilities that combine to make up that organization's attack surface, and changes in the threat environment will define the TTPTs that potential threat actors can apply to target those vulnerabilities.

Cyber intelligence professionals must not only understand the constantly changing dynamic between vulnerabilities and threats, they must also understand the security and intelligence capabilities they have in their tool kit. They must be able to engage in critical performance reviews of their tools as well as the manner and skill with which they are being applied, and they must seek to evolve and improve, or they will find themselves losing ground to threat actors.

This section presents a range of actionable concepts designed to provide cyber intelligence stakeholders with tools they can employ to establish and maintain a culture in which operational focus and continuous improvement are institutionalized. The section begins with two chapters that address driving continuous improvement through the application of self-learning and the creation of meaningful KPIs to measure performance, and it finishes with three chapters that present advanced concepts for framing analytic processes and for organizing and managing cyber intelligence operations:

Chapter 5.1 – *Institutionalizing Stakeholder Driven Process Improvements* presents a process review framework designed to help literate and educated stakeholders to contribute operational- and strategic-level feedback to cyber intelligence practitioners and to participate in processes designed to assess and refine cyber intelligence performance.

Chapter 5.2 – *Measuring Performance* presents a discussion of which cyber intelligence processes lend themselves to objective measurements and which have measureable attributes. The chapter develops sample KPIs to help readers to understand how they might design useful metrics.

Chapter 5.3 – *Analytic Frameworks* presents two analytic frameworks cyber intelligence analysts can employ to improve their understanding of the ecosystem in which cyber threat actors operate and how to apply that understanding to create richer context and to improve their ability to predict future threats more accurately.

> 5.3.1 – *System of Systems Analysis (SOSA)* presents an analytic framework for examining threat actor targeting options defined by the ecosystem in which they operate, and it offers an approach for identifying and understanding interdependencies among the subsystems that comprise that ecosystem. SOSA provides a handy approach for creating greater threat context and for building IT security resiliency for defense in depth.
>
> 5.3.2 – *Intelligence Preparation of the Business Environment* develops a four step analytic process for generating a greater understanding of the relationship between one's organization and the environment in which

it operates and how those factors shape threat actor perceptions and behaviors.

Chapter 5.4 – *Applied Intelligence* presents a case for developing cyber intelligence into a discipline within IT security that executes security actions. The concept of applied intelligence is based on the idea that there are a number of capabilities that could enhance threat understanding and support improved security that could either partner with or be aligned under cyber intelligence in ways that would transition cyber intelligence into an operational capability. The chapter discusses eight capabilities that have potential applicability as components of an applied intelligence service offering.

Chapter 5.5 – *Advanced Concepts for Cyber Intelligence Operations* presents four advanced concepts for leaders to consider as they seek to maximize their return on investment in cyber intelligence capabilities. The four concepts are capability enablers that do not fit neatly into any of the preceding sections of the book, but all four offer potential for improving intelligence outcomes by improving one's understanding of the factors that bear on intelligence operations from new perspectives.

For your consideration

The first four sections of this book focused on the fundamentals of cyber intelligence. They addressed questions dealing with what cyber intelligence is, what it does, how to talk about and analyze threats, how to define and acquire the cyber intelligence capabilities that the organization most needs, and how to conduct cyber intelligence operations.

The topics in this section move into the realm of advanced concepts. Some of the concepts (e.g. KPI development (Chapter 5.2), the analytic frameworks (Chapter 5.3), and proficiency matrices (topic 4 of Chapter 5.5)) will require that the organization conducting them have some amount of experience conducting cyber intelligence operations and access to an intelligence professional to guide stakeholders through the processes, but the remainder of the concepts do not require operational maturity or specific intelligence skills. The purpose of this section is to provide literate and educated stakeholders with additional options for organizing and managing cyber intelligence operations that they should consider once their initial cyber intelligence capabilities are in place.

Chapter 5.1
Institutionalizing Stakeholder Driven Process Improvements

Key Points

- Cyber intelligence organizations are either improving or losing ground to threat actors.
- The 4E process provides cyber intelligence practitioners with a solid framework for acquiring feedback from their actions in their support to security operations role, but it creates fewer incentives for customers of predictive threat warning and situational awareness products to offer constructive feedback.
- The PEAR cycle (Plan-Execute-Assess-Refine) offers a framework for acquiring and applying literate and educated stakeholder inputs that can be integrated into the 4E process to drive cyber intelligence process improvement:
    - Plan – define/prioritized leaders' cyber intelligence needs
    - Execute – conduct cyber intelligence operations that apply planning
    - Assess – evaluate performance of execution against the plan and identify issues that need to be addressed going forward
    - Refine – process outputs of the assess step and develop a coordinated list of planning issues with associated costs to drive the subsequent plan step
- The PEAR cycle will provide increasingly greater value to organizations as their cyber intelligence practices mature and stakeholder proficiency improves.

Stakeholder Roles

Literate Stakeholders	Educated Stakeholders	Intelligence Practitioners
• Update cyber intelligence team when organizational changes are likely to alter threat actor perceptions of the organization's attack surface • Understand PEAR • Participate in PEAR driven feedback evolutions	• Understand PEAR • Participate in PEAR driven feedback evolutions • Provide feedback without waiting to be asked • Lead by example	• Invest in key relationships • Develop customer outreach processes that minimize demands placed on customers • Be assertive • Be honest brokers • Accept criticism, apply what you can, be clear if something cannot be done

Context

One of the primary challenges associated with sustaining customer-driven intelligence operations in any field of endeavor is the variable nature of customer participation. Experience shows that the literate and educated stakeholders who constitute the body of intelligence customers will tend to provide feedback infrequently and with little depth during periods of routine/non-crisis operations, and they will tend to overwhelm the process with inputs during periods of high stress. This pattern is a practical application of the old adage that the squeaky wheel gets the grease, and as such, it is actually rational behavior, and it needs to be recognized as such.

The challenge facing cyber intelligence practitioners is that they must refine their processes during periods of routine operations, when customer feedback is scarce, and they need to be focused on operational execution during periods of high stress, which means that they will only have a limited capacity to respond to new guidance and feedback during periods where both are likely to be plentiful. The key to overcoming the challenges created by the mismatch in incentives between customers and practitioners is to recognize they exist and to establish separate but aligned process improvement cycles optimized for each group. The 4E process represents a robust process improvement cycle for intelligence practitioners and their peer-level customers in IT security. It stresses the importance of process feedback in all four phases of cyber intelligence operations; it has a phase focused on evaluating performance, and its circular design creates opportunities for organizations to leverage and apply experience-based learning within the existing operational flow.

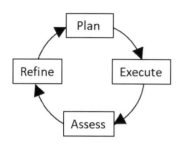

Figure 5.1.1 – The PEAR Cycle

The PEAR cycle (Plan-Execute - Assess - Refine) shown in Figure 5.1.1 is offered as a model for capturing experience-based learning from literate and educated stakeholders and applying it to cyber intelligence operations in the 4E process. The PEAR cycle has its roots in Dr. W. Edwards Deming's quality improvement PDCA cycle (Plan-Do-Check-Act)[43] and Colonel John Boyd's OODA loop (Observe-Orient-Decide-Act).[44] Figure 5.1.1 provides a visualization of the iterative PEAR process. The plan step involves actions design to translate organizational needs into cyber intelligence requirements and to allow stakeholders to articulate their performance expectations. Outputs from the plan step feed into the establish phase of the 4E process. Actions in the execute step are performed by cyber intelligence practitioners, they encompass actions associated with the *enable* and *execute phases* of 4E, and the outputs of those actions are intelligence products that stakeholders will address in the assess step. The assess step employs both objective and subjective measures of performance to identify issues to drive priorities in the refine step. Actions in the refine step consolidate issues identified in the assess step with issues identified in previous cycles that remain

---

[43] Mary W. Walton, The Deming Management Method, Berkley Publishing Group, 1986, pp 86-88.
[44] Mark Bonchek and Chris Fussell, *Decision Making, Top Gun Style,* Harvard Business Review, September 12, 2013.

unaddressed to provide priorities for the next iteration of the plan step. In actual practice, the line between refine and plan is very blurry, and actions associated with the two steps will often be ongoing concurrently.

One of the keys to applying PEAR is to recognize that it is a framework for organizing the acquisition of key elements of feedback from both individual stakeholders and groups of stakeholders. As such, organizations adopting this approach will find that they will not have a single macro-level PEAR process, but they will actually have a number of key stakeholder relationships in which they will apply the PEAR methodology as a means of collecting, processing, and applying feedback. Within the context of the 4E discussions in the previous section, PEAR is a customer outreach tool.

Successful application of PEAR is predicated on integration of PEAR and 4E into mutually supporting processes. There is not a one-for-one relationship between the phases of the two cycles, so knitting the two cycles together requires some skill. Figure 5.1.2 provides a visualization of relative relationships between the two processes.

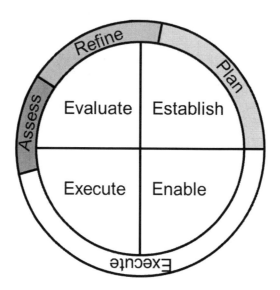

Figure 5.1.2 – Relationship Between the Steps of the PEAR Cycle and the 4E Process

Organizations that develop and apply the capabilities offered in the PEAR cycle will have two distinct advantages over organizations that do not. First, they will be able to provide their cyber intelligence practitioners with organizational understanding that will allow the practitioners to develop a range of threat actor courses of action informed by facts. Armed with that understanding, cyber intelligence will be able to conduct threat-driven IT security operations. Second, it provides stakeholders with a means to update their cyber intelligence requirements and performance expectations that can drive actions by cyber intelligence practitioners to prioritize customer needs and to define standards.

PEAR cycle application practices will vary from one organization to the next and strategies will evolve as cyber intelligence teams mature and gain proficiency. That said, individuals accountable for cyber intelligence contribution should push to develop monthly scheduled engagements for educated stakeholders and quarterly reviews for literate stakeholders in the first year of cyber intelligence operations. This structure will create opportunities to identify which stakeholders will provide the most frequent and/or meaningful feedback to bolster PEAR sustainability going forward.

Plan

Change is a constant factor for all organizations. As organizations move in anticipation of coming changes or in response to previous experience, they make decisions that affect variables with the potential to impact the priorities for cyber intelligence operations. Organizations that recognize this fact and develop practices designed to align cyber intelligence operations with changing organizational needs will make themselves more difficult targets for sophisticated threat actors who view organizational changes as vulnerabilities to be exploited.

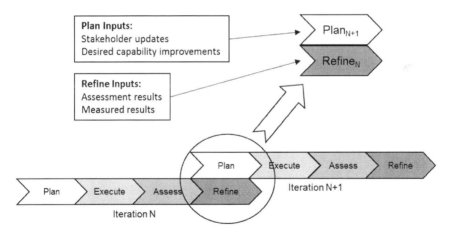

Figure 5.1.3 – Interrelationship of the Refine and Plan Steps in Sequential Iterations

Within the PEAR process, the plan step of any given iteration is closely tied to the refine step of the previous iteration (Figure 5.1.3). The component elements of the refine/plan continuum work in concert to improve cyber intelligence performance in the next iteration of operational execution by integrating the refined outputs of the assess step with stakeholder inputs.

The plan step for each iteration gives literate and educated stakeholders the opportunity to apply their performance feedback, to update cyber intelligence operational design elements [*Chapter 3.2*], and to review inputs that address desired changes to cyber intelligence capabilities. Examples of the types of stakeholder input intelligence planners should seek to acquire might include:

Literate Stakeholders' Inputs

- Future changes to the organization's operations: mergers, acquisitions, divestitures; new products and services; discontinuation of products and services; new partnerships; new physical locations; new regulatory requirements impacting IT security or intelligence, etc.
- Feedback on cyber intelligence performance: what they liked; what they did not like; what they saw that they did not expect; what they did not see that they expected to see; what they did not understand, etc.
- Inputs for an updated cyber intelligence mission statement to include operational priorities and areas of acceptable risk
- Updated intelligence needs and CODIs

Educated Stakeholders' Inputs

- Future changes to IT operations: new or retiring data centers; changes in vendors/partners; planned equipment upgrades; changes to the IT architecture; proposed changes in the IT security team; updated IT security risk assessment, etc.
- Feedback on cyber intelligence performance with emphasis on support to and integration with supported IT lines of operation: what they liked; what they did not like; what they saw that they did not expect; what they did not see that they expected to see; what they did not understand, what changes/improvements they would like to see, etc.

- Updated intelligence and information requirements

Combined, these inputs constitute updated planning considerations to be integrated with experience-based learning from the refine step to update the cyber intelligence planning outputs as inputs to the *establish phase* in the 4E process. To be clear, outputs from the plan step are at the big-picture/scheme of maneuver level, and they will need to be translated into execution-level actions by cyber intelligence practitioners performing *establish phase* tasks in the 4E cycle. Outputs address application of intelligence capabilities, stakeholder priorities, risk, and reporting responsibilities as guidance rather than as specifically directed actions. Examples might include goals addressing needs for new threat data sources (e.g. update sharing agreements with government agencies and industry partners), cost reduction (e.g. retire a system or a contract), or reducing reporting latency with new event driven products. Planning guidance might also prescribe greater levels of effort against specific classes of threats or in support of specific IT security functions. Regardless of content or format, plan outputs should address the following key considerations:

- **Desired outputs** – articulate the primary goals of cyber intelligence operations to include desired products and production timelines
- **Define supported processes** – provide a list of organization/IT processes that need to be addressed by cyber intelligence operations
- **Define intelligence role** – articulate expectations for intelligence in terms of how predictive threat warning, situational awareness and understanding, and support to security operations will contribute to organizational goals
- **List potential intelligence resources** – the plan should list all known intelligence resources available during execution of cyber intelligence operations; the list should include all existing internal and external capabilities and relationships

- **Identify shortfalls/unfunded capabilities** – plan integrity dictates that leaders document known shortfalls (e.g. people, skills, data, tools, and products) that planners could apply to address stated intelligence needs but that do not exist or are not funded
- **Articulate changes from the previous plan** – the plan is being updated in response to stakeholder inputs and lessons learned from assessing execution of the previous plan; the inputs and the changes should be clearly articulated so that intelligence practitioners can immediately identify changes to the plan

Regardless of the format or specific topics addressed, the goal is to provide cyber intelligence practitioners with the guidance necessary to adjust their operations to improve focus on key threats, provide more useful support, and to eliminate (or at least reduce) unproductive activities. Higher performing organizations will identify desired performance measures that can be used to develop metrics, and they will identify specific mitigation efforts and controls they can implement to address capability gaps identified in the planning process.

Execute

Cyber intelligence practitioners expend the vast majority of their time and effort executing intelligence operations designed to answer articulated intelligence requirements, enhance security, and to provide awareness and understanding of current threats and emerging threat trends. In the context of this chapter, however, the role of the execute step is to convert refined planning guidance into experience-based learning.

There are both objective and subjective components of learning that feed performance assessment in the assess step. Objective measures tend to address performance criteria like how long given products take to produce, or the percentage of intelligence requirements satisfied by the collection plan. Subjective inputs can address a broader range of topics involving things like the value of specific sources used in the analysis process and the quality or usefulness of the products generated from that analysis. Objective measure lend themselves to being codified as performance metrics. [*See Chapter 5.2.*]

Assess

The assess step encompasses actions designed to evaluate the performance of real-world cyber intelligence operations conducted in the execute step against the desired outputs articulated in the plan step. The goal of the assess step is to determine which elements of the plan were successfully addressed and which were not. Actions in the assess step evaluate the full range of intelligence operations holistically, but the value of the assess step is enhanced when the impacts of changes directed for the current PEAR cycle iteration are the point of emphasis. Cyber intelligence stakeholders must assess whether changes to the plan produced the expected results or the desired outcomes as an input to the refine step.

Consistent with the discussion in the previous section, analysts will have both objective and subjective inputs to support performance assessment.

Objective Measures

Objective measure offer empirical performance feedback, but they still require a fair amount of analytic scrutiny to provide meaningful value. Objective data needs to be viewed in the context of what it actually contributes to understanding, and it should lead to questions like: What does it actually measure, and is the statistical sample size relevant?

Objective approaches should be defined in the plan step, and where possible supported by metrics addressing cyber intelligence process outputs. Among the processes that lend themselves to objective measurement are the IIAM, production, and dissemination processes. Examples of objective measurement in each are:

- **IIAM** – effectiveness of intelligence collection across articulated requirements; advanced warning of key organizational changes prior to that information being made public; percentage of requirements generated by customers; percentage of support functions with three or more collectable requirements, etc.

- **Production** – labor hours/labor costs associated with standing production; elapsed time from alert of suspicious activity to an intelligence product being completed; percentage of time analysts are spending on production activities, etc.

- **Dissemination** – percentage of products with standard dissemination lists; time requirements for disseminating non-standard production; time delays between when a new person fills a position and they are added to appropriate distribution lists, etc.

Each of these examples provide topics that lend themselves to data collection and measurement, but data collected in most cases will have some degree of ambiguity associated with it. For example, what does it mean if an organization has five PIRs and 80% of all intelligence production addresses a single PIR and two PIRs have no production over the period being measured? Is a PIR with no intelligence produced a bad PIR? Did intelligence fail to develop a competent collection plan, or was the PIR narrow in scope and no activity actually occurred? Is the intelligence team overly focused in a single area? Is this an anomaly, or will similar results appear next time? What should the organization do, if anything, to address what appears to be an imbalance in operational focus? The assess step deals with identifying the kind of performance feedback cited in this example and determining whether the appearance of imbalance in intelligence operations is meaningful and something that can and should be addressed.

Subjective Measures

Subjective measures are an important component of cyber intelligence performance assessments, in large part because so few intelligence related activities lend themselves to meaningful objective measurement. While subjective measures provide valuable insights, they are not all valid or relevant, and they often reflect biases and perceptions rather than ground truth. There is an old adage in intelligence that addresses this challenge; the adage states that "perception is not reality but it is real." Useful employment of subjective measures can only take place in organizations that are willing to identify and acknowledge their own biases.

One of the key challenges in employing subjective inputs is acquiring the data set that one can use. The two primary sources of data are educated stakeholders and cyber intelligence practitioners.

Educated stakeholders are also the primary cyber intelligence customers, and as such, they represent one of the best sources of input for criteria by which intelligence performance can be measured. Examples of potential educated stakeholder driven subjective measures include:

- Information and intelligence requirements – both existing and proposed changes
- Defined list of processes cyber intelligence must support
- List of processes/decisions cyber intelligence is to address in each assigned security function
- Specified timeliness and format requirements

Intelligence practitioners also play a critical role in defining subjective performance measures by identifying where their efforts should be creating impact and assessing that impact in either absolute or relative terms. Every effort should be made to bring the full intelligence workforce into the discussion of key performance indicators to be measured. People in leadership positions tend to understand theory better than practice, whereas the analyst working directly with people in the functions cyber intelligence is charged with supporting will have actual experience providing examples of intelligence that contributed to greater security or improved decision making. Examples of potential intelligence practitioner subject measures might be:

- Self-assessment of intelligence operations for the ongoing execution period to include: ability to action existing intelligence and information requirements; performance of intelligence vendors (where germane); assessment of tools/equipment performance; intelligence process shortfalls; intelligence gaps; externally imposed policy challenges; performance against metrics
- Identify where additional feedback would be useful
- A list of which IT security functions the intelligence team feels it is contributing to positively
- What those positive contributions are
- A list of IT security functions the intelligence team feels it is not helping
- Identify gaps in intelligence capabilities to address articulated requirements and what solutions might exist to address those shortfalls

At the conclusion of the assess step, stakeholders should be able to articulate where intelligence operations are meeting (or exceeding) expectations and where they are not; what opportunities might exist to improve performance, and where redundancies may exist. Each performance issue identified as an output of this step needs to include a justification for why it is on the list, to include supporting evidence and source of that evidence. It is also important that the output identify gaps that need to be addressed in the refine and plan steps.

Refine

The refine step involves actions designed to apply experience-based learning from operational execution as a basis for driving continuous improvement of cyber intelligence operations. The primary inputs to this step are the issues identified in the assess step, but high performing organizations will also include unaddressed items from the previous PEAR iteration and evaluate whether conditions that prevented actions in earlier iterations (e.g. workforce proficiency, tools, budget, relative priority) have evolved to a point where those issues can be addressed and will be included going forward.

Actions in this step involve three types of refinement. The first involves refining all inputs into a prioritized list of issues that needs to be considered in the plan step. The second involves evaluating that list and seeking opportunities to combine similar and mutually supporting tasks into a single task. The third involves refining resource implications associated with every issue (both direct financial costs and opportunity costs) so that participants in the plan step have a basis for determining where the cut line will be drawn and which identified issues are not going to be addressed in the plan.

Chapter 5.2
Measuring Performance

Key Points

- Key performance indicators (KPIs) offer a means to generate objective performance data for a finite set of cyber intelligence processes.
- As a general rule, higher level cyber intelligence processes do not lend themselves to empirical performance measurement.
- Skillfully crafted KPIs can offer organizations a means to measure process performance within a subset of key processes to gain insights into actual performance against a pre-established set of standards.
- Of the 11 doctrinal intelligence processes integrated into the 4E model:
    - Three (production, dissemination, and integration) offer fertile opportunities for KPI employment.
    - Four (direction, collection, processing, and feedback) have subordinate tasks that lend themselves to KPI employment.
    - Four (planning, exploitation, analysis and evaluation) are so subjective in nature that they present very limited opportunities for KPI employment.

Stakeholder Roles

Literate Stakeholders	Educated Stakeholders	Intelligence Practitioners
• Be aware of your organizations cyber intelligence measurement processes	• Provide inputs to cyber intelligence practitioners regarding processes you need to have measured • Demonstrate proficiency in understanding the strengths and limitations of specific measures	• Recognize processes that lend themselves to measurement • Demonstrate proficiency in interpreting/applying results • Take advantage of opportunities to apply KPI data as inputs to decisions

Context

Building on the content from the previous chapter, this chapter presents an approach for developing and using KPIs as a means to generate objective measurement data from cyber intelligence operations that can provide performance feedback and can be employed to support efforts to drive continuous improvement. Any discussion of applying KPIs to cyber intelligence operations needs to begin with a disclaimer that the major processes that combine to constitute cyber intelligence operations do not lend themselves to empirical measurement at the macro level. Most of cyber intelligence processes have subordinate tasks that can be measured, and in most instances, organizations can use those measurements as surrogates for assessing performance trends for the higher level process the tasks support. The key point of this chapter is that skillfully crafted KPIs can offer organizations a means to measure process performance in a subset of key processes to gain insights into actual performance against a pre-established set of standards; they can provide indicators and trends to assist leaders in understanding performance issues and costs, but they will rarely create sufficient understanding to enable leaders to make real-time adjustments in ongoing operations.

Effective use of KPIs to create meaningful performance feedback begins with identifying which processes lend themselves to objective measurement then determining which performance elements one would like to measure. This chapter advances an approach that cyber intelligence activities can be broken into three broad categories with respect to how well they lend themselves to the application of KPIs:

- **Measurable processes** – include processes like production and dissemination that generate tangible outputs that can be measured in a manner that they will generally be able to provide meaningful performance feedback and identify performance trends as cyber intelligence operations evolve
- **Processes with measurable components** – include processes like IIAM and collection that have contributing actions that lend themselves to being measured objectively
- **Limited opportunity** – include processes with highly subjective outputs like exploitation and analysis; there are opportunities to measure some components of these processes, but few organizations will find value in doing so regularly

One of the benefits of this approach is that it offers a roadmap to cyber intelligence organizations as they mature. Newer service offerings will find value in developing KPIs for measurable processes but will accrue little benefit from trying to measure more complex processes. As cyber intelligence teams become deeper and better established, they will find some payoffs from measuring selected components of more complex processes. Few organizations will ever find great value in applying KPIs in the limited opportunity processes. Exceptions will be organizations that have a narrowly defined special focus that causes them to want to operate at a Zone 4 proficiency level as defined in Chapter 2.1.

The cyber intelligence processes evaluated for measurement in this chapter are derived from the list of doctrinal intelligence processes presented in Chapter 1.3. Those processes are all captured in 4E process model present, as shown in Figure 5.2.1.

Establish	Enable	Execute		Evaluate
Plan Direct Feedback	Collection (CRM) Feedback	Collection (COM) Exploit Produce Integrate	Process Analyze Disseminate Feedback	Evaluation Feedback

Figure 5.2.1 – Intelligence Processes – Doctrinal Processes by 4E Phase

Measurable Processes

In order for a cyber intelligence process to be a good candidate for objective measurement, it must meet two criteria. First, it has to produce an output that lends itself to some form of empirical measurement, and second, it has to be a process that does not depend upon inputs from outside organizations. Of the 11 doctrinal intelligence processes, only three meet both criteria: production, dissemination, and integration. Of the three, production is the process that offers the greatest potential for meaningful return, making it the process most organizations will want to focus on first.

Production KPIs

Cyber intelligence production is one of four functions (research, analysis, production, and customer outreach) intelligence analysts perform. Healthy cyber intelligence operations can only occur when individual analysts are able to allocate their time efficiently across all four functions. Experienced intelligence professionals recognize that customer demand for intelligence production can create unsustainable imbalances in analyst time allocation. Analysts can become so consumed in production activities that they have little time to conduct either research or analysis, and intelligence products can become little more than exercises in repackaging other peoples' work into the appropriate format. [*Chapter 4.2 [subtask 4.2.3.1] develops this challenge in greater depth, and Chapter 4.3 [subtask 4.3.3.2] addresses production management.]*

#	Description	Unit of Measure	Specification	Justification	Constraints
PM1	Measure time allocated to production activities across analyst workforce	% of time allocated to production activities	KPI is designed to create awareness of zero-sum relationship between research, analysis, production, and customer outreach	Provide leadership with empirical basis for measuring the impact of production requirements on overall cyber intelligence operations	Can be cumbersome to measure, and outputs can vary greatly over time
PM2	Measure specific costs of individual intelligence products	Average dollar cost per specified product over identified period of time	KPI is designed to create an understanding of what specific intelligence products cost to provide as a basis for measuring ROI	Many intelligence products, especially daily or weekly updates, create large, unrecognized financial costs. Leaders who have actual cost data will be able to make better informed choices about the value of individual intelligence products.	Determining actual costs can be difficult, particularly in cases where people feel threatened by change.

Table 5.2.1 – Potential Production KPIs

Production management is a critical component of sustained superior cyber intelligence operations, and there are multiple attributes that lend themselves to empirical measurement. Table 5.2.1 outlines two performance measures that organizations may want to consider: analyst workforce time allocated to production activities, and product costs for standard products in the production catalog. Both performance measures can be tailored to the specific needs of individual organizations. Variations of PM1 could be as simple as having all analysts report when they exceed an assigned threshold for production activity over a defined time increment and as complex as having all analysts submit daily timesheets that break their days into 15 minute intervals.

Dissemination KPIs

The two most common forms of dissemination are pushing and pulling/posting. Pushing refers to actions involved in delivering products to designated users, the most common forms of which are email, texting/office chat, and verbal. Pulling/posting should be self-explanatory, and for cyber intelligence operations, the most common forms of posting involve making products available to blogs, collaborative workspaces, or websites so that users can pull them whenever they need to review their content. Both forms of dissemination have strengths and weaknesses, and they are not mutually exclusive.

Measures of dissemination effectiveness and associated costs will be of increasing value to organizations as they mature. Organizations with a small number of products that they disseminate using tailored email distribution lists have no real incentive to measure dissemination process variables, but organizations with multiple products or that tailor specific products to unique audiences by maintaining single use dissemination paths will benefit from measuring the relative performance of each. Table 5.2.2 offers two measures organizations might consider tailoring to their specific needs.

#	Description	Unit of Measure	Specification	Justification	Constraints
PM3	Process maintenance costs	Labor/equipment costs over defined time period	KPI is designed to capture costs associated with the full range of dissemination activities from updating email distribution lists to maintaining blogs, wikis, collaboration sites and websites	Many organizations maintain multiple dissemination pathways without understanding costs involved, and in some cases lesser used pathways might have significant associated costs	Dissemination pathways may have multiple users, so isolating cyber intelligence product dissemination costs may be difficult
PM4	Dissemination planning proficiency	% of products in the product catalog that have developed dissemination plans	KPI provides feedback on planning process	Intelligence products developed in response to unusual events need to be delivered to all stakeholders in a timely manner. Products lacking dissemination plans will slow delivery and increase the likelihood that key customers will not get the product	KPI addresses the existence of dissemination plans but it does not address the quality or currency of those plans

Table 5.2.2 – Potential Dissemination KPIs

Integration KPIs

Intelligence integration involves updating analytic working tools and standing presentations with new intelligence. Organizations that employ in-house reference tools like cyber intelligence wikis and databases as knowledge management approaches to ensure the whole team is working from the same script, need to understand how well those tools are being maintained and how much it is costing the organization to maintain them. Standing capability briefing slides and executive threat briefings must also be updated at regular intervals, and there are cost associated with those updates that should be measured.

While integration KPIs are fairly straight forward, the insights they will provide are probably less useful than production and dissemination KPIs. Table 5.2.3 offers two potential measures that lend themselves to KPI development that might add value.

#	Description	Unit of Measure	Specification	Justification	Constraints
PM5	Process maintenance costs	Labor/ equipment costs over defined time period	KPI is designed to capture costs maintaining analytic resources associated with intelligence integration standards. Many organizations will find overlaps with PM3	Maintenance of analytic resources can impose significant costs, and organizations that track those costs can identify opportunities to eliminate high cost/low payoff activities	Analysts tend to be very protective of their pet projects, so acquiring accurate costing data can be difficult in environments in which analysts think that their inputs might contribute to the demise of their favorite products.
PM6	Timeliness of updates	% of products updated according to an established standard	KPI provides an indicator for how much stress intelligence integration is placing on cyber intelligence execution	In any cyber intelligence operation in which this measure is not at or near 100% there are either too many products, overly restrictive update policies, or a workforce that is not accountable to their	Same constraint as PM5. Most data will come from people who have incentives to protect the status quo and will tend to provide data accordingly

Table 5.2.3 – Potential Integration KPIs

Processes with Measurable Components

While none of the remaining eight doctrinal processes lend themselves to being measured using KPIs as effectively as production, dissemination, and integration, four processes (direction, collection, processing, and feedback) do offer some opportunities worth exploring. These four processes offer outputs that can be measured, but the insights those measures would provide would often say more about the quality of inputs from stakeholders or the actions by threat actors than about the proficiency or effectiveness of cyber intelligence operations. In all four cases, however, it is possible to identify contributing subtasks that can measure cyber intelligence performance isolated from contributions by other participants in the ecosystem.

Direction KPIs

The most significant outputs of the direction process are planning guidance and intelligence needs. While neither of these outputs comes from the cyber intelligence team, the quality and timely delivery of both outputs provides useful feedback on stakeholder relationships and the relative priority of cyber intelligence within IT and IT security operations. Effective cyber intelligence leaders should be able to drive timely guidance and updated requirements with compelling data and trust. KPIs addressing direction outputs should focus on timeliness of stakeholder responses to proposed process changes and requirement updates, and track that data over time to look for trends.

Collection KPIs

Direct measurement of collection performance is made difficult by the fact that one cannot detect an action that did not occur, so absence of collection does not necessarily equate to a poor collection approach. Collection actions associated with the collection discipline CRM can provide useful feedback regarding the depth and breadth of actions designed to refine intelligence and information requirements into actionable collection strategies. Collection KPIs will provide data to support trend analysis and their ability to contribute to understanding will likely increase in value over time, but they will have very limited applicability as a real time indicators of operational performance.

Processing KPIs

Processing actions encompass both converting machine readable data into formats that can be exploited by human analysts and automation efforts that cue analysts to the existence of data to be exploited. Among the more useful processing actions are logging of events of interest and alerts that a defined event of interest has occurred. Useful processing KPIs will deal with whether key processing actions are in place, how long it takes to update alerts, the latency between when an event occurs and the correct cyber intelligence analyst is working it, clarity of alerts, and false alarm rates. In many organizations, actions outlined for potential KPI development are not conducted by the cyber intelligence team, and priorities for updates to security systems are outside of the span of control for the cyber intelligence leader. People need to be aware of who the stakeholders are in cases in which multiple organizations contribute to a process being measured by a KPI.

Feedback KPIs

Many people think of intelligence feedback solely in terms customer feedback at the end of the process, but that is just one type of feedback. People engaged in each cyber intelligence process within any given cyber intelligence operation have an obligation to provide regular feedback to the people who performed the actions that preceded them. Collection managers need to tell the people who provide them with requirements when the requirements do not make sense or are unlikely to generate collection. The better they understand what the customer needs, the more likely they are to be able to provide it. The same goes for analysts talking to collection managers, and analysts engaged in integration talking to analysts engaged in production activities. KPIs designed to measure feedback will likely have greater value when applied over longer periods of time to help recognize performance trends.

Limited Opportunity

The four remaining cyber intelligence processes (planning, exploitation, analysis, and evaluation) offer only limited opportunities for applying objective criteria that would support KPI development. Measurements like frequency of occurrence of specific tasks are easy enough to put in place, but they are unlikely to provide meaningful insights that can be used to support decision making. Organizations seeking to develop a very high level of proficiency in a specifically identified exploitation or analysis function will normally make that decision in response to a specific need. In those instance, it is possible to develop KPIs associated with whether actions designed to provide the additional proficiency contributed to the desired outcome and what the costs associated with achieving that outcome were.

Chapter 5.3
Analytic Frameworks

Key Points

- This chapter presents two analytic frameworks that offer cyber intelligence teams pathways to tracking/presenting cyber-threats with greater contextual richness.
- System of system analysis (SOSA) provides an analytic approach for creating a greater understanding of threats and threat actors by modeling the ecosystem in which they operate, the subsystems within that ecosystem, and the interdependencies between those subsystems that conspire to shape threat actor perceptions of the ecosystem.
    - The two primary applications of SOSA are to generate greater threat context and to support IT security defense in depth.
    - SOSA illuminates threat actor actions and support mechanisms (nodes) and the communications/ interrelationships (links) between them, both of which provide network defenders with awareness they can apply to detect and/or disrupt threats.
- Intelligence preparation of the business environment (IPBE) adopts and adapts the analytic approach and rigor of one of the more universally successful military intelligence planning tools, intelligence preparation of the operational environment (IPOE).
    - IPOE provides a structured analytic approach for developing likely "enemy courses of action" based on opportunities and constraints imposed by the environment in which all participants operate.

- The principles of IPOE are applicable to private sector cyber intelligence programs, but the doctrinal IPOE process is not.
- The IPBE approach presented in this chapter represents an effort to adapt the key elements of process flow of IPOE, and the actions that enable them, to make them more applicable to private sector cyber intelligence operations.
- The goal of IPBE is to develop "most likely" and "most dangerous" threat actor courses of action that can be applied as planning factors for IT security operations.

Stakeholder Roles

Literate Stakeholders	Educated Stakeholders	Intelligence Practitioners
• Demonstrate awareness of systems-based approaches	• Drive decisions regarding when and how to apply these analytic frameworks • Make time for process updates • Wargame analytics and preplanned responses	• Master internals of the analytic frameworks • Learn to teach them to stakeholders • Continually refine systems models • Stress most likely and most dangerous methodologies

5.3.1 – System of Systems Analysis

Context

System of systems analysis (SOSA) provides an analytic framework for examining specific operational capabilities as components of the larger ecosystem in which they operate, and it is useful for developing and understanding the interdependencies that different components of that ecosystem have on one another. In the hands of skilled cyber intelligence analysts, SOSA can be applied to provide greater insights into the full range of challenges threat actors will need to negotiate successfully to achieve their goals. SOSA can provide analysts with deeper insights into the constraints facing threat actors and enable them to recommend changes in organizational security design that can both benefit network defenders and complicate approaches for threat actors.

SOSA supports two worthwhile goals for any cyber intelligence program:

Threat Context – Intelligence analysis that focuses on intentions, capabilities, and opportunities but neglects the physical laws that govern the ecosystems in which threat actors operate, will tend to produce worst case analysis. While worst case outcomes should always be addressed as a component of a thorough analytic process, they will rarely be the most likely outcome. Intelligence products become progressively less credible with every unrealized dire threat warning they produce, and credibility is a prerequisite to relevance. SOSA allows cyber intelligence analysts to evaluate new intelligence within an operational framework that more accurately represents the world in which threat actors and network defenders operate, and that improved accuracy will enable analyst to produce more realistic threat assessments.

Defense in Depth – One of the goals for any IT security team should be to maximize the number of opportunities it has to defeat threats targeting its networks and data. SOSA provides cyber intelligence teams with a structured process for analyzing threat actor methods and for identifying potentially detectable actions that threat actors will have to take as they advance through the succession of steps necessary to conduct successful attacks. Each potentially detectable step represents an opportunity for the IT security team to shape and layer their security operations in ways to promote more favorable outcomes.

This section presents a three step approach for conducting SOSA in support of cyber intelligence operations: (1) develop a process model for characterizing threats; (2) refine threat models, and (3) apply threat models to cyber intelligence operations

Step One – Develop a Process Model for Characterizing Threats

Most firms offering services in the IT security and cyber intelligence fields have developed models of threat actor behaviors that they employ in their service offerings. One of the more common and effective approaches is the kill-chain. The primary contribution of the kill-chain approach is that it creates a mindset that malicious actors targeting one's organization must work through a series of definable actions to accomplish their goals. Once network defenders understand what those actions are, they can begin to look for opportunities to impose costs on threat actors by complicating their tasks (e.g. multi-factor authentication and network segmentation) and increasing the likelihood that malicious actions will be detected.

Among the better known and more highly respected threat frameworks is the Lockheed Martin kill-chain. The authors applied the US Department of Defense's doctrinal targeting kill-chain construct (find, fix, track, target, engage, and assess, or F2T2EA) to the process of computer network intrusions. The resultant seven step intrusion kill-chain (reconnaissance, weaponize, delivery, exploitation, installation, command and control, and actions on objective) has become a standard reference for most IT security and cyber intelligence professionals.[45]

Figure 5.3.1.1 – Lockheed Martin Kill-Chain

The Lockheed Martin kill-chain provides a good starting point for developing a process model, but it is incomplete. The authors did

---

[45] Eric M. Hutchins, , Michael J. Cloppert, and Rohan M. Amin, Ph.D., <u>Intelligence-Driven Computer Network Defense Informed by Analysis of Adversary Campaigns and Intrusion Kill Chains</u>, Lockheed Martin White Paper, pp. 4, 5.

an outstanding job of describing the steps threat actors must progress through between their efforts to gain intelligence on the networks they are attacking and the execution of their desired actions on objective, but reconnaissance is not the first step, and actions on objective is not the last.

Before malicious actors begin conducting reconnaissance for the purposes of gathering intelligence on their intended target, they will have already had to go through a target selection process. Actors will have made a decision to conduct some action (e.g. steal, manipulate, deny access) to a given network or data set to accomplish a desired outcome. Likewise, once the perpetrators have conducted their actions on objective, they still have more work to do in most cases. Actors will need to assess whether they achieved their desired goals, and if one of their goals is persistent presence, whether they were detected. If their action on objective was data theft or extortion, then, they will need to conduct actions to monetize their theft or collect their extortion payments.

The Intelligence and National Security Alliance (INSA) recognized the importance of the actions not addressed in the Lockheed Martin kill-chain, and citing Lockheed Martin's work as a point of reference, they published their own version of an intrusion kill-chain, which is presented below as Figure 5.3.1.2.[46]

Figure 5.3.1.2 – INSA Kill-chain

INSA's paper and kill-chain model are more complete, but they do not address activities to monetize actions on objective. Both Lockheed Martin and INSA did superb jobs of modeling threat actor behaviors that mattered most to their organizations, but the

---

[46] George Bamford, John Felker, and Troy Mattern, Operational Levels of Cyber Intelligence, INSA, September 2013, p. 5.

fact that neither is complete reinforces the importance of individual organizations tailoring a threat model to their specific needs.

Figure 5.3.1.3 presents a simplified kill-chain that consolidates the 15 steps of the Lockheed Martin and INSA kill-chains into four steps (plan and lead, stage, gain access, and exploit access).

> **Plan and lead** has both pre-attack (e.g. develop concept, identify targets, and define TTPTs) and post-attack (e.g. assess performance and determine follow up actions) tasks.
>
> **Stage** addresses pre-attack actions designed to acquire the capabilities to conduct the attack (e.g. infrastructure, malware, coders, and obfuscation.)
>
> Actions supporting the **gain access** step might include delivering malware, spear phishing, exploiting insider(s), and exploiting security seams in 3rd party relationships.
>
> Examples of actions threat actors might take to **exploit access** include move laterally, escalate privileges, install backdoors, command and control, exfiltrate data, and encrypt or erase data to support actions on objective.

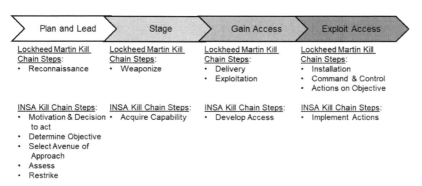

Figure 5.3.1.3 – Simplified 4-Step Kill-chain

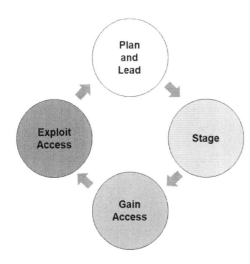

Figure 5.3.1.4 – Process View

Given that the plan and lead step has both pre-attack and post-attack options, a more accurate way to visualize the four steps in the simplified kill-chain is to arrange the steps into a circular process view like Figure 5.3.1.4. This arrangement stresses that sophisticated attacks are seldom one-shot fire and forget operations. Attackers will frequently have to go through several iterations before achieving their desired outcome and will generally make adjustments in their restrike based on learning from previous iterations.

The Lockheed Martin and INSA kill-chains were both optimized to address threats from state actors, and while some private sector organizations are targets of state actors, most organizations will see their primary external threats coming cybercriminals. Cybercrime threat models need to have steps to account for crime-as-a-service (CAAS) and monetization of actions on objectives. CAAS covers a wide range of products and services available malicious actor on criminal forums and marketplaces, many of which are hosted on the dark web. Cyber intelligence analysts who recognize CAAS trends will be able to anticipate evolving threats targeting their organizations in the form of mass spam campaigns, watering holes, or malvertising. Understanding which vulnerabilities are being exploited by the most popular exploit kits is useful intelligence for the patching team.

Monetization addresses the steps involved in generating financial return from actions on objective, and they vary depending upon what the actions on objective were. Stolen user and customer credentials might be sold to other malicious actors or used to conduct frauds. Stolen payment card data can be monetized through purchasing and reselling goods or by selling blocks of card data in "carder forums." Of note, most of the major payment card breaches from point-of-sale attacks on large retail firms in recent years were not discovered until the criminals sought to monetize their thefts. Rapid response to intelligence generated by analysis of similarities in purchases on stolen cards led to attackers being detected, their malware being removed, and their attacks being disrupted.

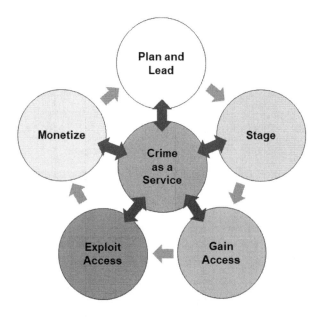

Figure 5.3.1.5 – Cybercrime Threat Model

Figure 5.3.1.5 presents a visualization of a cybercrime threat model that businesses in the retail, hospitality, and financial services industry might adopt or refine. It adds actions for monetize and CAAS to process view of the simplified kill-chain. CAAS is placed in the middle, because CAAS marketplaces offer goods and services that can support actions in all of the other five bubbles.

Step Two – Refining Threat Models

SOSA provides an analytic framework for addressing the interrelationships and interdependencies between all of the subsystems of the larger ecosystem. The cybercrime threat model in Figure 5.3.1.5 is actually a visualization of the cybercrime ecosystem, and each of the six circles are the subsystems of that ecosystem.

In order to apply SOSA, cyber intelligence analysts must first refine the level of detail in their threat models from a macro-level to an execution-level by identifying actions within each subsystem that potential threat actors are likely to carry out to produce the desired output from that subsystem. Once analysts have developed a working list of supporting actions within each subsystem, they need to work through how those actions support one another and identify artifacts of each action that may generate detectable indicators.

This level of detail supports what traditional signals intelligence professionals refer to as link analysis. Link analysis views process actions as nodes that are tied together through some means of communication, which are called links. In traditional intelligence operations, links represent collection opportunities that can provide a range of outcomes from tactical threat warning to insights on future intensions. Within the context of contemporary cyber warfare approaches, these links also represent opportunities to disrupt attacks. Skillful execution requires organizations to be able to understand whether the benefits of disrupting a link outweigh the loss of intelligence that will result from the action.

Table 5.3.1.1 offers an example of what a first generation execution-level analysis matrix might look like. The content is

Sub-system	Subordinate Nodes	Actions Creating Vulnerabilities	Detection Strategies	Disruption Strategies
Plan and Lead	Motivation to act	None	None	None
	Determine objective	None	None	None
	Select avenues of approach	None	None	None
	Intelligence and reconnaissance	Scanning	Monitor scanning	None
		Develop insiders	Insider threat program	Honeypots
		Research 3rd Parties	None	None
		Rehearsals	Anomaly detection	None
		Open source research	None	Information security program
		Human collection	Awareness and reporting	Information security program
	Assess	None	None	None
	Restrike	None	None	None
Stage	Acquire capabilities	Participate in criminal forums	Cyber intelligence	None
		Register domains	Cyber intelligence	Shut down/block access
		Move money	None	None
	Weaponize	None	None	None
Gain Access	Develop Access	Hack accounts	Various/system dependent	IIAM
		Social engineering	Awareness and reporting	Employee action
	Deliver weapon	Spear phishing	Awareness and reporting	Block replies/links
		Infected media	Awareness and reporting	Removable media policies
		Infected email attachments	Mail guards/endpoint security	Various
Exploit Access	Maintain access	RAT/Backdoor installation	Signature/Behavioral monitoring	Clean infection
	Move laterally	Access other internal networks	Behavioral monitoring	IIAM/Network Segmentation
	Escalate privileges	Gain new access	Various controls	IIAM
	Actions on objective	Exfiltrate stolen data	Extrusion detection	Various controls
		Corrupt data	User Report	Back up data
		Deny access to data	User Report	Back up data

Table 5.3.1.1 – Nodes, Vulnerabilities, Detection, and Disruption

neither complete nor is it fully actionable, but it provides an example of the kinds of information a SOSA would use, and it illustrates two important points: threat actors will take actions that cyber intelligence has no reasonable expectation of ever detecting, and just because one can detect something does not mean that one can disrupt it.

A refined version of Table 5.3.1.1 will address the actions creating vulnerabilities in far greater detail, which will afford organizations the ability develop more specific detection and disruption strategies. As an example, threat actors register domains for a variety of purposes. Two examples are: (1) actors register domains that look like they belong to the targeted organization so that they can divert traffic to those domains without causing people to suspect that they are not on a legitimate site, and (2) mass malware distributors register large numbers of domains to complicate security organizations ability to block traffic to their downloaders. Each approach has a different detection and disruption strategy. Organizations can monitor domain registrations to detect registration of domains using the organization's name. Those domains can be shutdown, served with cease and desist letters, or in some cases bought from the registrant. Organizations will want to monitor content on suspicious sites and warn customers of their existence. Cyber intelligence can be applied to identify personas who register domains for suspicious purposes, which can provide another tool for detecting suspicious sites one might want to block. Mass registrations often use domain generation algorithms, and if one can break the algorithm, one can block or sinkhole domains generated by the algorithm. Actionable detection and disruption strategies require some degree of understanding of malicious actor TTPTs to generate sufficient detail to be effective.

Like so many other cyber intelligence tools, threat models (and their content) need to be updated and refined continuously once they are put into actual application. Changes in organizational threat profile, evolution of threat actor capabilities, and self-learning from experience using the models should all drive updates and refinements.

Step Three – Apply Threat Models to Cyber Intelligence Operations

Skillful application of SOSA to create defense in depth begins with determining which of the links and nodes present the greatest vulnerabilities to threat actors and the greatest opportunities for cyber intelligence and IT security. Once those links and nodes have been selected, cyber intelligence efforts need to place emphasis on improving their ability to detect indicators of activity, and the IT security team needs to develop and exercise preplanned responses to respond when specific threat indicators are active.

The decision to disrupt actions one perceives to be threat related should never be taken lightly. All actions have consequences, and the second order effects and unintended consequences associated with showing one's hand to an attacker can have greater costs than not acting. The decision to act represents the classic intelligence conundrum of determining when the organization is better off leaving a known threat in place (because it is known and can be exploited) and when it is time to eliminate the threat (knowing that the adversary will now have a better idea of one's capabilities and will likely respond in a different manner that will be harder to detect using the capabilities one just gave away.)

In most cases, the need to disrupt increases and the negative consequences decrease the farther into the kill-chain one gets. Disrupting the sale of stolen credentials in the monetize phase or blocking exfiltration of data associated with action of objectives are easy decisions to make. The skill comes in deciding whether to shut down an account early in the kill-chain that one knows has been compromised. If the IT security team has the capability and skills to track actions taken on the compromised account, leaders will have to evaluate the potential gains from additional intelligence on the attacker and his/her TTPTs versus the risks of leaving a known malicious actor on their network. Other factors, like how the account was compromised, and the likelihood that the attacker may have access to multiple accounts need to be addressed in the decision whether to respond. There are no universal right or wrong answers, but organizations that have developed and exercised preplanned responses will make better decisions under the pressure from real-world threats than those that have not.

Most threat actors will not be defeated by a single disruption, and they will work to overcome disruptions by either countering the security applied to their link or bypassing security with a new link. Cyber intelligence leaders need to analyze threat actors' most likely responses to security actions, before those actions are applied, and have collection strategies in place to look for indicators of threat actors countering security. Lesser skilled or determined attackers and opportunistic actors can be encouraged to move on fairly quickly, but more highly motivated threat actors will only be put off once their own risk versus gain calculus tells them that costs being imposed by security disruptions make abandoning their course of action the financially prudent decision.

5.3.2 – Intelligence Preparation of the Business Environment

Context

Environmental understanding is a prerequisite to enlightened application of intelligence. Over the last several decades, the US military has evolved the term "operational environment" or OE to expand on the usability of and to replace the previous term "battlespace." OE includes both internal and external factors that both empower and constrain operations. Factors considered in military definitions of OE include political, military, economic, social, infrastructure, and information.

Military intelligence operations employ a construct called the "intelligence preparation of the operational environment" process, more commonly referred to by its acronym IPOE. In simplified terms, IPOE provides a structured process for the intelligence team to develop predictions for threat actors, which they refer to as enemy courses of action. Skilled professionals are able to employ IPOE as an interactive tool to evaluate the likely impact of their own decisions on the behavior of their adversaries. Leaders can employ IPOE outputs for environmental "shaping" operations designed to align environmental factors in their favor for the purposes of denying an opponent information they might want or need, or deceiving malicious actors to slow down their decision-making processes. [*Environmental shaping is covered in depth in Chapter 5.5.*]

This chapter builds a construct for a private sector analog for IPOE, intelligence preparation of the business environment (IPBE), that optimizes the key components of IPOE in a manner that allows them to be performed to address cyber threats in a sustainable fashion.

Operational Definition for Business Environment

A sampling of existing definitions for the term business environment demonstrate strong commonalities among different sources. Among the sources reviewed, there was universal agreement that business environment encompasses both internal and external factors impacting business operations, but there was some variation between them on what those factors were. For the purposes of discussions in this chapter and beyond, factors applied will be:

- Internal:
    - Culture
    - Leadership/Ownership
    - Employees
    - Network
    - Critical Information

- External
  - Customer/Clients
  - Partners/Suppliers
  - Competition
  - Technology
  - Legal/Regulatory
  - Political
  - Economic/Market
  - Social/Popular Culture

Intelligence Preparation of the Business Environment (IPBE)

The military IPOE process has many attributes that lend themselves in application to private sector needs, but the IPOE process described in doctrine is human capital intensive and requires some very specialized skills. This presentation develops an IPBE process that takes the best elements from the IPOE process and applies them to a more business friendly approach. It retains a four-step approach that begins with defining the environment and ends with developing courses of action for threat actors, but the internals are simplified considerably. The proposed IPBE is optimized as a sustainable activity in contrast to the IPOE process described in military doctrine, which is optimized to support plan development in response to a crisis response and tends to bog down during routine operations.

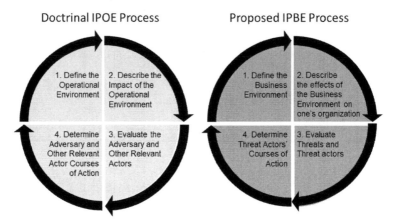

Figure 5.3.2.1 – IPOE versus IPBE[47]

Step One – Define the Business Environment

Process Summary: This step begins by defining the problem or problems that one is trying to solve then by defining the contribution one expects cyber intelligence to make in solving the problem(s). The next step is to identify factors in the business environment that have the potential to impact cyber intelligence operations (positive, negative, and neutral). During this process, it is also necessary to identify gaps in one's understanding and to develop strategies to acquire information to address those gaps.

Process Initiation: Two activities should initiate this process: new business initiatives and new discoveries of changes the threat environment. New business initiatives with the potential to change the business' attack surface (e.g. new markets, products or partners) require that the organizations reassess their business environment in the context of the new business initiatives. Changes in the threat environment detected during the execution of cyber intelligence operations need to be analyzed in the context

---

[47] Joint Publication 2-01-3, Joint Intelligence Preparation of the Operational Environment, May 2014, p I-25.

of how the new intelligence impacts organizational understanding of the problem(s) to be solved or alters operational prerogatives.

Key Similarities and Differences Between IPOE and IPBE: The IPOE process endeavors to define the operational environment from the perspective of accomplishing specifically assigned missions constrained by a finite geographic area. The hierarchal military culture and the unique attributes of the concept of command shape the IPOE approach in a manner that cannot be replicated in the private sector, and the geographical components are not applicable to the cyber domain. In addition, the military process starts with the problem and the physical geography being defined by a higher echelon of command, while the IPBE process begins with the adopting organization defining the problem(s) to be solved themselves, and it is dominated by environment factors involving culture and organization rather than physical geography.

Step One: Define the Operational Environment	Step One: Define the Business Environment
1. Identify the joint force's operational area 2. Analyze the mission and Joint Force Commander's intent 3. Determine the significant characteristics of the operational environment 4. Establish the limits of the joint force's area of interest 5. Determine the level of detail required and feasible within the time available 6. Determine intelligence gaps, shortfalls, and priorities 7. Submit requests for information to support further analysis	1. Define the problem(s) to be solved 2. Define the role cyber intelligence must play to solve the problem 3. Identify the characteristics of the business environment that both enable and limit cyber intelligence operations 4. Identify gaps/shortfalls in understanding and establish priorities to address them 5. Initiate collection actions to address identified gaps/shortfalls

Table 5.3.2.1 – Defining the Business Environment[48]

Step Two – Describe the Effects of the Business Environment on One's Organization

---

[48] *Ibid*, p II-2.

Process Summary: This step in the IPBE process applies organizational understanding to the business environment established in the previous step and creates a common framework for defining the critical strengths and weakness for both one's organization and the actors who pose threats (actual and potential) to the organization.

Process Initiation: Analysis conducted in support of step two is triggered by updated outputs from step one.

Step Two: Describe the Impact of the Operational Environment	Step Two: Describe the effects of the Business Environment on your organization
1. Develop a geospatial perspective of the operational environment 2. Develop a systems perspective of the operational environment 3. Describe the impact of the operational environment on adversary and friendly capabilities and broad courses of action	1. Develop visualizations for the business environment 2. Conduct systems of systems analysis of critical elements in the business environment 3. Describe how the business environment either supports or inhibits courses of action available to both your organization and real and potential threat actors

Table 5.3.2.2 – Describing the Effects of the Business Environment on One's Organization[49]

Key Similarities and Differences Between IPOE and IPBE: The geographic component of the IPOE process carries over into step two with its first step being to develop a geospatial perspective. The value of the geospatial perspective is that it provides a common visualization of the physical domain, so while it not a reasonable step for the IPBE, the concept of a threat visualization has merit. The IPOE and IPBE share common second and third actions in this step, although the IPBE step has been rewritten to a non-military description.

---

[49] *Ibid*, p. III-1.

Step Three – Evaluate Threats and Threat Actors

Process Summary: Actions in this step are designed to identify specific threats then to analyze the capabilities/vulnerabilities associated with those threats based on previous analysis of the business environment. The step concludes with a net assessment of strengths and weaknesses of both potential threat actors with respect to one's organization. This net assessment forms the basis for analysis in step four.

Process Initiation: Intelligence responding to an organization's cyber intelligence requirements is the primary trigger for initiating new analysis.

Key Similarities and Differences Between IPOE and IPBE: The primary difference between the two constructs is the addition of a fifth step in IPBE to identify one's own strengths and weaknesses. IPOE is a component of a larger military planning process in which operational planners provide organizational self-analysis to the intelligence team, while IPBE is an independent process within intelligence, thus making this analysis an intelligence function.

Step Three: Evaluate the Adversary and Other Relevant Threat Actors	Step Three: Evaluate Threats and Threat Actors
1. Update or create adversary models 2. Determine the current adversary situation 3. Identify adversary capabilities and vulnerabilities 4. Identify adversary centers of gravity and decisive points	1. Create and update threat actor behavioral models 2. Assess threat actors' current situation 3. Identify threat actor capabilities/vulnerabilities 4. Identifying threat actors' core strengths 5. Identify your own organization's critical weaknesses and core strengths

Table 5.3.2.3 – Evaluating Threats and Threat Actors[50]

---

[50] *Ibid*, p IV-1.

Step Four – Determine Threat Actors' Courses of Action

Process Summary: This step supports analytic processes designed to identify the most likely and the most dangerous threat actor courses of action available to actors targeting one's organization. Once these perspective courses of action are identified, analysts can identify indicators for each that can be employed to improve one's ability to detect threat activity consistent with identified courses of action. Once these courses of action are developed, they can be employed to initiate predictive threat warning problems [*see Chapter 4.2, subtask 4.2.2.2.*]

Process Initiation: Threat actor course of action development requires that analysts understand the capabilities of both potential adversaries and their own organization. The most common stimuli for course of action reviews will be assessed changes to threats or threat actors and changes in business operations (e.g. business development actions, leadership changes, and shifts in product and/or service offerings.)

Key Similarities and Differences Between IPOE and IPBE: Differences listed in Table 5.3.2.4 are relatively minor and mostly semantic.

Step Four: Determine Adversary and Other Relevant Actor Courses of Action	Step Four: Determine Threat Actors' Courses of Action
1. Identify the adversary's likely objectives and desired end state 2. Identify the full set of adversary courses of action 3. Evaluate and prioritizing each course of action 4. Develop each course of action in the amount of detail that time allows 5. Identify initial collection requirements	1. Identify threat actors' likely objectives/goals 2. Identify most likely and most dangerous threat actor courses of action for each actor 3. Evaluate and prioritize each course of action 4. Develop potentially detectable indicators for each course of action 5. Integrate indicators into the collection requirements management process

Table 5.3.2.4 – Determine Threat Actors' Courses of Action[51]

Cautionary Note on Appling IPBE

IPBE is an advanced concept that supports cyber intelligence planning and execution at the operational- and strategic-levels of operation. When executed by skilled intelligence professionals, IPBE will be able to keep cyber intelligence operations focused on the threats of greatest relevance to the organization, and it will provide stakeholders with critical insights into how organizational behavior can either inhibit or enable threat actor behaviors. Analysts who adhere to the rigor provided by the framework can produce intelligence in which all analytic judgements are clearly documented and can be applied to future analysis as process inputs and analytic assumptions change.

Organizations that lack intelligence professionals who have experience working with IPOE or IPBE should exercise caution if they decide to apply IPBE. In the wrong hands, IPBE has the potential to become the ultimate form of intelligence for intelligence sake (IFIS). Many analysts can become fully consumed in developing intelligence analysis support products and elegant databases, and others will convince themselves that the

---

[51] *Ibid*, p V-1.

methodology has broader applications and try to apply it inappropriately.

At the end of the day, IPBE's contribution to cyber intelligence operations will be directly related to leaders keeping processes lean and focused on the outputs it was commissioned to produce.

Chapter 5.4
Applied Intelligence

Key Points

- Applied intelligence represents an advanced approach to cyber intelligence operations that moves intelligence beyond its traditional role as a support capability to an expanded role as an operational capability.
- Applied intelligence operations require the combination of relatively mature IT security and cyber intelligence capabilities and an organizational culture in which individual and team performances are evaluated on the basis of their contribution to desired organizational outcomes.
- Organizations seeking to move to an applied intelligence construct will have to drive high degrees of interoperability between their cyber intelligence team and other key security functions to include: detection/sensor and logging management; the CIRT/SOC, network hunters, the red team, domain protection, counter intelligence, incident response, and the fraud team.

Stakeholder Roles

Literate Stakeholders	Educated Stakeholders	Intelligence Practitioners
• Be aware of alternative organizational constructs and the opportunities/challenges they present	• Evaluate potential of an applied intelligence construct • Identify organizational construct that best serves the team dynamic • Create incentives for success	• Advocate for relationships that optimize the potential of cyber intelligence to be of greatest value to the organization • Learn to influence what you cannot direct • Challenge "no" with data

Context

The opening section this book presented a case that the three primary roles for cyber intelligence in most private sector organizations will be predictive threat warning, threat awareness, and support to security operations, and those three roles have continued to be highlighted throughout the discussions in the first four sections. These three roles represent a conventional approach to the conduct of intelligence operations applied to the cyber intelligence field. This conventional approach views intelligence as a support function designed to provide leaders and people engaged in operational functions with threat awareness, knowledge, and understanding they can apply to make better informed decisions.

The problem with conventional cyber intelligence operations is that they do not address the critical seam between threat understanding and security actions. The cyber intelligence team may understand a specific threat, and they may have articulated their understanding in intelligence products to other members of the IT security team, but they will consistently lack visibility into whether the people they disseminated the intelligence to either read their products or take actions in response to the intelligence. Applied intelligence represents an advanced use case for cyber intelligence in organizations in which leaders have begun to question whether a passive form of cyber intelligence (i.e. inform but do not act) is the best model for their organization.

Applied intelligence is not so much a departure from conventional cyber intelligence constructs as it is an advance application. Applied intelligence operations require a level of maturity and teamwork across the entire IT security team, not just the cyber intelligence team. Organizations in which status is defined by control/ownership will struggle with applied intelligence, but organizations that embrace teamwork as a core value and that have leaders who do not feel that they need to own a process as long as they can influence it, should take a hard look at applied intelligence as an approach for closing seams and reducing time lags between threat awareness and IT security team response.

This chapter develops eight functions that organizations should consider either integrating into or achieving high levels of interoperability with applied intelligence:

    (1) Detection/sensor and logging management
    (2) SOC exploitation
    (3) Network hunters
    (4) Red team
    (5) Domain protection
    (6) Counter intelligence
    (7) Incident response
    (8) Fraud

All eight functions represent opportunities for mutually beneficial relationships. Tailored cyber intelligence can improve outcomes in all eight areas, and all eight functions can contribute to cyber intelligence proficiency. Levels of integration and organizational alignment can vary greatly between different organizations, but one can make strong arguments that network hunters, domain protection, and counter intelligence all lend themselves to being aligned under the cyber intelligence in a high percentage of cases. Detection and red team functions will also lend themselves to being aligned within the applied intelligence team in many organizations, and CIRT/SOC, incident response, and fraud functions will remain independent service offerings outside of the applied intelligence construct in almost any imaginable scenario.

The remainder chapter presents a discussion of how stronger interrelationships and interoperability between cyber intelligence and the eight supported functions will benefit both the cyber intelligence team and the function being highlighted. The section header for each section offers an assessment of likely potential for aligning the function into applied intelligence.

(1) Detection/Sensor and Logging Management – Medium/High Integration Potential

Applied intelligence does not just provide the teams managing the components of the organization's detection operations (e.g. teams that manage Internet facing sensors, proxy servers, mail guards, and logging systems) with threat indicators and threat actor TTPTs, it also works with those teams to optimize their capabilities and enhance their contribution to actions to defend the network and to provide cyber intelligence collection operations with indicators of malicious activity. In applied intelligence, the scope of CRM is expanded to include developing operational strategies for applying the organization's sensor grid to detect indicators of threat activity and to provide threat warning. COM evolves into a system of systems management effort, i.e. each component of the detection system is optimized to detect actions at different points along the kill-chain to create defense in depth.

Integrating elements of one's detection system into an applied intelligence concept will change the culture of the security professionals in those roles. Within most existing security cultures, actions like anti-virus software detecting and cleaning malware, proxy blocks preventing endpoints from connecting to malicious sites, and quarantined emails or email attachments are seen as wins that require no further action, but in applied intelligence, those actions offer potentially valuable intelligence. The malicious actors behind the actions one successfully defended today are evaluating their effectiveness and are likely to apply their learning to future probes or attacks. Security organizations that do not seek to keep pace with threat actors are losing ground to those actors.

The applied intelligence team must master their understanding of the systems they can leverage to collect intelligence within their networks and to develop strong partnerships with the teams that own those systems to ensure that they have full visibility into the health and performance of critical systems so they can measure the effectiveness of intelligence contributions toward achieving specific desired outcomes. Applied intelligence teams will need to have people capable of providing inputs in the required formats or have access to people who can be tasked to perform that role.

(2) SOC Exploitation – Low Integration Potential

Security operations centers (SOC) are a commonly used naming convention for describing the functions associated with monitoring network security and responding to suspicious activities. SOC capabilities and operational priorities can vary widely, but from the perspective of applied intelligence, SOCs represent the location where indications of malicious activity on the network are flagged to human operators for their evaluation and action. Within the framework of the cyber intelligence processes proposed in this book, that human intervention constitutes threat data exploitation.

The cognitive human input to SOC operations can generally be characterized as triaging security alerts. Analysts are confronted by large volumes of data that populate their consoles resulting from rules applied to sensor and logging systems. Their job is to recognize signals of interest in large noise fields and to take predefined actions in response to the detected activity. In most operations, only a small subset of alerts are worked, and the rest fall below the cut line and timeout and are deleted from the console.

The applied intelligence construct recognizes the intelligence potential in alerts upon which non-intelligence watch team members are not acting. In some cases unworked alerts may be actual threat intelligence, and in other cases they may be feedback on the performance of alerts that the intelligence team put into the system. The intelligence can be present in logged activities like those covered in the previous section, i.e. an alert that a specific endpoint tried to connect with blocked criminal infrastructure might be an indication the endpoint is infected. If that is true, then the team needs to determine if the infection is unique or the first discovery of a larger problem.

Over time, organizations can write a lot of security rules, and rules that are no longer contributing to threat detection are likely adding to the noise field and reducing clarity. If the cyber intelligence team is not exploiting the outputs of their rules, they will have no basis for updating or deleting dated, obsolete, and/or ineffective rules they wrote.

Where possible, applied intelligence teams should have technical intelligence analysts on duty in the SOC as a component of support to security operations. When that is not possible, applied intelligence should establish a mechanism for reviewing triggered events in a timely manner. SOC leadership needs to view themselves as a critical component of threat indications and warning, meaning they have strong incentives to develop a mutually supporting relationship with cyber intelligence.

(3) Network Hunters – High Integration Potential

Network hunting is a security field that has grown significantly over the last five years. Hunters are highly trained IT security professionals who can supplement automated and signature-based detection approaches by actively searching for specific threat indicators to look for evidence of malicious activity on the network. Hunter operations (referred to as hunting) can be initiated in a variety of ways. The most common and effective hunting operations are those cued by intelligence, either new threat reporting or outputs of intelligence research.

Hunting, like cyber intelligence, is evolving rapidly and in multiple directions simultaneously. While there are some commonly recognized best practices and a growing number of practitioners contributing to the professionalization of network hunting, the field is still very open for experimentation.

In many ways, hunting is the critical skill of applied intelligence. Traditional intelligence operations analyze newly detected/reported threats in terms of what they might mean to the organization and how they relate to what was previously reported. Network hunters view newly detected/reported threats as the catalyst for determining whether the organization has already been attacked using the new capability, and for determining whether existing collection capabilities will detect the threat if the organization were to be attacked in the future. They can apply what they learn from their actions to increase the effectiveness of future cyber intelligence operations and to update IT security processes.

One can make the case for aligning hunting activities under the applied intelligence team because their research provides intelligence, but one could also argue that hunting is the human, non-signature-based component of the detection process. Regardless of who has tasking priorities and who writes performance reviews, network hunters need to be tightly tied into the applied intelligence effort. Hunters should look for cyber intelligence to cue their research, and cyber intelligence practitioners should view the output of hunting activities as intelligence.

(4) Red Teams – Medium/High Integration Potential

Red teams are groups of highly skilled IT professionals who are organized to test the effectiveness of their parent organizations' network and data security programs. While there is broad agreement about what a red team is, there is a great deal of variation from one organization to the next regarding how red teams are organized, tasked, operate, and to whom they answer. Red team employment models generally involve teams being assigned a set number of tasked engagements over a specified period of time. Each engagement will have predetermined learning objectives and the red teams will have rules of engagement designed to make the tests realistic. The red team will then run the engagement and provide feedback to both their leadership and the group they tested. That feedback will include weaknesses they encountered/exploited, strengths that challenged them that can be built on, and recommendations for improving system design, security processes, and user performance.

Red teams are an important component to any IT security operation, but they could be even more valuable if the TTPTs they employed in their engagements were guided by intelligence. Too often, red team engagements focus the teams' efforts on a small segment of the kill-chain, and teams are unconstrained in their TTPT and free to employ their insiders' knowledge of the network. These engagements can produce useful feedback, but they also limit the scope of the learning that can take place. By skipping steps in the kill-chain, the engagement will miss opportunities to identify potential opportunities to detect threat actors or to prevent them from moving to the next step. While red teams should not be constrained to the TTPTs of known threat actors, their engagements need to test the effectiveness of intelligence-driven signature or behavioral detection capabilities established to address those TTPTs.

Red team engagements, both design and rules of engagement, should be shaped by cyber intelligence, and the learning that takes place within those engagements can provide valuable intelligence. Applied intelligence teams will recognize the mutually beneficial nature of a tight relationship with their red teams and will work to provide those teams with accurate real-world threat data and TTPTs that can be employed to generate lessons learned based on realistically designed engagements. Red team rules of engagement should still allow them the freedom to employ alternate TTPTs, and the vulnerabilities and deficiencies identified from those actions should be identified as possible future threats from a learning adversary.

A highly functioning applied intelligence team should be supporting new detection strategies and security processes, and red teams offer the most realistic way to test whether those changes are achieving their desired outcomes.

(5) Domain Protection – High Integration Potential

Malicious actors regularly register domains to support a wide range of malicious activities, and their actions can provide cyber intelligence teams with indicators of potential future threat vectors that can be used to develop detection signatures. In addition, cyber intelligence analysts can develop databases of registrants with histories of registering domains employed in attacks and/or frauds against one's organization or organizations in one's industry as sources of threat intelligence. The concept of domain protection programs does not stop at monitoring; it can involve developing policies and capabilities designed to combat domain misuse targeting one's organization. Domain protection activities range from offering to buy domain names all the way to having domains shut down. Two examples of activities domain protection teams will need to be able to address include:

Domain squatting, the act of registering domains that might be of value to somebody or that can easily be mistaken for a domain of an organization for which the registrant is not associated, is a common problem across all business and nonprofit sectors. In some cases, the registrant is behaving as an entrepreneur and will seek to make a profit by selling registered domain names to organizations that would want to own those domain names. In other cases, those domain names will be employed in misrepresentation attacks and frauds. Domain protection analysts will need to determine how the domain is being used to understand what the policies for purchasing, sending a cease and desist letter, or shutting down the domain are. Not all domain names are associated with active sites, so in many cases, the team will need to monitor for activities that indicate when a potentially malicious domain becomes active.

Indirect attacks employ look alike domain names to execute frauds that do not target one's organization but target people who think they are dealing with one's organization. This type of fraud activity is common in the retail and financial industries, although there is a great deal of variation in the actual frauds used to monetize the phony domain. Look alike webpages might be used to entice people to enter credentials or to get them to apply for a service or purchase a product that involves an advance payment. In other cases, clicking on the link will expose the user to an exploit kit and malware installation. Regardless of how the frauds are executed, they generate reputational damage.

Conventionally organized cyber intelligence operations can monitor domain name registration activity as a key source of indicators of future threats, but applied intelligence operations go a step further by developing/executing actions designed to deny malicious actors access to domains that can be used to attack one's organization and/or reputation.

(6) Counter Intelligence (CI) – High Integration Potential

In traditional intelligence parlance, counter intelligence (CI) is a discipline designed to detect and disrupt intelligence collection against one's organization. CI can include a wide range of programs running the gamut from physical security, to information security, to operational security, to employee vetting. Few contemporary private sector organizations have concentrated the elements of CI into a single distinguishable program, but most are performing all of the associated functions.

CI is a critical component for any IT security program, because two of the most insidious threat actor types that target networks and data come from malicious insiders and advanced threat actors.

Both actor groups operate on one's network in a manner designed to look like legitimate users doing normal business, thus they complicate detection efforts that rely on traditional signature-based sensors and evolving behavioral analytic approaches.

Insiders, by definition, have legitimate login credentials and account accesses. In the contemporary office environment, many will also have mobile devices approved for use on the organization's network that will allow them to connect at almost any time from almost any place. They are trusted users who can operate with impunity as long as they follow the rules of their user agreements, and they have opportunities to steal the credentials of coworkers or to escalate privileges/accesses by volunteering to take on additional responsibilities within their job scopes. In worst case scenarios, malicious insiders are already super users who can create new accounts and grant new accesses.

Advanced threat actors will seek to gain and maintain access to networks they target and to operate like legitimate users. Once these actors are on the network, they are indistinguishable from malicious insiders in terms of how they behave.

Because these classes of threat actor are already on the organization's network, the IT security team needs to have capabilities to recognize and detect user actions that may be indicators of malicious activities. CI is one of those capabilities. Working in concert with identity and access management (IAM), data loss prevention (DLP), and cyber intelligence, CI can develop indicators that constitute suspicious activity on the network and can ensure that activity consistent with those indicators is logged. CI operations are increasingly employing behavioral-based techniques for identifying suspicious activity, but skilled threat actors are aware of this trend and will do everything possible not to engage in behaviors that will trigger detection.

The case for a strong partnership between cyber intelligence and CI is self-evident, but cases for integration or subordination of CI with or into an applied intelligence construct will generate a good deal of resistance in many organizations. Western cultures place great importance on employee privacy rights, and those values are reflected in both organizational policies and laws. Most private sector organizations with cyber intelligence and insider threat programs have created firewalls between those programs to avoid the appearance they are spying on their own employees, but those firewalls can be self-inflicted vulnerabilities that advanced threat actors can employing to great effect.

Effective intelligence/CI relationships are possible within legal, ethical, and cultural norms of behavior, but they require long-term commitment and principled application. The organization owns the network and the data residing on it, and employee network access should only be granted to employees who have signed a user agreement in which they acknowledge that their access to the network is contingent upon their compliance with the rules. Malicious insiders are violating their user agreements, and external advanced threat actors are not employees and have no privacy rights.

(7) Incidence Response – Low Integration Potential

The case for a relationship between applied intelligence and CIRTs is that both benefit from regular and robust interactions. Incidents requiring response can provide valuable intelligence regarding threat actor TTPTs that applied intelligence can use to help the IT security team detect and defeat similar incidents in the future. Technical intelligence analysts, particularly those with hunting skills can support incident response teams' efforts to determine the scope of incidents they are working. Most organizations will benefit from developing and testing processes by which intelligence analysts can add value to the incident response process and streamline learning that can be applied to provide greater threat understanding.

Cyber intelligence can apply lessons from post-event analysis of incidents to update actions in the *enable phase* of the 4E process, like preplanned responses. CIRT members can play a critical role in ensuring threat characterizations are accurate and in offering additional feedback on threat vectors of concern.

Although it is theoretically possible to develop scenarios in which aligning the CIRT inside of an applied intelligence team might make sense, in the vast majority of real-world use cases, that relationship is not a realistic organizing model. More realistic models will generally have the CIRT director and the cyber intelligence leader as peers, and aligned in the IT security organization in a manner in which there are few barriers between their teams. Collocation of teams is desirable in almost all cases.

(8) Fraud – Low Integration Potential

Fraud and cyber intelligence are two completely separate disciplines, but there is a fair amount of overlap between the two as people engaged in fraud increasingly employ IT as an enabler for their fraud activities. From a cyber intelligence perspective, fraud is a primary means by which cybercriminals monetize stolen data, and as such, it represents an additional opportunity to detect and/or disrupt a cyber-attack. Cyber intelligence and fraud teams will tend to have different sources for detecting organizational data, but both will benefit from information about employee security credentials, logon/passwords, and customer data being in dump sites or being sold in criminal markets.

One of the keys for developing a healthy relationship is for organizations to be able to define roles/divisions of labor between the two disciplines across the full range of cyber enabled frauds and for frauds employed as components of cybercrime. Given fraud teams, in industries where fraud is common, will generally be larger, more experienced, and have more external contacts than the cyber intelligence team, it makes sense in most cases to give the fraud team the lead.

Applied intelligence teams might find value in modeling their relationships with fraud teams on those they have with their SOC and CIRT. Like those relationships, the keys to success are a shared understanding of what is important to all process participants and established practices for sharing information.

Chapter 5.5
Advanced Concepts for Cyber Intelligence Operations

Key Points

- This chapter develops four advanced concepts stakeholders can apply to cyber intelligence operations to improve outcomes, regardless of the maturity of their cyber intelligence practice.
- **Environmental shaping** addresses using design to create or preserve organizational advantages over malicious actors by limiting their options or forcing them to act in ways that makes them easier to detect and defeat.
- The application of **profit center** approaches to cyber intelligence can impose process rigor and identify where cyber intelligence is providing real value and what demands are imposing friction on cyber intelligence operations.
- **DOTMLPF** provides an organizational schema for understanding the contribution of the component parts of cyber intelligence operations and providing leaders with a disciplined approach for examining where under investment in unexciting components of cyber intelligence operations might be limiting performance.
- **Proficiency matrices** are variants of maturity models that can be applied both as planning and resource management tools.

Stakeholder Roles

Literate Stakeholders	Educated Stakeholders	Intelligence Practitioners
• Recognize opportunities present in the four advanced concepts • Ask hard questions	• Gain an understanding of the potential contribution of each of the four concepts • Advocate for timely application as opportunities arise • Push people out of their comfort zones	• Master the tasks associated with each advanced concept • Learn by doing – experiment with potential high payoff elements of these concepts and advocate for what you think will work in your organization

Context

This chapter presents four advanced concepts for leaders to consider as they seek to maximize their return on investment in cyber intelligence capabilities. All four concepts are outliers in the sense that none fits neatly into any of the other processes presented thus far, but all four offer potential for improving cyber intelligence outcomes by improving one's understanding of the factors that bear on cyber intelligence operations from new perspectives. These approaches can accelerate development of cyber intelligence operations in organizations entering the field and kick start new ways of thinking in established cyber intelligence practices. The four advanced concepts are:

(1) Environmental shaping
(2) Profit center approach
(3) DOTMLPF
(4) Proficiency matrices

(1) Environmental Shaping

The term "shaping" is borrowed from US Army doctrine, where it is used to describe operations in the physical world that are designed to create or maintain conditions favorable to the organization employing them. Shaping actions are designed to limit the options available to an opponent, deny them a capability they might want to use, or force them to act prematurely. Deception is a primary shaping tool, and it is used both to create confusion and to complicate decision-making.

Shaping operations in the cyber domain share the same purpose as their counterparts in physical domains; they are deliberate actions designed to create or preserve advantages belonging to the organization executing the actions. Environmental shaping is a cornerstone of threat-driven IT security operations, and it can create additional opportunities to detect and defeat malicious actions, thus enhancing defense in-depth approaches. The starting point for shaping operations is threat understanding. That understanding is applied to questions that address how potential threat actors view one's organization; what actions attackers might take, and what actions are available to the IT security team that might deter attacks, or reduce the likelihood that attackers might be able to achieve their actions on objective should deterrence fail.

Most mature IT security practices are already conducting actions consistent with the principles of shaping operations; common examples are network segmentation, data classification policies, and IAM practices. Applying threat understanding generated by cyber intelligence can increase the effectiveness of these actions and identify additional opportunities. The two critical inputs to any effective environmental shaping effort are self-knowledge and threat knowledge. Although there are many potential sources of self-knowledge, the best place to start is with the CODI input provided during the *establish phase* and updated in PEAR. The threat knowledge of greatest value to this process includes the outputs of IPBE analysis (e.g. threat actor most likely and most dangerous courses of actions), and threat understanding resulting from SOSA (e.g. links and node, kill-chain imposed limitations, and interrelationships between multiple required actions.)

In its simplest form, an environmental shaping strategy should have four goals: (1) reduce the organization's attack surface; (2) increase complexity for perspective threat actors; (3) elevate transparency; and (4) deceive and distract threat actors.

(1) Reduce the Organization's Attack Surface

One of the primary takeaways from the nine case studies present in Chapter 2.2 is that in each case, the targeted organization created conditions that motivated or enabled the attackers' actions. Given that the attack surface both defines the art of the possible for malicious actors and the range of threat vectors one's IT security program needs to address, every reduction in the attack surface represents a double payoff: fewer options for attackers, and fewer vulnerabilities for defenders to cover. Table 5.5.1.1 offers three shaping actions organizations might consider to assist in reducing their attack surfaces.

(2) Increase Complexity for Perspective Threat Actors

With the exception of state actors charged with carrying out specifically tasked assignments, the vast majority of cyber-attacks are subject to some kind of internal cost versus benefit calculation known only to the threat actors. This means that increasing complexity by creating additional process steps or requiring addition access credentials will add to threat actor workload and impose costs. In some cases, if organizations can introduce a sufficient level of complexity, they might also be able to increase costs enough to deter potential attackers and cause them to turn their energies elsewhere. The primary challenge in implementing actions in support of this goal is figuring out how to increase complexity to threat actors without increasing burdens and costs on one's workforce. Table 5.5.1.1 proposes four shaping actions with potential for maximizing attacker complexity while minimizing self-inflicted pain.

(3) Elevate Transparency

A key takeaway from the SOSA discussion in Chapter 5.3 is that threat actors have to accomplish a range of actions to move through the kill-chain. Any action on the target's network represents a detection opportunity for the IT security team. Organizations should use this fact to their advantage and do everything possible to increase their ability to recognize that actions dangerous to the security of their networks and data are occurring. Almost any shaping action taken to support the previous two goals is also likely to support this goal as well. Actions required to bypass tighter data access controls or to escalate privileges to gain access to additional network segments will increase the number of actions threat actors must take, and each action is an additional opportunity to detect the malicious activity. Table 5.5.1.1 develops behavioral-based analytics as a shaping tool for increasing the likelihood of detecting malicious actions and recognizing them for what they are.

(4) Deceive and Distract Threat Actors

Actions associated with this goal are closely related to and can often enhance actions in goal (2). Actions designed to deceive represent very high-end use cases, and many have potential downsides, so they should be thoroughly vetted prior to being implemented. Table 5.5.1.1 offers two examples of deception.

Environmental shaping is an advanced concept that requires the presence of a reasonable mature cyber intelligence practice that it is integrated into a highly capable IT security team. Shaping operations provide organizations with a range of options for building on their advantages and for imposing cost on potential attackers. Truly effective environmental shaping operations require the buy-in of most literate and educated stakeholders.

Shaping Goal	Shaping Action	Examples	Intended Effects
Goal (1): Reduce the Organization's Attack Surface	Manage Internet facing profile by restricting website content on people and contact information	Limit personal data on leadership biographies; control the number of publically visible phone numbers and email addresses	Reduce the intelligence value of the information you put into the public domain to make social engineering attacks more difficult
	Reduce potential attack vectors by eliminating or isolating non-critical systems from business critical software and data	Strictly control 3rd party connections and vendor/contractor accesses; require strong business cases before any new systems are connected to the network	Do not allow your least proficient partner to establish your security posture. Make threat actors play on a playing field you control. Do not connect unproven technology because it is cool.
	Develop data access control policies that limit both how and when critical data can be accessed	Prohibit access to customer PII from employees' personal devices; restrict access to financial transition software to specific business hours; only allow changes to detection rules to be made from specifically designated network devices in a controlled physical location	Reduce the value of any single attack vector a threat actor may employ.
Goal (2): Increase Complexity for Perspective Threat Actors	Network segmentation	Separate financial, personnel, business development, proprietary, security, and customer data into specific network segments each of which has specific access controls	Increase the complexity of both locating and gaining access to organizational CODI. Do not allow any single account or password to provide universal access.
	Encryption policies	Encrypt data on internal drives of mobile endpoints; encrypt password databases	Add an additional layer of complexity to being able to exploit access to critical databases or stolen devices
	Intrusive administrator control policies	Two person control policies for gaining or granting access to highly sensitive hardware, software, or databases	Limit the potential damage from the compromise of single systems administrator's account
	Multifactor authentication	Employ biometrics or one-time use passwords/pins as access controls for highly sensitive network segments containing CODI	Multifactor authentication increases the workload of and costs imposed on threat actors
Goal (3): Elevate Transparency	Behavior-based analytics	Incorporate keystroke pattern analysis, login locational history, user preferences, and time patterns as behavioral indicators	Behavioral analytics supports detection of account takeovers; no threat actor is going to behave exactly the same way as the legitimate account owner
Goal (4): Deceive and Distract Threat Actors	Legends	Create an artificial position or project that will likely be of interest to threat actors	Distract threat actors by providing them with a high payoff target that may cause them to expend effort and elevate their presence on the network
	Honeypots/Honeynets	Build a virtual network segment that appears to host high value content and monitor efforts to gain access to it	Skillfully constructed honeypots offer the potential to deceive threat actors into investing time and revealing their presence and their TTPTs

Table 5.5.1.1 – Environmental Shaping Goals and Actions

(2) Employ a Profit Center Mentality

This management concept advances the idea that it is possible to combine the best elements of both the cost center and profit center funding models while simultaneously minimizing the negative qualities of each. For those not familiar with the two models, here is a quick overview:

What is cost centers? Cost center schemes vary slightly from one organization to the next, but for the purposes of this discussion, the central elements are that the business function is funded by fees paid by other work centers. In the case of IT security functions, managers in other parts of the organization are charged some fixed amount for each of their employees who operate a network device, and for each device they have that connects to the network. These fees constitute the budget of the cost center, which then delivers a predetermined set of services for those fees.

What are the advantages of cost centers? The cost center approach is an efficient way to fund IT services, because it provides a stable budget source across multiple fiscal periods, and because risk-based decisions are made using enterprise-level risk calculations.

What are the negatives? The downside of the cost center approach is that it creates a protected monopoly, and people who work in protected monopolies have few incentives to provide responsive customer service or to manage costs. IT professionals do not refer to the people in their own organization with access to their network as customers; they call them users. Customers can take their business elsewhere, but users must accept the service they get.

What is profit centers? The profit center approach flips the cost center paradigm on its head. Profit centers must produce income by providing goods and services for which customers are willing to pay.

What are the advantages of profit centers? Profit centers offer customers a menu of products and services with associated costs, and customers determine which products and services they want, and what they are willing to spend to get them. Unlike cost centers, poor product quality, non-competitive pricing, and unresponsive service have directly measureable consequence. Profit centers that can deliver outputs efficiently and gain economies of scale can increase their profitability and provide workers with financial rewards, which generates incentives for the workforce to perform at a high level, exercise initiative, and treat users as valued customers.

What are the negatives? There are several downsides to applying a profit center model to IT security/cyber intelligence services, but the primary one is that it is difficult to align the desired outcome for the enterprise to customer purchasing decisions. Individual work centers will seek to maximize their financial benefit, and in so doing, many will accept risks on behalf of their function and assume somebody else is paying for products or services the enterprise needs but for which they are unwilling to pay.

To be clear, with the exception of companies in the security or consulting sectors that sell cyber intelligence products and services to external customers, <u>it is hard to imagine a scenario in which operating one's cyber intelligence practice as a profit center rather than a cost center would ever make sense</u>. The purpose of talking about the profit center construct is not to advocate for it as a viable approach; rather, it is to encourage cyber intelligence stakeholders to employ some profit center management practices to create greater visibility into costs and value. Profit center operations impose a high degree of rigor and discipline on cyber intelligence operations, because they create an imperative to develop product and service catalogs supported by costing data and pricing structures. Product catalogs define what intelligence products customers can buy and how much each costs. Services are normally packaged a multi-tiered service level agreements (SLA) that will define what customers can expect for whatever level of service they are purchasing.

Several benefits accrue to cost center operations that emulate this approach. The first benefit is that it provides leadership with a financial basis for establishing priorities and for calculating budget requirements for future operations. The second benefit is that it gives managers a basis for evaluating analysts' time utilization against a pre-established set of workforce priorities. A third benefit is that it can contribute to a more refined understanding of what customers really want and how much it costs to provide it to them.

Cyber intelligence leaders can learn a good deal from their counterparts who sell IT security and cyber intelligence services as their core business. These firms tend to conform to traditional consulting firm models for calculating the price structure for either a fixed-price package of products and services defined by an SLA or for individual products and services that can be sold independently.

One of the more challenging elements of this approach is developing prices. At the simplest level, the cost of providing a given product or service is a function of labor rates multiplied by labor hours multiplied again by a variable that captures overhead costs. Those costs can range from costs associated with non-salaried portions of workers' compensation packages, to costs for leasing the office in which work is done. They also include IT seat licenses, lights, electricity, and supporting cost centers like HR; most importantly, they must include a markup for profit. Most firms develop a variable that they can apply that captures all of these non-direct labor charges. That number is normally 2.0 plus or minus 0.2. Firms operating in areas with high costs of living, real estate costs, and taxes will tend to add to the 2.0 multiple while firms in low cost areas can subtract from it.

A good example of how to apply a consulting firm model would be to calculate the cost of producing a daily intelligence summary. In this example the daily summary is produced by a team of three people, a junior analyst, a senior analyst, and the cyber intelligence leader. The junior analyst spends an average of three hours a day, the senior analyst an hour and a half, and the leader spends 15 minutes editing and disseminating the product. The junior analyst has a $60K salary; the senior analyst has a $90K price point, and the leader is at $150K. Using a nominal labor figure of 2000 hours a year means that $60K a year is $30 an hour, and $90K a year is $45 hour, but if one takes advantage of the 2.0 multiplier, the calculation gets really simple. Labor hours times two is annual salary divided by 1000, so $60K is $60 an hour; $90K is $90 an hour, and $150K is $150 an hour. If the product is published 250 days a year, its cost is calculated as follows:

$$250 \times ((0.25 \times \$150) + (1.5 \times \$90) + (3.0 \times \$60)) =$$
$$250 \times (\$37.50 + \$135.00 + \$180) =$$
$$250 \times \$352.50 =$$
$$\$88,125 / \text{Year}$$

Leaders who demand that their cyber intelligence team develop product and service catalogs and who apply basic cost modeling analysis are better positioned to understand the actual cost of doing business. In some cases, the data will provide a compelling rational argument to outsource certain products and/or services or to cut them all together. In cases where costly production requirements offer little customer value, this approach can lead to cutting waste.

(3) DOTMLPF

DOTMLPF stands for doctrine, organization, training, materiel, leadership (and education), personnel, and facilities. In application, DOTMLPF is a management framework that can be applied to complex service offerings like cyber intelligence as a tool for viewing the capability as a sum of its component parts. DOTMLPF provides managers and planners with a framework for evaluating the relative maturity of factors contributing to the creation of a sustainable and effective cyber intelligence capability and for identifying shortfalls that need to be addressed in upcoming budget cycles or through broadening of external relationships.

Given that DOMLPF is a somewhat clumsy acronym it is worth digressing to develop a common understanding of and application for each of the component terms.

- **Doctrine**, in this application, refers to processes and policies; it specifically addressed whether they exist, and if they exist, whether they have been formally codified in documents or published instructions. Do the key stakeholders know that processes, policies, and relationships have been formalized? Are they being used? When was the last time they were updated?

- **Organization** covers a multitude of variables but in the context of a leadership assessment, the primary variables involve the cyber intelligence organization and the functions it directly supports. Does the cyber intelligence organization make sense? Is it aligned functionally to cyber intelligence requirements? Are there gaps and/or redundancies? Are the functions supported by intelligence organized in a manner that allows them to employ cyber intelligence?

- **Training** is pretty self-explanatory. Is there training in place within the organization, or do cyber intelligence practitioners have access to external sources of training to help them develop their skills? Is training aligned to processes highlighted in doctrine? Does training support critical skill development for skills identified in doctrine?

- **Materiel** is a great military catchall word that covers almost anything that exists in the physical world. In the context of assessing cyber intelligence capabilities, materiel should be thought of as the IT tools cyber intelligence requires to operate.

What detection sensors are on the network? Can they be programmed responsively? Is there a logging system that can support detection, alerting, and hunting operations? Does the intelligence team have the server space and dissemination tools it needs?

- **Leadership and education** addresses whether key stakeholders understand cyber intelligence sufficiently well to task, direct, and execute operations. This is essentially a self-assessment in this application. Stakeholders need to ask themselves if they understand their roles and are able to provide the meaningful requirements and feedback that effective cyber intelligence operations require. They also need to ask whether the people they have hired to perform cyber intelligence roles have the capabilities to lead and the backgrounds to perform their roles.

- **Personnel** in this assessment process refers primarily to the people working on the cyber intelligence team. The primary questions involve whether the organization has positions filled with people possessing the background and skills to be successful in those positions, and whether there are sufficient numbers of people to perform all of the tasks assigned to the cyber intelligence function by the organization's literate and educated stakeholders.

- **Facilities**, in the context of assessing the ability of cyber intelligence to perform its assigned roles, include not just the quality of physical workspaces but also proximity of people who should be collocated and collaboration tools in instances where teams and functions are spread across multiple locations. It is important that any facilities assessment address actual capabilities rather than advertised capabilities.

The DOTMLPF framework provides leaders with an approach for identifying the root causes of shortfalls in cyber intelligence performance, thus enabling them to apply effort and resources where they will have the greatest positive impact. Organizations with immature cyber intelligence practices tend to focus on hiring more people and contracting for more intelligence as their primary strategies for accelerating capability growth, but the potential return on those investments is often limited by things like the absence of refined, repeatable analytic processes, the inability to ingest externally provided intelligence indicators, and the lack of institutional standards for what actions constitute threats that matter to the organization. Failure to identify and address these limiting factors will likely result in purchasing capabilities one cannot fully utilize.

(4) Proficiency Matrices

A proficiency matrix is a variant of a maturity model. It is a tool to help stakeholders to define the attributes and measurement standards for specifically identified tasks at multiple performance or proficiency levels. Although organizations can develop and use proficiency matrices for a variety of applications, the three primary variants and applications recommended are: (1) an executive-level proficiency matrix; (2) an execution-level proficiency matrix; and (3) a time-phased proficiency implementation matrix.

(a) Executive-level Proficiency Matrices

As the name implies, the executive-level proficiency matrix offers a high level view of the cyber intelligence process that addresses proficiency attributes at the process phase level. Table 5.5.4.1 (parts one and two) provides a sample of an executive-level proficiency matrix that employs the four proficiency standards developed in Chapter 3.1 (baseline, developing, safe to operate, and highly capable) to define proficiency levels, and the 4E process (establish, enable, execute, and evaluate) defined in Section 4 as the processes being measured. The content in each of the 16 corresponding squares defines performance attributes for each process at each proficiency level with sufficient specificity to support some degree of measurement.

	Baseline	Developing
Establish	All stakeholders acknowledge their roles. Processes are under development.	Intelligence practitioners drive the requirements processes, but they are not getting questions and feedback is limited. Cyber intelligence processes are being developed and tested.
Enable	Key tasks are defined and are assigned to specific individuals for execution. A basic understanding of capabilities is in place.	Intelligence practitioners are able to assign collection to each registered requirement. Elements of execution planning are in place and execution templates are under development.
Execute	Key execution processes are defined and assigned to intelligence analysts who understand their tasks and know who they need to interact with to perform those tasks. Very little original analysis is conducted. Dominant activities are research and repackaging of other peoples' analysis.	A finite number of specific intelligence products has been defined and can be produced. Analysts can provide key performance metrics manually. The majority of intelligence analysis involves tailoring other peoples' analysis to meet organizational requirements.
Evaluate	Elements of performance feedback are under development and product quality assessments are being performed. PIR satisfaction can be tracked manually.	A subset of key performance milestones have been identified and can be tracked. Process feedback is dominated by practitioner driven actions.

Table 5.5.4.1 (Part I) – Sample Executive-level Proficiency Matrix

	Safe to Operate	Highly Capable
Establish	Educated stakeholders are driving the intelligence requirements process. A cyber intelligence TTPT is developed and documented in a shareable format. TTPTs are being updated in response to real-world experiences.	Literate stakeholders' intelligence needs are captured. Major organizational decision trigger intelligence threat assessments. Changes in IIAM inputs trigger automated notifications to affected stakeholders.
Enable	A CRM process is in place, and collection managers routinely engage stakeholders to refine specific elements of requirements prior to assigning collection. Templates, preplanned responses and warning problems are being employed. Performance targets are in place for key intelligence execution functions.	IIAM processes are highly automated. Warning problems are fully aligned to intelligence requirements and indicators identified in each problem drive logging and alerting. Performance measures can be monitored during execution to provide rapid feedback on performance factors.
Execute	Collection performance is well documented during execution. COM practices are driving feedback to CRM. All eight execution tasks are in place and can be executed proficiently. Performance can be monitored and KPIs are being tracked by cyber intelligence leadership.	Real-world collection proficiency is driving requirements feedback all the way back to the establish phase. Cyber intelligence and supported security disciplines are increasingly interdependent and are generating new ways of doing business. KPIs are highly automated and displayed in real time on performance dashboards.
Evaluate	Execution performance against priority targets is being tracked in a timely fashion and is being provided as feedback to people in the execution phase. Intelligence impact is being measured in a timely fashion.	Evaluate tasks are driving process updates across the other three operational phases at all times. Costing information is be tracked continuously.

Table 5.5.4.1 (Part II) – Sample Executive-level Proficiency Matrix

The executive-level proficiency matrix is useful for coordinating leadership buy-in on decisions regarding how the organization will define the proficiency attributes in the process/proficiency pairings that will serve as the targeted capabilities for developing execution-level proficiency matrices.

(b) Execution-Level Proficiency Matrices

Execution-level matrices require a substantial amount of thought and effort to build and a fair amount of work to maintain, so people should be cautious at the design phase to select the key tasks/subtasks for each phase that they want to emphasize in their future cyber intelligence operations. The number of tasks/subtasks developed and the level of detail for each should be directly proportional the size of the cyber intelligence workforce envisioned. Smaller intelligence organizations, e.g. no more than 6-8 people, may want to forego the process all together. Modestly sized intelligence organizations, e.g. fewer than 20 people, may choose to only develop proficiency descriptions for the safe to operate proficiency level. Larger organizations and enterprises that plan to rely heavily on outsourcing strategies will find value in developing highly detailed matrices or each line of operation in all four phases and at all four proficiency levels. This level of detail will allow leaders to make tradeoffs at different points in their development cycle between acquiring additional organic capabilities, purchasing products from external sources, and accepting an understood measure of risk for a finite period of time.

Execution-level proficiency matrices can be standalone planning tools or they can be used to spinoff short duration tactical plans. Regardless of how one employs them, it is important to maintain the appropriate perspective that proficiency matrices are planning and management tools; they are not products and should not be driving continuous updates and reviews. Once cyber intelligence operations are established and being conducted, proficiency matrices reviews should probably not occur more frequently than quarterly.

Table 5.5.4.2 provides a generic format for an execution-level proficiency matrix. Readers can find a fully developed execution-level proficiency matrix, with sample inputs for all 48 data fields in Appendix C. The inputs in that sample matrix provide a good starting point that people can adapt and apply to develop a matrix that reflects their organization's unique needs.

	Tasks	Baseline	Developing	Safe to Operate	Highly Capable
Establish	IIAM	1	2	3	4
Establish	Plan and Execute Intelligence Operations	5	6	7	8
Establish	Intelligence Management	9	10	11	12
Enable	IIAM	13	14	15	16
Enable	Plan and Execute Intelligence Operations	17	18	19	20
Enable	Intelligence Management	21	22	23	24
Execute	IIAM	25	26	27	28
Execute	Plan and Execute Intelligence Operations	29	30	31	32
Execute	Intelligence Management	33	34	35	36
Evaluate	IIAM	37	38	39	40
Evaluate	Plan and Execute Intelligence Operations	41	42	43	44
Evaluate	Intelligence Management	45	46	47	48

Table 5.5.4.2 Execution-level Matrix Guide for Appendix C

(c) Time-Phased Proficiency Implementation Matrices (TPPIMs)

As the name suggests, TPPIMs support a time-phased implementation of actions described in the process/proficiency pairings of proficiency matrices as a basis for creating a roadmap for developing the capability to execute mature cyber intelligence operations. This concept supports the ability of organizations to tailor both desired outcomes and implementation priorities for which process/proficiency pairings should be achieved, and in so doing, develop an actionable roadmap for acquiring the cyber intelligence capabilities necessary to meet leaders' desired end-state.

There are three types of TPPIMs that organizations will want to consider developing: process focused, task focused, and subtask focused.

Process focused TPPIMs will employ executive-level proficiency matrices, and they can be used for macro-level planning and executive updates. Interdependencies between the higher level cyber intelligence processes dictate that as a general rule, all four processes should be within one proficiency level of one another.

Q1

	Baseline	Developing	Safe to Operate	Highly Capable
Establish		✓		
Enable	✓			
Execute		✓		
Evaluate	✓			

Q2

	Baseline	Developing	Safe to Operate	Highly Capable
Establish		✓		
Enable		✓		
Execute		✓		
Evaluate		✓		

Q3

	Baseline	Developing	Safe to Operate	Highly Capable
Establish		✓		
Enable		✓		
Execute			✓	
Evaluate		✓		

Q4

	Baseline	Developing	Safe to Operate	Highly Capable
Establish			✓	
Enable		✓		
Execute			✓	
Evaluate		✓		

Figure 5.5.4.1 – Sample Process Focused Time-Phased Proficiency Implementation Matrix

Figure 5.5.4.1 provides a sample process focused TPPIM employing an executive-level proficiency matrix. The figure provides an example of an evolutionary process that prioritizes proficiency development order of execute, establish, enable, and evaluate in that order. Q3 is the only quarter in which more than one process moves up a level of proficiency.

Task focused TPPIMs will employ execution-level proficiency matrices to break processes into component tasks. This level of detail can allow leaders to focus efforts and resources on specific tasks that matter most to their operations. Figure 5.5.4.2 provides a task focused TPPIM that expands on the Q3 process focused TTPIM (presented on Figure 5.5.4.1) by adding the tasks associated with each of the three lines of intelligence operations in each of the four phases to create a planning tool that supports maturity/proficiency development for all 12 tasks.

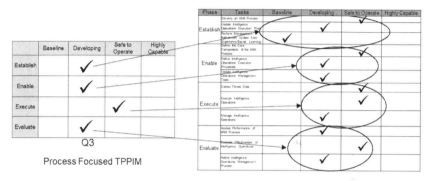

Figure 5.5.4.2 – Drill Down from Process Focused to Task Focused TPPIM

Subtask focused TPPIMs are the most detailed of the three, and they support highly detailed execution-level planning. They are especially useful because they empower leaders to develop cyber intelligence capabilities in a non-linear fashion, thus enabling them to make tradeoffs between capabilities in a manner that allows them to recognize the consequences of their decisions. Figure 5.5.4.3 drills down to the subtask level for the "execute intelligence operations" task developed in Chapter 4.3.

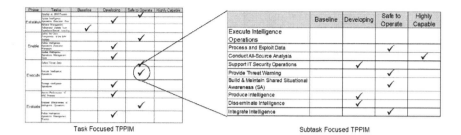

Figure 5.5.4.3 – Drill Down from Task Focused to Subtask Focused TPPIM

This subtask focused TPPIM establishes the analytic workforces priorities at the subtask level. It prioritizes all-source analysis as the most important capability, followed by process and exploit, provide threat warning, build shared situational awareness, and integrate intelligence. In this example, planners are accepting risks associated with performing the subtasks execution of intelligence support to IT security operations, intelligence production, and dissemination at the developing level for Q3. A matrix at this level of detail is a useful tool for both planning and for measuring performance against a plan, and it can be used to demonstrate to stakeholders both what tradeoffs are being made, and what the impact of those tradeoffs are.

Analysis supported by this level of detail will become increasingly useful as cyber intelligence capabilities mature, because it provides a good visualization for budgeting decisions. Leaders can see specific tradeoffs between risks and costs. This will allow them to understand the impact of shifting budget between capabilities or adding/subtracting money from the projected budget.

Afterword

My Journey

This book represents a major milestone in a journey that began with my first exposure to the ideas that would one day become cyber intelligence in the early 1990s. I was fortunate enough to be selected to attend a series of professional forums sponsored by the offices of the Chairman of the Joint Chiefs of Staff and the Secretary of Defense in 1992 and 1993 that were designed to develop new military concepts. Thought leaders in the sponsoring offices recognized that other nations were studying the US military's operations in Desert Storm (aka the First Gulf War) and that they were developing tactics and weapons to counter US successes. They recognized that the only way to stay ahead of future adversaries was join them and study our own performance in a critical manner and to identify and address performance deficiencies identified in real-world operations.

One of the deficiencies they identified was the limitations in existing approaches for identifying and targeting vulnerabilities created by adversaries' centralized command and control doctrine and the technologies they employed to execute it. I attended two week-long forums in which participants began applying network topologies to combat systems and started asking hard questions about what kinds of intelligence was needed to understand the links, nodes, and interdependent relationships within any given ecosystem to be able to create desired military effects with the minimal amount of effort. While initial discussions focused on kinetic options (i.e. physical destruction of physical targets), it did not take long before intellectual concepts addressing ideas like exploiting links for intelligence or disrupting data flow and/or user confidence in data began to compete for equal levels of effort with destructive effects. The existing warfighting concept called command, control, and communications counter-measures (C3CM) was replaced by command and control warfare (C2W), which was intended to characterize a shift in approach to warfighting focused on providing commanders with a broader menu of options for exploiting vulnerabilities in an adversary's command and control networks.

The concept of C2W proved to be a catalyst for a good deal of innovation in the 1990s, and with each new idea came a new naming convention. C2W morphed into network-centric warfare, which begat information operations and information warfare, which eventually gave way to cyber warfare. By the time I got to the Naval War College in 1999, I decided to use the term "warfare in the information age" when referring to emerging cyber warfare constructs and capabilities in my academic writings, because I recognized the future was far from sorted out, and I did not want my ideas to be locked into a single transient doctrinal concept.

Each of the naming conventions reflected a somewhat different focus of effort, but there were consistent themes running across all of the concepts being advanced. The intent in all cases was to leverage an adversary's dependence on communications and computers as a means to create specific effects. Intelligence support was initially focused on being able to understand what was connected to the network, but over time it broadened to include the human dynamics for how networks were being employed. At some point in the process, people began to discuss how potential adversaries might employ cyber warfare against us, and the concept of what we now call cyber intelligence was born.

I was totally focused on military applications until I took a graduate school seminar in the winter of 2000 that addressed the legal and ethical complexities of militaries and intelligence services employing commercial networks. It was my first exposure to a variety of new ideas ranging from commercial cryptography to the conflicting roles of protecting one's citizens while honoring their privacy rights in the Internet era. Sitting in that classroom, I began to realize that the world had fundamentally changed in the previous decade and that the implication of those changes on me as a military intelligence professional were quite profound. The emerging concept of a cyber domain represented a brave new world in which individuals, like-minded groups, corporations, and governments were all on a largely equal footing and had the means to target whomever they wanted for whatever reasons motivated them to act.

After graduating from the Naval War College, I spent three years each as the senior intelligence officer for US Navy Forces Europe and the US Transportation Command, before completing my navy career with two years as head of the Information Dominance Division at the Navy Warfare Development Command. With each passing year, I watched the military increase its attack surface by moving more of its daily business correspondence, administrative and personnel related functions, logistical planning and execution, and programing and budgeting processes onto unclassified networks riding on commercial communications backbones. Malicious cyber events, many created by poor user decisions and inadequate network security, increased throughout that period, and each event provided me with new data points for addressing the challenges associated with developing an understanding of threats to one's networks and information. My final years in the navy were focused more on theory and architecture than on developing practical applications for cyber intelligence, but I was building the requisite knowledge to establish and run a cyber intelligence operation, and that became a post-navy career goal.

I spent the first four year of my post-navy career as a client facing consultant for navy commands charged with developing and fielding cyber capabilities in the fleet. The navy was moving in the right direction, and my experiences added to my education, but I am a doer, and as a consultant, I could only recommend and hope that others would take action. Furthermore, I was also frustrated by a public sector culture in which penalties for making mistakes were greater than rewards for doing the right thing.

During the late summer of 2012, GE Capital's CISO reached out to me to discuss the possibility of me joining his team and heading up efforts to establish a cyber intelligence capability. GE Capital was in the process of being designated as a Systemically Important Financial Institution (SIFI) by the Financial Stability Oversight Council (FSOC) created by Dodd-Frank, and among the regulatory requirements associated with the SIFI designation was that the company needed to have a cyber intelligence capability. GE Capital's IT leadership recognized that it would take both time and resources to bring a functioning cyber intelligence capability on line, and they were determined to integrate it with detection and response functions at the design phase.

I joined GE Capital in November 2012 and ran their cyber intelligence and incident detection programs until they were disestablished in September 2016 following the company's successful petitioning of the FSOC to be decertified as a SIFI. I spent the first 30 months at GE Capital building an applied intelligence team designed to enable threat-driven IT security operations and the last 16 months trying to find a home for my team and developing transition plans for moving the servicing of the company's remaining cyber intelligence needs to GE Digital.

While I am disappointed that I did not have more time at GE Capital, I look back on the experience positively and I am thankful for the opportunities I was given. I was able to achieve my primary post-navy career goal; I got to apply my ideas for cyber intelligence in a private sector company that wanted to develop threat-driven IT security operations. I am thankful to the people at GE Capital gave me an opportunity to achieve that goal.

This book represents an after action review of what I learned, not just in my four years at GE Capital but in the twenty year run up to taking that job. My goal in writing this book is to share what I learned with others as a means of adding to the collective knowledge of the cyber intelligence field. I hope that this book can be used as a catalyst for accelerating capability development in organizations investing in cyber intelligence competencies. The content represents experience-based learning; the concepts and practices presented have shown promise in real-world application, and they represent a solid foundation on which to build repeatable and responsive cyber intelligence capabilities that can enable threat-based IT security operations.

Appendix A
List of Acronyms

API	Automation Programming Interface
BEC	Business Email Compromise
C2W	Command and Control Warfare
C3CM	Command, Control, and Communications Counter-Measures
CAAS	Crime-as-a-Service
CI	Counter-Intelligence
CIO	Chief Information Officer
CIRT	Computer Incident Response Team
CISO	Chief Information Security Officer
COA	Course of Action
CODI	Critical Organizational Data and Information
COM	Collection Operations Management
CRM	Collection Requirements Management
CTO	Chief Technology Officer
CTOE	Cyber-Threat Operating Environment
DDoS	Distributed Denial of Service
DLP	Data Loss Prevention
DOTMLPF	Doctrine, Organization, Training, Materiel, Leadership and Education, Personnel, and Facilities
EEI	Essential Element of Information
FSOC	Financial Stability Oversight Council
FRBNY	Federal Reserve Bank of New York
HR	Human Resources
IAM	Identity and Access Management
IFIS	Intelligence for Intelligence Sake
IIAM	Intelligence and Information Acquisition Management
INSA	Intelligence and National Security Alliance
IPBE	Intelligence Preparation of the Business Environment

IPOE	Intelligence Preparation of the Operating Environment
ISAC	Information Sharing and Analysis Center
IoT	Internet of Things
IP	Internet Protocol
IT	Information Technology
KPI	Key Performance Indicator
NSA	National Security Agency
OODA	Observe-Orient-Decide-Act
OPM	Office of Personnel Management
PDCA	Plan-Do-Check-Act
PEAR	Plan-Execute-Assess-Refine
PII	Personally Identifiable Information
PIR	Prioritized Intelligence Requirement
POS	Point of Sale
PPR	Pre-Planned Response
RAM	Random Access Memory
RFI	Request for Information
RMA	Revolution in Military Affairs
SA	Situational Awareness
SIEM	Security Information and Event Management
SIFI	Systemically Important Financial Institution
STIX	Structured Threat Information Exchange
SWIFT	Society for Worldwide Interbank Financial Telecommunications
SLA	Service Level Agreement
SOC	Security Operations Center
SOSA	Systems of Systems Analysis
TASII	Trusted Automated Exchange of Indicator Information
TPPIM	Time-Phased Proficiency Implementation Matrices
TTPT	Tactics, Techniques, Procedures, and Tools
VOIP	Voice Over Internet Protocol

Appendix B
Contemplating Future Threats

My first working title for this book was "*Hope is not a Course of Action: Conducting Successful Cyber Intelligence Operations to Counter Fifth Generation Threats.*" The title captured two of the key points of the book; cyber intelligence success is a byproduct of design and threats to one's networks, data, and information are omnipresent. Unfortunately, the title created a compelling need to begin the book by explaining what it meant, and in the end, it just made more sense to come up with a simpler title.

The phrase "hope is not a course of action" is drawn from joint military planning. Military planners do not have the luxury of wishing or assuming away problems, and it is common for people conducting plan reviews to cite weak or poorly developed planning elements as being evidence of planners applying hope as a course of action. The stimulus for me to use the phrase in the title, however, came from a graduate school engineering professor who described the technology integration strategy of a specific navy engineering bureau as "squirting a money hose at their problems and hoping the dollars would wash them away." The professor's money hose analogy is an apt description of one of the dominant behaviors I witnessed throughout my tenure as a private sector cyber intelligence leader, i.e. organizations funding capabilities they neither understood nor could employ in the hope that the mere presence of additional capabilities would prove to be game-changing actions. One of the goals of this book is to call out that behavior so that people engaging in it recognize its futility.

The concept of fifth generation threats is one of my own making. Military historians use the term revolutions in military affairs (RMAs) to characterize changes in warfare capabilities that fundamentally change how warfare is conducted and that are sufficiently decisive that countries that do not adopt the RMA are hugely disadvantaged or become militarily inconsequential. Despite the existence of a prolific body of work on RMAs, there is no universal agreement on what historical events constitute RMAs, and none of the models I studied in my research were very useful in helping to frame contemporary events. Undeterred, I developed my own five generation threat model, which is presented in Table B-1. The model characterizes the key attributes of each generation, addresses the critical technologies applied, and presents intelligence capabilities developed to exploit vulnerabilities created those technologies.

There are several factors that set the fifth generation apart. The biggest is that it is the first generation in which the cutting edge technologies employed by first world militaries and intelligence services are not only available to lesser developed states, but also to non-state actors, both organizations and individuals. This flat playing field has created the threat environment characterized in Chapter 2.1 in which states, criminals, and hacktivists can attack people and organizations in any of the three threat categories and in which all must worry about insider threats. In addition, the fifth generation is unique because the cyber domain makes factors like time and geographic separation all but irrelevant.

The five generation threat model supports two conclusions that people seeking to drive long-term successes must both recognize and address. First, the forces of technological innovation are continuing, so fifth generation threats are a phase, not an end-state. Second, the rate of technological development is accelerating, so the length of each succeeding generation is shorter than the one that preceded it. Together, these two conclusions create an imperative for thoughtful people to ask what sixth generation will look like, and how long before we transition to a sixth generation regime.

	Timeframe	Characterization	Technical Innovation	Intelligence Developments
Gen-1	Ancient times to mid-19th Century	Low technology; written codes, couriers, visual reconnaissance, and interrogation	Written language, codes, signal fires and flags, cavalry for battlefield reconnaissance	Linguists, code breakers, mapping/battlefield visualization, concept of intelligence requirements
Gen-2	Mid-19th Century to the beginning of World War Two	Increased application of intelligence to transportation and communications technologies	Communications (telegraph, telephone, and wireless); airborne reconnaissance (balloons and airplanes); cameras	Signals intelligence (wire tapping and intercept); radio direction finding; imagery intelligence
Gen-3	Early 1940s to mid-1960s	Centralized command and control, long haul communications, high altitude and high speed air breathing platforms, low earth orbit satellites; nuclear weapons and propulsion	Code machines and early computers; RADAR; improved long-range communications; low probability of intercept communications	Digital code breaking; satellite/denied area access; electronic intelligence; growth in national intelligence agencies; long range acoustic intelligence
Gen-4	Mid-1960s to late 1990s	Proliferation of space-based communications and sensors; massive gains in processing power; shift to digital systems; enormous grow in processing speeds and communications bandwidth	Space-based communications and intelligence collection systems; digital, multispectral, and radar imagery; cell phones; personal computers; distributed networks; email	Revolution in all-source fused intelligence capabilities; near real time intelligence from remote sensors, day/night capabilities, strategic products available to tactical users
Gen-5	Late 1990s to present	The Internet; the rise of social media; nation-state capabilities in the hands of non-state actors; irrelevance of geography; commercial cryptography; commercial imagery; GPS; smart systems	Ubiquitous use of IP and cellular communications; embedded sensors/ smart systems, mobile high-speed computing supported by near continuous broadband access; GPS embedded smart devices	Cyber Intelligence, anticipate and detect threats to one's networks and information from the full range of potential threat actors. Develop models for detecting and sharing threat intelligence that do no harm to benign actors in the cyber domain.

Table B-1: The Five Generation Threat Matrix

Many of the technical innovations that will define the sixth generation already exist and are being fielded. Learning machines, artificial intelligence, the industrial Internet/Internet of Things, blockchain technology, and self-operating equipment represent key attributes for defining the playing field on which sixth generation threat actors will practice their craft. It is not yet clear how sixth generation threats will come together, but it seems likely that cyber to physical threats will increase dramatically.

While the ideas and concepts advanced in this book are artifacts of the fifth generation threat period, they will provide a solid foundation for characterizing future threats as creative threat actors continue to push the art of the possible, and for organizing sixth generation threat-driven IT security operations. Forward thinking people can begin preparing for logical manifestations of sixth generation threats by recognizing how to avoid enlarging their organizations' attack surfaces to predictable future threats, and they can also apply emerging technologies, like machine learning and artificial intelligence, to IT security practices to keep pace with threat actors.

Appendix C
Sample Execution-Level Proficiency Matrix

Chapter 5.5, Section (4)(b) introduces the concept of an execution-level proficiency matrix. This appendix presents a detailed example of an executive-level proficiency matrix with sample inputs for all 48 data fields. The matrix has been broken into eight tables so that all of the inputs are readable. Table C0 below provides a key for reading the eight tables.

	Tasks	Baseline	Developing	Safe to Operate	Highly Capable
Establish	IIAM	Table C1	Table C3	Table C5	Table C7
Establish	Plan and Execute Intelligence Operations	Table C1	Table C3	Table C5	Table C7
Establish	Intelligence Management	Table C1	Table C3	Table C5	Table C7
Enable	IIAM	Table C1	Table C3	Table C5	Table C7
Enable	Plan and Execute Intelligence Operations	Table C1	Table C3	Table C5	Table C7
Enable	Intelligence Management	Table C1	Table C3	Table C5	Table C7
Execute	IIAM	Table C2	Table C4	Table C6	Table C8
Execute	Plan and Execute Intelligence Operations	Table C2	Table C4	Table C6	Table C8
Execute	Intelligence Management	Table C2	Table C4	Table C6	Table C8
Evaluate	IIAM	Table C2	Table C4	Table C6	Table C8
Evaluate	Plan and Execute Intelligence Operations	Table C2	Table C4	Table C6	Table C8
Evaluate	Intelligence Management	Table C2	Table C4	Table C6	Table C8

Table C0 – Key

	Tasks	Baseline
Establish	Develop an IIAM Strategy	Need for IIAM process identified and representative products are under development. Limited participation outside of the cyber intelligence team.
	Update Intelligence Operations Execution Plan	Cyber intelligence operations are more a byproduct of evolution than of planning. Basic cyber intelligence tasks are identified and being performed. Learning and process evolution are occurring at the individual level.
	Refine Intelligence Operations Management Process	Need for process is recognized and is driving development as management processes come on line.
Enable	Define the Core Components of an IIAM Strategy	Intelligence and information requirements are collected and shared. Collection planning is generally driven by the art of the possible rather than the relative priority of existing requirements.
	Refine Intelligence Operations Execution Processes	Intelligence products are under development and while not fully standardized, they have a degree of consistency. Dissemination execution defaults to a quantity has a quality of its own approach, i.e. when in doubt transmit and people can choose whether they want to read it or not.
	Update Intelligence Operations Management Tools	Intelligence management is a function of the leadership team and consists primarily of periodic assessments of performance against expectations.

Table C1 – Establish and Enable Phases at the Baseline Proficiency-Level

	Tasks	Baseline
Execute	Collect Threat Data	Heavy dependence upon external sources for threat data. Organic collection capabilities exist but require human intervention.
	Execute Intelligence Operations	Open source article sharing is primary source of reporting, and each intelligence report is viewed as a unique event. Analysis is characterized by application of logic but seldom cites precedents or trends.
	Manage Intelligence Operations	Rudimentary tracking mechanisms are in place to monitor intelligence outputs, with emphasis on tracking reports that bear directly on known intelligence requirements.
Evaluate	Assess Performance of IIAM Process	Intelligence relevant to specific IIAM requirements is identified and is tracked. Intelligence team has few insights into how products are being used and practitioners tends to update processes and requirements based on perceptions of customer satisfaction rather than on actual feedback.
	Evaluate Effectiveness of Intelligence Operations	Effectiveness measures are internally developed and tend to focus on execution rather than operational impact. Analysts do seek feedback in efforts to improve their value, but those efforts tend to drive individual performance and have limited impact on the team.
	Refine Intelligence Operations Management Process	Cyber intelligence leaders take note of what is working and seek to apply successes more broadly.

Table C2 – Execute and Evaluate Phases at the Baseline Proficiency-Level

	Tasks	Developing
Establish	Develop an IIAM Strategy	Intelligence and information requirements exist, and customer review and feedback processes are in place.
	Update Intelligence Operations Execution Plan	Core processes have been documented, and group learning is occurring. Intelligence practitioners are seeking and employing feedback from customers to refine plans for future operations.
	Refine Intelligence Operations Management Process	Initial binary metrics are being used to identify process gaps and redundancies. Management process remains internal to the cyber intelligence team.
Enable	Define the Core Components of an IIAM Strategy	PIRs and EEIs exist and are widely shared. Processes for translating information and intelligence requirements into collection requirements exist but are immature and evolving.
	Refine Intelligence Operations Execution Processes	Product templates exist for routine production, but special production is handled on a case-by-case approach. Threat warning problems are under development, as are preplanned responses; plans tend to be in checklist formats and lack depth.
	Update Intelligence Operations Management Tools	Management has established analyst time utilization goals and expects analysts to report when prescribed thresholds are out of design tolerance. Contributions of intelligence partners and vendors are tracked.

Table C3 – Establish and Enable Phases at the Developing Proficiency-Level

	Tasks	Developing
Execute	Collect Threat Data	A relationship exists between cyber intelligence and other security function that manage logging, network sensors, and mail guards as well as monitoring and alerting.
	Execute Intelligence Operations	Analysts have awareness of previous reporting on a given threat and on similar threats, and they include context in their reports and develop their own analysis of threat impact to the organization. Single source reporting still dominates but analysts routinely seek additional sources to confirm or deny information.
	Manage Intelligence Operations	Product standardization has led to an understanding of process elements to be tracked. Processes are manual and non real-time, but managers can track trends and adjust processes in response to performance issues. External sources are also being tracked, and intelligence analysts have some capability to provide feedback to customers on the art of the possible and to provide alternative options for providing desired cyber intelligence.
Evaluate	Assess Performance of IIAM Process	IIAM requirements are being tracked as addressed or not addressed. Gaps in collection and reporting are assessed for opportunities to improve outcomes. Feedback conversations are taking place and are driving changes in IIAM processes.
	Evaluate Effectiveness of Intelligence Operations	Analysts are actively engaged in seeking to understand how to provide greater value to their customers, and they are sharing learning with their teammates. Managers conduct critical reviews of intelligence products and provide analysts with feedback. Unusual events generate feedback sessions and lessons learned are collected and used to update processes.
	Refine Intelligence Operations Management Process	Cyber intelligence leaders are able to apply experience and learning as feedback to stakeholders and external customers for the purpose of driving increased understanding of critical processes. This understanding can be applied to refine and improve KPIs and to identify process gaps.

Table C4 – Execute and Evaluate Phases at the Developing Proficiency-Level

	Tasks	Safe to Operate
Establish	Develop an IIAM Strategy	Educated stakeholders actively contribute to the intelligence requirements process and provide clear inputs on relative priorities among requirements. They also provide CODI to the intelligence team.
	Update Intelligence Operations Execution Plan	Critical intelligence processes have been published and shared with all stakeholders. Organizational updates and evolving stakeholder concerns are driving execution planning priorities and defining measures of effectiveness.
	Refine Intelligence Operations Management Process	Management plan is in place and being used to update key stakeholders and drive more refined KPIs. CISO team updates and professional interactions generate actionable feedback that is being used to update execution plans.
Enable	Define the Core Components of an IIAM Strategy	A mature CRM process is in place, and updates to content or priorities of requirements are mapped to collection quickly in alignment with relative priorities. IIAM processes and associated actions are highly transparent to all stakeholders.
	Refine Intelligence Operations Execution Processes	All intelligence products have developed templates that include standardized dissemination lists. Templates are available to all analysts and employed unless leadership directs otherwise. Threat warning problems have been built to address critical strategic warning events identified in PIRs, and preplanned responses have been built to address most likely threats.
	Update Intelligence Operations Management Tools	Analyst time utilization templates exist and are being employed. Contributions of intelligence partners and venders are being measured with emphasis on whether they offer unique access or address gaps in organic intelligence operations.

Table C5 – Establish and Enable Phases at the Safe to Operate Proficiency-Level

	Tasks	Safe to Operate
Execute	Collect Threat Data	A COM function is in place, and intelligence practitioners are able to leverage multiple sources for threat data collection. Alerts are in place to automate notification of activities of interest detected on organic sensors or logged in the logging system. Collection strategies are dynamic.
	Execute Intelligence Operations	Analysts seek to report new threats in the context of existing understanding based on previous intelligence reporting, and they routinely cite precedent and how a new report modifies existing understanding. A high awareness of source biases is in place and multiple source reporting is the accepted standard. Threat context drives analyst production schedules and dissemination decisions. The absence of evidence that should exist is reported as evidence.
	Manage Intelligence Operations	Analyst workflows are in place, and managers have the ability to track competing processes and make adjustments to keep operations on track. External intelligence sources are also being managed and requirements are being tracked and shortfalls being addressed. Meaningful KPIs are in place and they provide managers with warning that processes are moving outside of desired tolerances. Intelligence team is both providing and receiving meaningful feedback to/from stakeholders.
Evaluate	Assess Performance of IIAM Process	IIAM requirements are tracked for satisfaction (i.e. was the question answered, and did the answer provide the requestor with the information they were looking to get), and intelligence operations are adjusted accordingly. Customer outreach plans are being executed and are driving process refinement and changes in IIAM requirements and priorities.
	Evaluate Effectiveness of Intelligence Operations	Cyber intelligence team has a solid understanding of how its products are impacting operations of key supported functions and can adjust operations accordingly. Quality assurance processes are in place and analysts are receiving feedback on both product quality and analytic biases. Team leverages unusual events as learning opportunities and conducts post-event analysis of intelligence performance to drive lessons learned and process improvements.
	Refine Intelligence Operations Management Process	Operational effectiveness assessments provide the basis for identifying effectiveness of existing management processes and where improvements are warranted. KPI effectiveness reviews are common, as are reviews of management controls on external relationships.

Table C6 – Execute and Evaluate Phases at the Safe to Operate Proficiency-Level

	Tasks	Highly Capable
Establish	Develop an IIAM Strategy	Literate and educated stakeholders routinely initiate proposed changes to intelligence requirements and request intelligence threat assessments to support major organizational decisions.
	Update Intelligence Operations Execution Plan	Execution planning process is very stable, and updates can generally be characterized as adding new options rather than replacing processes that are not meeting standards.
	Refine Intelligence Operations Management Process	Cyber intelligence operations are characterized by highly automated performance measures and proactive feedback. Management processes are highly stable and require infrequent updates.
Enable	Define the Core Components of an IIAM Strategy	Processes are highly automated, and key components can be tracked in real time and displayed on dashboards. Organic sensors, external intelligence sources, and network hunting can be fully leveraged.
	Refine Intelligence Operations Execution Processes	PIRs and threat research drive the production of threat warning problems and preplanned responses. Preplanned responses have all been exercised across multiple scenarios and have been tested by red team and alternative analysis processes.
	Update Intelligence Operations Management Tools	Tools exist to track analyst time utilization and to provide leadership with accurate costing data for intelligence products. External contributions are tracked in a manner that supports ROI analysis.

Table C7 – Establish and Enable Phases at the Highly Capable Proficiency-Level

	Tasks	Highly Capable
Execute	Collect Threat Data	Collection processes are highly automated and operators have real time visibility into collection activity and sensor performance/health. Organization has access to threat feeds from multiple external sources, and can filter those streams so that irrelevant and redundant reporting is not populating analysts queues or being maintained in threat databases.
	Execute Intelligence Operations	All-source reporting dominates, and the absence of more than one source is reported along with source reliability and historic reporting biases. Analysts have a sufficiently capable knowledge management system that they can cite previous published threat reports and can provide the context of how the new report adds additional context and/or understanding. Production/ dissemination processes enable highly tailorable intelligence support to specific subsets of customers.
	Manage Intelligence Operations	Analyst workflows are automated and provide tailorable feedback to both the analysts and managers. Critical cyber intelligence processes are identified and automated collection relevant to many KPIs is in place and is populating performance dashboards. Processes are in place to provide accurate measurements of ROI for external sources, which enable efficient management of those relationships.
Evaluate	Assess Performance of IIAM Process	Cyber intelligence leaders have deep and timely insights into the impact of specific elements of their operations and can anticipate future needs and recommend changes in IIAM requirements to customers based on performance.
	Evaluate Effectiveness of Intelligence Operations	Cyber intelligence team has a red cell function to perform alternative analysis of a significant subset of intelligence products to identify analytic biases. Analysts receive feedback and training based on trends identified by the red cell. Post-event analysis drives updates to preplanned responses and lessons learned performance shortfalls drive training programs. Exercise programs exist for individual and team training.
	Refine Intelligence Operations Management Process	High levels of process stability are exhibited that reflect deep understanding of critical management functions and process maturity.

Table C8 – Execute and Evaluate Phases at the Highly Capable Proficiency-Level

Made in the USA
Middletown, DE
30 August 2024

59999523R00219